ETHICS IN THE ANTHROPOLOGY OF BUSINESS

Ethics in business is a major topic both in the social sciences and in business itself. Anthropologists, long attendant to the intersection of ethics and practice, are particularly well suited to offer vital insights on the subject.

This timely collection considers a range of ethical issues in business through the examination of anthropologically informed theory and case examples. The meaning of ethical values, practices, and education are explored, as well as practical ways of implementing them, while the specific ethical challenges of industries such as advertising, market research, and design are considered. Contributions from anthropologists in business and academia promise a broad range of perspectives and add to the growing discussion on the ways anthropologists study, work, teach, and engage in a variety of industry settings.

Engagingly written, *Ethics in the Anthropology of Business* will be of interest to a wide variety of audiences, including practicing anthropologists, current and future business leaders, and scholars and students from a range of social sciences.

Timothy de Waal Malefyt is a Clinical Associate Professor of Marketing at the Gabelli School of Business, Fordham University, USA. A trained anthropologist, he has over 15 years of business experience working in advertising firms.

Robert J. Morais is Principal Emeritus of Weinman Schnee Morais Inc. and an Adjunct Professor at Columbia Business School, USA. A trained anthropologist, he has 35 years of experience working for a range of global businesses.

ANTHROPOLOGY AND BUSINESS

Crossing Boundaries, Innovating Praxis
Series Editor: Timothy de Waal Malefyt

Both anthropology and business work at the forefront of culture and change. As anthropology brings its concerns with cultural organization and patterns of human behavior to multiple forms of business, a new dynamic of engagement is created. In addition to expanding interest in business as an object of study, anthropologists increasingly hold positions within corporations or work as independent consultants to businesses. In these roles, anthropologists are both redefining the discipline and innovating in industries around the world. These shifts are creating exciting cross-fertilizations and advances in both realms: challenging traditional categories of scholarship and practice, pushing methodological boundaries, and generating new theoretical entanglements. This series advances anthropology's multifaceted work in enterprise, from marketing, design, and technology to user experience research, work practice studies, finance, and many other realms.

Titles in series

The Business of Creativity: Toward an Anthropology of Worth
Brian Moeran

The Magic of Fashion: Ritual, Commodity, Glamour
Brian Moeran

Intimacy at Work: How Digital Media Bring Private Life to the Workplace
Stefana Broadbent

Ethics in the Anthropology of Business: Explorations in Theory, Practice, and Pedagogy
Timothy de Waal Malefyt and Robert J. Morais

ETHICS IN THE ANTHROPOLOGY OF BUSINESS

Explorations in Theory, Practice, and Pedagogy

Edited by Timothy de Waal Malefyt and Robert J. Morais

Routledge
Taylor & Francis Group

NEW YORK AND LONDON

First published 2017
by Routledge
711 Third Avenue, New York, NY 10017

and by Routledge
2 Park Square, Milton Park, Abingdon, Oxon OX14 4RN

Routledge is an imprint of the Taylor & Francis Group, an informa business

British Library Cataloguing in Publication Data
A catalogue record for this book is available from the British Library

Library of Congress Cataloging in Publication Data
A catalogue record for this book has been requested

ISBN: 978-1-62958-526-0 (hbk)
ISBN: 978-1-62958-527-7 (pbk)
ISBN: 978-1-315-19709-8 (ebk)

Typeset in Bembo
by Out of House Publishing

MIX
Paper from
responsible sources
FSC
www.fsc.org   FSC™ C013985

Printed in the United Kingdom
by Henry Ling Limited

CONTENTS

CONTRIBUTORS

Jo Aiken, Ph.D. candidate in Anthropology, University College London, focuses her research on material culture and design anthropology. She received her M.A. in Applied Anthropology from the University of North Texas in 2014. She works full time in organizational development at the NASA Johnson Space Center while conducting research for her thesis on human-robotic interaction with NASA's Human Research Program.

Allen W. Batteau, Professor of Anthropology, Wayne State University, worked in the software industry for ten years before returning to an academic career. His research has focused on organizational culture, human-computer interaction, and flight safety. Dr. Batteau is the author of *Technology and Culture* and co-author of *The Dragon in the Cockpit* (senior author, Jing Hyung-Sing), and "Negations and Ambiguities in the Cultures of Organization" in *Classics in Critical Management Studies* (edited by Mats Alvesson). His current research examines *l'imaginaire* of high speed rail in the United States.

Elizabeth K. Briody, Principal, Cultural Keys LLC, is a cultural anthropologist who has been engaged in cultural change efforts for over 30 years. Cultural Keys helps organizations transform their culture, reach their potential, and attract and retain new customers. Dr. Briody has worked in health care, aerospace, aging, manufacturing, consumer products, service industries, research institutions, and other industries in the United States and abroad. Recent books include *The Cultural Dimension of Global Business*, with Gary P. Ferraro, 8th edition in press, and the award-winning *Transforming Culture*, with Robert T. Trotter II and Tracy L. Meerwarth.

Julia C. Gluesing, Professor, Global Executive Track, Wayne State University, is a business and organizational anthropologist and President of Cultural Connections,

Inc. She teaches engineers about global perspectives, global leadership, and mixed methods research. Dr. Gluesing is a speaker about ethics in cross-cultural interactions and is a consultant in teaming and product development in global networked organizations.

Dawn Lerman, Professor of Marketing and Executive Director, Center for Positive Marketing, Gabelli School of Business, Fordham University, studies the impact of words and other aspects of language on brand perceptions, consumer-brand relationships and memory for brands. She serves on the editorial review boards of the *Journal of Business Research* and the *International Marketing Review*, and is a member of the board of directors of the Advertising Educational Foundation. Dr. Lerman is also a co-author of the forthcoming book, *The Language of Branding*.

Timothy de Waal Malefyt, Clinical Associate Professor, Gabelli School of Business, Fordham University, worked in advertising for over 15 years before joining Fordham, leading strategic insights for brands such as FedEx, Campbell's, GE, Hyatt, M&Ms/Mars and Gillette at BBDO, and for Cadillac at D'Arcy in Detroit. Dr. Malefyt has authored numerous publications, including the books, *Advertising Cultures* (co-editor) and *Advertising and Anthropology* (co-author).

Tracy Meerwarth Pester, Corporate Officer at Consolidated Bearings Co., is a business anthropologist with interests in cultural modeling, cognitive anthropology, and symbolic anthropology. She co-authored the award-winning book *Transforming Culture* with Elizabeth Briody and Robert Trotter II. With Julia C. Gluesing and Brigitte Jordan, she co-edited *Mobile Work, Mobile Lives*, NAPA Bulletin 30. Her work appears in a variety of publications including *Human Organization*, *Journal of Manufacturing Management*, and *Space and Culture*.

Christine Miller, Associate Clinical Professor and Assistant Director, M.B.A. Program, Stuart School of Business, Illinois Institute of Technology, works at the intersection of anthropology, design, and business. Her research interests include socio-technical systems (STS) and the ways in which sociality and culture influence the design of new products, processes, and technologies. Dr. Miller studies technology-mediated communication and knowledge flows within pluridisciplinary groups and teams and the emergence of co-located and technology-enabled collaborative innovation networks (COINs).

Robert J. Morais, Principal Emeritus, Weinman Schnee Morais and Adjunct Professor, Columbia Business School, spent 25 years in advertising before joining Weinman Schnee Morais, a marketing research firm, in 2006. Dr. Morais has worked in health and wellness, food and beverages, household cleaners, luxury hotels, and industrial lubricants, among many other categories. He is the author of numerous publications including the books *Refocusing Focus Groups* (author), and *Advertising and Anthropology* (co-author).

Victoria Schlieder, a Research Associate at WBA Research, received her M.S. in Applied Anthropology from the University of North Texas in 2014. She has conducted research on declining retail establishments and what can be done to revitalize them, including a study of a "dead mall" and her master's thesis research on retail businesses in downtown Bloomsburg, Pennsylvania. As a full-time Research Associate at WBA Research she manages the day-to-day activities of a number of consumer satisfaction studies, with a focus on the healthcare industry.

John F. Sherry, Jr. is Herrick Professor of Marketing and Concurrent Professor of Anthropology, University of Notre Dame. He investigates brand strategy, experiential consumption, and retail atmospherics. Dr. Sherry is a Fellow of the American Anthropological Association and the Society for Applied Anthropology, a past President of the Association for Consumer Research and the Consumer Culture Theory Consortium, and a former Associate Editor of the *Journal of Consumer Research*.

Bradley J. Trainor, Veterans Health Administration, 2016 Patient Safety Fellow, has worked in government or government related contractor positions since 2003. His work has mostly involved program and policy evaluation or needs assessments. Dr. Trainor worked for the Department of Army in Afghanistan in 2010–2011 and again in 2013–2014. He is the author of "Mitigating Kuchi Settlement Issues in Kandahar" in *Practicing Anthropology*.

Christina Wasson is Professor of Anthropology at the University of North Texas. She developed the only design anthropology course offered through an anthropology department, as part of UNT's focus on business anthropology. A linguistic anthropologist, Dr. Wasson's passion is investigating communication, collaboration, and community-building, both face-to-face and online.

ACKNOWLEDGMENTS

Ethics in the Anthropology of Business is based, in part, upon a set of papers presented in a session entitled "Ethics in Business Anthropology" at the 2012 meeting of the American Anthropological Association in San Francisco, California, USA and a special 2014 issue of the Journal of Business Anthropology. This book contains revisions of several of the JBA papers along with new papers by the editors and additional contributors. We want to express our gratitude to Brian Moeran, editor in chief of the *Journal of Business Anthropology*, who encouraged the special JBA issue and development of this book.

We thank Vanessa Zapata, who assisted us with formatting and related editorial tasks and also express our appreciation to Louisa Vahtrick, Marc Stratton, Amy Kirkham, Eleri Pipien, Gail Welsh and Susan Boxall for their able assistance and expertise.

Finally, Timothy Malefyt acknowledges the influence on his thinking about ethics by his children, Emily, Paul and Matthew, as does Robert Morais by his children, Daniel and Betsy. They have inspired us to think deeply about how to live an ethical life both personally and professionally.

1

INTRODUCTION

Capitalism, Work, and Ethics

Timothy de Waal Malefyt and Robert J. Morais

Over the years, ethics has become a highly topical issue, encompassing the social sciences, philosophy, a wide array of university courses, and business practices. The focus on ethics has grown dramatically as business has expanded globally, and scholarly discussions on capitalism have become increasingly vigorous. Anthropologists, aware of ethics for decades, have written extensively about ethical issues from an increasingly broad range of perspectives.[1] The greater attention to the study of ethics within corporate environments is apparent, with ethical discussions frequently appearing on business anthropology blog posts.[2] Indeed, this broadening interest in ethics reflects Cefkin's observation that "Ethical issues infuse every aspect of corporate ethnography ... from the very constitution and formation of the research agenda to the nature of fieldwork encounters" (2010, 18).

Ethical concerns are more relevant than ever as anthropologists are increasingly employed in business endeavors and other forms of capitalistic enterprises. Nevertheless, Marietta Baba identifies "an uneasiness that some anthropologists feel in the use of their work in ethically questionable sales of products and services (Baba 2006, 47), and notes the "aversion to (anthropologists) applying knowledge in the domain of business" (Baba 2012, 55). This sensibility presents challenges for anthropologists who believe they have a "moral obligation to act and make this world a better place" (attributed to Genevieve Bell in Sinatti 2015), or concur with the Society for Applied Anthropology's "commitment to making an impact on the quality of life in the world" (www.sfaa.net).

This volume encompasses a variety of ethical circumstances and examples of the work of anthropologists in business and academia, and discusses what ethical practice and education mean in terms of shared or contrasting values and how such values should be implemented.[3] We propose that ethics for anthropologists working in and for business are complex, and differ fundamentally from academic and other practicing non-business anthropologists. This difference can be traced to capitalism and the nature of exchanges, encounters, and interactions and practices, which form myriad relationships in these associations. We examine such difference of relations in terms of what it means to work in and for capitalistic enterprises, since, as we suggest, the very nature of capitalism assumes an alternate ontology for ethical considerations. First, we provide a background to the challenges of anthropologists in corporate work, and then discuss the complexities of capitalism as an orientation for employment, and then spell out our thoughts on capitalistic ontology as a distinct ethical environment for anthropologists to navigate, followed by a discussion on the Code of Ethics of the American Anthropological Association.

Confronting Controversy Over Anthropologists in Business

There is a range of responses in reaction to anthropologists employed in or for businesses. At one end of the spectrum, there are anthropologists who advocate greater involvement in investigations of capitalism, consumption and production, organizational development, and business education as alternatives to academic practice of anthropology and to better inform the myriad modern social practices, theories and peoples involved in these areas. At the other end, there are anthropologists who denounce any sort of involvement by anthropologists or social scientists in capitalistic enterprises. Some argue that anthropologists typically study "less advantaged people" precisely because they are not in positions to demand something in return. Marilyn Strathern, for instance, claims that the local people with whom anthropologists engage have no agency when they experience exploitation and that others have the power to turn data collected into materials whose value cannot be shared with the subjects of study (Strathern 1987, 20). Laura Nader questions the extent of "power relationships" in anthropological research and whether such dominant-subordinate relationships of inequality may be affecting the kinds of theories anthropologists produce (1974, 289).

Nevertheless, this widespread Boasian perspective typically implicates more abstract moral concerns than specific ethical quandaries. As Lucas (2009,13) writes of anthropologists in the military, ethics should be reserved for specific groups or organizational norms and principles, while morality applies more broadly to shared principles or guidelines of human behavior. Moreover, there is widespread practice, notes Lucas, in Geertz's comments (1973) on moral philosophers, "to resort to very focused, narrowly-defined, and quite frequently hypothetical or fictionalized cases … to focus on precisely the elements of a controversy that are most in dispute, while relegating other, perhaps confusing and less relevant details to the background" (Lucas 2009, 14). This is often the case for anthropologists employed in businesses that are critiqued for working on "bad" products (such as tobacco and liquor) while products that are benign or healthy are less likely to raise critical attention. The issues we discuss in this opening chapter have direct ethical bearing on business anthropology practices that are debated and discussed as ethical issues for all anthropologists – "clandestine and secret research," "transparency," and the question of full disclosure with informants – how open and available should and can business anthropology be. More importantly, we consider how can and should anthropological work be framed within the larger business context of capitalism, corporate competition and responsibility. We posit that ethics are best applied with relativism to business and *from within* business rather than through moral judgments outside and across fields, since capitalism implies a different ontology for the framing of ethics.

Business Anthropology: Capitalism, Customer Insights, and Ethics

For anthropologists employed in and for corporations there are many ways to frame their work in a capitalist system, depending on context and use (Miller 1997). What does it mean to work in or for profit-driven marketers, for instance, gathering customer insights for product design, brands, or to help advance organizational efficiencies within a corporation when employment in capitalistic organizations is a matter of framing what is ethical and what is not (Borofsky 2016)? While economists would define capitalism as an economic system based on private ownership and as the means of production and operation for profit, other social scholars posit capitalism as more mercurial where, "its definition shows a chameleon-like tendency to vary with the ideological bias of the user" (Deane 1996, 71). Daniel Miller applies a practical ethnographic approach to what he calls "organic capitalism" (1997, 9) in describing his work with consumers in day-to-day practices of commerce, shopping exchanges, and human relationships of consumption. Nigel Thrift and other cultural theorists emphasize capitalism's transient and malleable nature, defining it as "a series of relations of relationships" that are adapted by actors, intervened by objects and instituted by practices (2005, 1–2).

In light of these issues, we discuss four conditions of capitalism that situate our analysis of ethics relative to anthropologists' work in firms today. These conditions contain the inherent difficulties and complexities in vetting out ethical issues for anthropologists. First, capitalism itself represents a fluid field of strategic possibilities with a high degree of instability and uncertainty. Second, since capitalism operates under such uncertain conditions, it draws for its effect on what can be conceptualized as a kind of magical enchantment. Third, capitalism increasingly blurs the distinction between production and consumption by building off co-operative relations between consumers and firms, so that assigning agency, power and responsibility to specific parties is increasingly complex. Fourth, "innovation" is an ever more essential mandate that continuously calls for change in relations between consumers and producers, seeking novelty as a cultural imperative. These perspectives, increasingly narrow their focus from top down to the groundwork of ethnography, to detail the conditions and implications of what it means to work in or for capitalistic industries, and they necessitate new ethical considerations.

First, a fundamental challenge for anthropologists working in and for business is that capitalism creates highly unstable conditions under which work transpires, where ethics are not absolute but shift according to cultural, organizational, staff, and working conditions. Capitalism, Thrift contends, does not consist of neat whole systems of "unities and totalities" (2005, 2), but rather is highly unstable, "unfinished," in constant flux, changing in form and practice as it is uncertain about the future, and yet depends upon it. Like works of art that shift in value through symbolic power (Bourdieu 1993), capitalism develops subjective value via a shifting network of relations. As such, economies, both global and local, exist within a field of "strategic possibilities" and "position-taking" (Bourdieu 1993), relative to other cultural forms and processes, so "that every position, even the dominant one, depends for its very existence on the other positions constituting the field" (1993, 30). Any new redistribution of capital describes a change in a "field of forces" at work, as much as a shift in a "field of struggles" (Bourdieu 1993, 30). Since corporations are comprised of such malleable fields and shifting networks, which are only "partly in control" as "constantly mutating entities" (Thrift 2005, 4), business anthropologists employed in such domains are faced with endlessly more challenging and emergent contingencies, as they, themselves, comprise the "relations of relationships."

This performative yet transient context presents business anthropologists with numerous and complex ethical choices since capitalism is "perpetually unfinished" (Thrift 2005, 3). As such, capitalistic products and processes and the myriad working relations that unfold must be understood, not in terms of fixed structural relations or behavioral models that economists might follow and attempt to predict, but more as an *assemblage* (Latour 2005) or a way of *coming into being* (Ingold 2013), that brings into play particular combinations of populations (target audiences), territories (markets), brands and services, and corporate initiatives. The unpredictable quality of such assemblages requires continual rethinking and updating of ethical behavior. In a world of shifting ground, such relations continually unfold under potential conditions of manipulation and oppression, but also contain "little spaces of joy and generosity" (Thrift 2005, 2) that are part of its products and processes. This affirms the claim that most ethical crises that anthropologists encounter are likewise, even more emergent, "unplanned, unanticipated, and revolve around conflicts between ethical principles rather than the violation of them" (Whiteford and Trotter 2008, 97). How then do anthropologists respond in such a shifting environment, in which ethical implications are emergent, unplanned, and unanticipated?

Second, since capitalism is a network of relations that operates under conditions of uncertainty and instability, it also inhabits what we interpret as a magical world of enchantment (Thrift 1997, 2005; Holmes 2014; Moeran 2015; Moeran and Malefyt 2016). Magic thrives under conditions of uncertainty, since it is employed in "the domain of the unaccountable and adverse influences, as well as the great unearned increment of fortunate coincidence" (Malinowski 1954, 29). In other words, multiple forms of capitalism use magical practices and ideology to *deal with uncertainty* – from the uncertainty of fishing under open sea conditions (Malinowski 1954, 31), to the modern-day profit-making activity of central bankers (Appadurai 2015, 32), to the practices of financial trading floors (Zaloom 2006), and the marketing of cultural products in fashion and advertising (Moeran 2015, 219–222). Even economic forecasting reveals that the rise and fall of central banks of commerce hinges on the magical language and spoken words of its "magicians," like Alan Greenspan (Holmes 2014, 21–22). Because magic "speaks to realms other than material reality" (Greenwood 2009, 8), it engenders a sense of enchantment in our modern world. A "magical consciousness" accesses hidden, unseen forces, or acts at a distance, as a prime vehicle for firing the imagination and rallying purposeful capitalistic practices that seek to achieve specific ends. Magical rites and affirmative language are designed to effect *transformations* (in share prices, advertising, and "fashion" trends), and so tend to be strictly prescribed in terms of time; they are performed regularly at particular times of the year (fashion "week" or advertising awards ceremonies) or, if daily, within strictly controlled time limits (e.g., the opening and closing bell at the New York Stock Exchange). To be effective and to *do* things (Mauss 1972, 19), these events occur in specially qualified places such as the World Economic Forum in Davos (Mauss 1972, 46) or as set rituals in advertising agency and corporate offices before a client pitch of creative work (Malefyt and Morais 2010). All of this creates the necessary conditions for an emergent awareness of "magical capitalism" which flourishes under enchantments (Moeran and Malefyt 2016). The world of capitalism thus resembles less a rational or intellectual world of proper checks and balances and more an "imaginary of the medieval world of dark superstitions and religious bliss than we fondly choose to believe" (Thrift 2005, 2; cf. Miyazki 2003).

Some argue that magical language and enchantment in the objective and affective forms that capitalism produces may be invaluable to ethical life. Bennett (2001) presents the concept of "enchantment" as a feeling of being connected to existence in an affirmative affective way and represents an overlooked feature of contemporary experience. Capitalism can energize ethical and political life in positive ways. Enchanted capitalism can be a powerful force that motivates people to engage "more positively" in intense relationships with other people, life, and the cosmos at large. The "positive effects" of capitalism are evidenced, for instance, in advertising messages (Malefyt 2015), which can enhance consumer's social bonds and worldview. As philosophers Deleuze and Guattari (1987) write, an enchanted lens can foster transformations with a "catalytic function" that increases the speed of exchanges, relations and reactions around it, so as to enter into new potentialities, new connections and settings (1987, 348). We situate our consideration of ethics in capitalism within this enchanted worldview from which meaning is derived, "within a process of cross-cultural interaction," as it designates an impassioned form of conceptualizing the world, "apart from the 'rational' West" (Wax and Wax 1963, 503).

Third, the increasing emphasis on interaction between consumers and corporations and new forms of hybrid marketing make it increasingly difficult to demark classic divisions between production and consumption. What happens to our evaluation of ethical agency when our analysis of capitalism moves from binary notions of "exchanges," which can be scrutinized for unequal relations of power and difference (Faier and Rofel 2014), to, for instance, the modern form of blurred boundaries of customer–manufacturer co-creation? As Thrift notes, "Consumers are expected to make more and more extravagant investments in the act of consumption itself, through collecting, subscribing, experiencing and, in general, participating in all manner of collective acts of sense making" (Thrift 2005, 7). Daniel Miller re-examines traditional divisions between consumption and production in questioning, "What is a relationship?" (2007) by looking at the complexity in relations between goods and people, and the multiple types of inter- and intra-connections they create. David Graeber (2011) further questions the binary divisions between consumption and production in examining the widely used term "consumption," which casts a negative, moralistic sense of wasting, burning, or destroying something that did not need to be destroyed. "Consumption" aggregates myriad forms of people's relationships, self-expression, and even enjoyment with material objects, such as cooking dinner, applying eyeliner, or even watching television, into one negative term. "Consumer society" becomes equivalent to a society of wastrels and destroyers. When anthropologists view consumption and production as two opposing poles of capitalism a dualism is forced. One state exists in opposition to the other as two spheres of a world; when a person is not working then she must be consuming (Graeber 2011).

Further challenging the binary of consumption and production, recent research examines other factors in material culture, such as the range of relationships both human and non-human and their agency that complicates precise assignment of agency and power. From the work of Bourdieu, Latour, and Miller, "exchange" is not reduced to privileging a world of only social bonds among or between human relations, since social relations themselves are premised on a material order of things (Horst and Miller 2012).

> It is impossible to become human other than through socializing within a material world of cultural artifacts that include order, agency and relationships between things themselves and not just their relationship to persons. Artifacts (goods and services) do far more than just express human intention.
>
> *(2012, 24)*

Miller shows that people are not alienated by superficial or shallow relations in an "exchange" of goods, but rather enhanced and fortified through continued interactions with and among them. Goods as possessions, then, are highly meaningful agents and "try to turn the alienable back into the inalienable" (Horst and Miller 2012, 7). Everyday acts of shopping and domestic consumption practices utilize commodities to facilitate and express meaningful relationships between people (Miller 1997, 1998, 2007). Co-created hybrid relations in consumption and production and their entanglements with goods and services as agents of change, reveal that capitalism can serve multiple agents, and demonstrates the difficulty in assigning ethical responsibility to one party or another.

In addition, some academic anthropologists have shifted their perspectives from capitalism as a monolith of power to examine instead the contingent, hybrid, and interactive ways cultural meanings are produced through relations of value creation. These anthropologists find that "encounters" between and among researchers and locals are not unidirectional and necessarily one-way exploitative, but increasingly involved in processes of "negotiation, resistance, awkward resonance, misunderstanding, and unexpected convergence" (Faier and Rofel 2014, 365). The specificity of circulating objects and subjects that link local to global transnational corporations to consumers are traced, for example, in the moral geography of value creation in Coca-Cola's international "brand building enterprises" (Foster 2008). These global interactions forge linkages among corporate officials, marketing personnel, consumers and consumer activists and "locals" into caring relations from an "economy of qualities" (Callon et al. 2002). Yet, other global interactions create "friction" (Tsing 2005) from global connections and tensions among environmental encounters, cultural diversity, and capitalistic goals. Such engagements between capitalism, power, and difference are neither all good nor all bad, but reflect the contingent ways that relationships and networks of interactions with goods and services, and anthropologists studying them on behalf of corporations, can act along with material factors as agents of change themselves.

Finally, adding to the complexity of co-creation in capitalism, recent mandates in industry and business schools call for innovative practices and creativity as a lifelong process of learning and adapting to changing markets and services. Capitalism seeks ever-changing forms of networks, and innovation is viewed as the key to corporate growth, economic prosperity, and social well-being (Ingold and Hallam 2007, 1). Innovation ideology contributes to increased competitiveness such that if organizations do not continually change what they offer in products and services and how they create and deliver them to customers, they risk being overtaken by companies that do (Bessant and Tidd 2007). Nevertheless, the process of innovation is complex, and the failure of marketplace projects is more common than success. In many instances, innovation is subject to strong technical and commercial uncertainties and failure rates are high; economist Edwin Mansfield suggests that about half of all US private business R&D is dedicated to projects that ultimately fail (cited in Tidd and Bessant 2009). Innovation ideology means that "knowledge" as a resource in business is not "passively stored" or structured in models, but at the ready to activate "technical-artistic" transformations of life (Thrift 2006, 281). Active knowledge is a way for firms to boost their difference from and competitiveness with other organizations. *Innovation* becomes built into a continuous and inexhaustible process of emergence that goes beyond capital accumulation (Thrift 2006, 281).

One source that business draws on innovation and inspiration includes institutionalized forms of critique or what Thrift (2005) calls "Cultural Circuits." These cultural circuits are comprised of business schools, management consultants, and media, which keep capitalism continuously on the edge, making it fast-moving, ambivalent, and difficult to predict. Students in business schools, for instance, are taught new approaches to engaging consumers and practicing corporate responsibility, from *purpose marketing* or *pro-social marketing* (Elliot 2013), to sustainable practices, to ethical behavior of firms, corporate social responsibility, and so forth. Teaching ethics in business schools stresses the need for "mindfulness of society" and spurs new pedagogical curricula in business education (Peterson 2012, 9). This knowledge makes its way into firms when they hire graduates as managers, and it instills an awareness of innovation and entrepreneurial ideas as agents of change. Media enterprises inspire change by inventing terms such as "the knowledge economy," "the dot.com" or "digital economy," "the information economy," and so forth (cf. Cassidy 2002; Gadrey 2003), which boost ideas about productivity and the reach of capitalism in the current era (Thrift 2005, 11). Cultural circuits then assume roles in commodity production as capitalistic tools of innovation through which information technologies (e.g., Big Data, crowd-sourcing, networks, and communities in social media) create new venues for consumer and corporate interaction. Business anthropologists are often charged with mediating these emerging conditions and may teach in business schools, incubating knowledge practices and bringing "Thought leadership" to a productive process as the forefront of possibilities change (Thrift 2006, 2014).

Today, innovation is often sourced from meaning and fresh ideas created by consumers and producers. In practices of open or "user-centered" innovation, organizations are tapping into consumer trends in commodity involvement and from user-based communities that thrive on branded products and services (i.e., Apple communities, Harley-Davidson "hog" rallies) that make it easier for firms to follow product adaptations to customer needs and desires, and for them to flourish in the marketplace. The business obsession with innovation, knowledge, and creativity is applied to communities of practice in metaphors of performance, such as the value of spontaneous decision-making in "Blink" (Gladwell 2005), and draws consumer knowledge of commodities to feed back into systems of consumer experience to continuously perpetuate engagement. Such economies of innovation are seen as co-created along with use of information technology. As Von Hippel states:

> Users of products and services – both firms and individual consumers – are increasingly able to innovate for themselves. User-centered innovation processes offer great advantages over the manufacturer-centric development systems that have been the mainstay of commerce over hundreds of years. Users that innovate can develop exactly what they want, rather than rely on manufacturers to act as their (very often imperfect) agents. Moreover, users do not have to develop everything they need on their own: they can benefit from innovations developed and freely shared by others.
>
> *(2005, 1)*

Firms are even more likely today to reward consumer innovation, and some offer payments to consumers for their ideas. For instance, Google challenges and even rewards coders and hackers to infiltrate their software, which helps educate Google on how to improve their products. Many corporations hire "mystery shoppers" who visit stores, showrooms, and restaurants, and answer surveys based upon their experience in the interest of both basic service improvements and more expansive service innovation. If capitalism is adaptable (Miller 1997) and has "always been experimental" (Thrift 2006), then the call for more innovative practices reflects an open discourse making possible new configurations as opposed to fixed and formal structures. This so-called "experimental event" of capitalism as continuously reforming itself, reveals a process of continual movement and reconfiguring assemblages as part of the "economization" of the world (Latour 2005; Çalışkan and Callon 2009).

What does all this mean for business anthropologists? At the very least, business anthropologists are mediators of knowledge practices and apply learning first-hand to business situations. Since innovation is a key agenda for businesses to boost difference among corporations and establish identity with consumers, business anthropologists become intermediaries in integrating such "difference and identity" into cycles of production and reproduction of capitalism in their work.

A Call for a New Ethical Model for Anthropologists in Business

Business anthropologists work within the environment of capitalism, embracing capital fluidity, cultural circuits of critique, rising demand for innovation, and engaging in co-creation between consumers and producers in an enchanted field of uncertainty and change. Such dynamics affect not only their ethics, but also involve the products and processes that anthropologists study. Business anthropologists are mediators of relationships, practices, and processes that are in flux and so confront capitalism in the myriad ways it *comes into being* (Ingold 2013), which non-business anthropologists do not. The challenge of business anthropologists employed in this movement of goods and services locally and globally is to confront an alternative ontology. This new ontology is predicated neither on static or structural models that predict change, as economists might follow, nor on restricted or occasional conditions of "exchanges" or "encounters" that academic anthropologists use to discuss issues of agency, power, and difference (Faier and Rofel 2014). Rather, business anthropologists work in an interactive field of consumer–producer co-creation in continual change that presents a substantial ethical challenge. Not only are issues of causality, power, and agency less clearly assigned, but also anthropologists in business are, themselves, agents of change, since they investigate products, brands, and new technologies that bring about newness and change for communities and individuals that adopt them. This challenge is explored in design research by Blomberg and colleagues (Blomberg et al. 1993) and Wasson (2000), and acknowledged by Ehn (1988) when she states that "what we design is not just artifacts but by intervention a changed or reformed practice" (1988, 128). Capitalism works with an agenda, with specific goals in mind. The practice of business anthropology itself is thus something fluid, dynamic and essentially "comes into being" (Ingold 2013) as an agent *of* change and an agent *for* change that is "goal directed" in its ontology, such that ethical considerations are central to its purpose and to relations with others.

Working in a Goal-directed Ontology

If capitalism is always in the process of becoming in the form of "relations of relationships" with consumers, commodity products and services, and seeks definitive ends, what are the implications of such networks and relations for business anthropologists? If capitalism is "goal directed" while academic anthropology is open ended, exploratory and neutral to affecting change, how do we evaluate comparable circumstances for ethical considerations, such as "do no harm," "informed consent," "full disclosure," and "transparency" that revolve around different types of relationships and ends for business anthropologists and academic anthropologists? If, for business anthropologists, change is implicated in any goal-directed involvement, and for academic anthropologists "do no harm" implies minimizing change, how do we reconcile such divergent agendas? Do different ontologies impact what and how we evaluate ethical considerations for business anthropologists versus academic anthropologists?

Anthropologists have written about ethical consumption as the collective effort of concerned people to influence the economic realm by instilling in it values and norms from the social realm of home and family (Carrier and Luetchford 2012). Ethical concerns by impassioned people view human relations with care, then suggest acting collectively for the common good and join movements, organizations, and behave in ways that benefit others; otherwise, personal desire of a sole individual can be idiosyncratic and ineffective (Murphy and Sherry 2014). The forces of capitalism can be both positive and negative, and continuously generate change. As Sherry notes, "For better and for worse, marketing has become perhaps the greatest force of cultural stability and change at work in the contemporary world" (2008, 85). Business anthropologists extend the reach of goal-directed interactions into all types of relationships they engage, with expected and unanticipated consequences. As Brenkert states of the way interactions and relationships are conveyed differently:

> People sitting around a campfire or at the dinner table, or even hanging out at a coffee shop, may engage in (conversational) exchanges of which no one knows (beforehand) the likely outcome. In contrast, in marketing exchanges marketers intentionally and actively seek to bring about an exchange which is designed to attain an end they seek.
>
> *(Brenkert 2008, 14)*

Brenkert's comments draw a comparison between the way academic anthropologists might conduct fieldwork in open-ended participant observation conversations, with how business anthropologists work on behalf of capitalistic objectives. Even open-ended conversations and "exploratory research" in marketing have specific ends in mind for the relationships they develop with consumers, which in turn have organizational and/or design implications. Further, such interactions are premised on continuing relationships, since "marketers are interested in developing explicit, ongoing relationships with customers in which individual transactions may occur and consumers play a role in creating these exchanges" (Brenkert 2008, 14). Ethical implications then are not mere appurtenances to the work of marketing research, but central to business practices and anthropological ideology in corporate work.

Business Anthropology: At the Heart of Capitalism, Consumption, and Power

Ethical action is, or at least should be, integral to business practices and to the individual projects, practices, and outcomes of anthropologists at work in business. In recent years business ethics in the marketing world, for example, has moved beyond the so-called marketing principle of delivering what consumers claim they need and want for maximum profit, to designing activities that recognize a company's competencies, resources, respecting cultural values and norms and providing the greatest value to consumers (McDonough and Braungart 2002; Brenkert 2008, 53). Marketers no longer ask, "How can we influence our customers," but rather ask, "How can our customers influence us," and even, "How can our customers influence each other?" (Kotler and Armstrong 2016). Ethics lies at the heart of goal-oriented relationships on which marketing is based. Marketers, for instance, parse out the term engagement in much more sophisticated and nuanced understandings of their customers. Some marketers (Maslowskaa et al. 2016) propose the term *engagement* as a *customer engagement ecosystem*, a conceptual model that encompasses brand actions, other actors, customer brand experience, shopping behaviors, brand consumption and brand-dialog behaviors. This model suggests that interactions between elements are non-linear and reactive, and extend beyond immediate engagement; each action causes a reaction that affects the ecosystem. It reflects the interconnected character of today's marketing environment, such as the growing importance of empowered consumers through the Internet in different forms of "brand dialog behaviors."

Other analyses of capitalism and consumption that implicate ethics have demonstrated growing awareness among corporations regarding earth's limits and environmental sustainability, fair trade, calls for transparency in operations, and corporate social and humanistic responsibility. These concerns have led to the rise of "Conscious Capitalism" (Hollender and Breen 2010), the "Age of Accountability" (Savitz and Weber 2007), and corporate initiatives in positive and social marketing (Murphy and Sherry 2014). The movement towards corporate social responsibility (CSR) is closely aligned with, and at times overlaps, ethics in advertising, marketing, and other consumer-facing enterprises. CSR encompasses "the obligations of the firm to society, or more specifically, the firm's stakeholders – those affected by corporate policies and practices" (Smith 2003, 53). The interrelatedness of CSR and ethics is such that internal policies and processes ensure a CSR oriented company conducts its operations in a responsible and ethical manner. Its external initiatives contribute to and improve the communities in which it operates through, for example, corporate philanthropy and employee volunteerism, with close attention paid to the impact of these initiatives on society. If the difference in the work of business anthropologists and academic anthropologists is between directed and non-directed forms of engagement with subjects, then issues of transparency, accountability, conscientiousness, and social responsibility come to the forefront of business anthropologists' actions with and in corporations, and imply an ethical critique of such actions which have ramifications for all involved.

Code(s) of Ethics for Anthropologists

For practitioners of anthropology in business, determining ethical courses of action is not only contingent on corporate actions in the marketplace, but also depends on guidance from sources close to anthropologists, such as from the Code of Ethics of the American Anthropological Association (AAA). The Code of Ethics, initially formulated in 1971, would seem to be the place to seek direction and guidance on ethical issues. The AAA code underwent a multi-year process of revisions, and was approved in 2012 by 93 percent of those who voted (Kelsey 2012; see Plemmons and Barker 2016 for essays on the changes to the AAA code by members of the taskforce). Although the revised ethics code aimed to consider applied anthropology in its latest version, it is silent and, at times problematic, concerning *business* anthropology. Consequently, the 2012 version of the AAA Code of Ethics presents many challenges for business anthropologists, much as did the previous code.

Several of the "disconnects" between the code and business anthropology practice will continue to vex business anthropologists unless the AAA once again revises the code to reflect the realities of industrial practice. Until that occurs, anthropologists who work in business can elect to use the AAA ethics code as a general guide where applicable, and rely on personal ethical standards, the input of professional colleagues, or consult the RICE Guide to help them evaluate the ethics of their business engagements (Bohren and Whiteford 2013; also see Whiteford and Trotter 2008). As Hammershøy and Madsen (2012) suggest in a thoughtful critique of the AAA Code of Ethics, the code makes it "clear to us as business anthropologists that we must first and foremost protect the subjects we study; however, we are quite left to our own devices in regards to figuring out how we position ourselves towards the larger project and aim of business anthropology" (Hammershøy and Madsen 2012, 3).

Taking a directed approach, Elizabeth K. Briody and Tracy Meerwarth Pester challenged the AAA's apparent "hands off" guidelines to "do no harm," with a call to action: "Do some good" in efforts to "improve the human condition" (Briody and Meerwarth Pester 2015). Their argument has been repeated elsewhere (Hammershøy and Madsen 2012; Borofsky 2016). We agree that an engaged anthropology should promote and emphasize actions toward "doing good." As Briody and Meerwarth Pester contend, "Professional anthropologists work *inside* some cultural system – whether as employees, consultants, contractors, or volunteers – and typically work toward a more effective system" and go on to ask, "Why doesn't the code value the use of anthropological theories and methods to help improve the human condition?" Yet while the case for doing good internally within a system of production sounds promising, practicing anthropologists in other less tangibly associated fields, such as finance, advertising, and fashion industries, face more opaque challenges.

A central issue for anthropologists employed in service industry jobs – such as advertising, for example – is the indirect way they work on actual consumer goods. Anthropologists in advertising do not manufacture products or work directly with teams of people that do (designers, engineers, assembly line workers, production managers, etc.). Rather, they generate insights that enable advertising agencies to communicate the benefits of products to audiences in persuasive ways. Thus, they do not make anything concrete; they help create ads that depict lifestyles, values, and ideals in which brands provide consumers with perceptible benefits. In other words, "The specificity of advertising is defined by the fact that it produces no durable or tangible goods but rather ideas evaluated by others" (Malefyt 2012, 219). Anthropologists in advertising deal with the abstracts of "value creation" in producing advertisements; they also collaborate concretely and consequently with the corporate executives who run these companies and select advertisements (or not). In such tenuous "one-off" positions, anthropologists in advertising are responsible for the success of intangible ad creation, and for the corporate relations and consumers' relations that enhance their position within an advertising agency, between the product and consumer, and most importantly between agency and client. So to influence positively this "relationships of relations" is to deal not directly with products that are beneficial or harmful, but rather with the subjectivities of human inconsistencies and fickle engagements that qualify these products. It is possible for anthropologists in advertising to work on "bad" products (soda, cake mixes, liquor) but have excellent relations with their clients, or champion beneficial products but have tenuous client relationships. From our perspective, ethical behavior for anthropologists in business entails selecting projects that are inherently ethical (e.g., not working on products that overtly cause harm to people or society) and acting with integrity on behalf of the subjects of anthropologist's study and the sponsors of our research. It also means honoring contractual arrangements such as non-disclosure of commercially sensitive information. Nevertheless, upholding ethical action in business anthropology is problematic at times. For example, which and how certain products cause harm is not always clear – consider liquor, cake mix, and gas powered automobiles – and corporate sponsors own the research findings and can use them as they see appropriate.

Some non-applied anthropologists would disagree with Briody and Meerwarth Pester's activist stance, believing that the field anthropologist should maintain the status quo, make no waves, in other words, and leave little impact. But the AAA recognizes – and sees major employment opportunities in – the work of applied anthropology, and this is one of the reasons that the revised ethics code acknowledged applied anthropology. And yet for one realm of applied anthropology, business anthropology, the same components of the code are incompatible. Perhaps this traces to Baba's (2006, 2012) contention that the role of business anthropologists in advancing corporate profit does not sit well with many members of the AAA. The AAA's embrace of applied anthropology, we posit, is counterproductive to anthropologists in business because of the conditions of capitalism previously outlined, and as such, the current Code of Ethics is untenable. The Code requires revisiting again with cognizance of anthropology's positive role in capitalism and with attention paid to the particular requirements of ethical anthropologists in business practice.

The challenges of the AAA Code of Ethics for anthropologists who operate in the business world require that anthropologists crafting a code that business anthropologists can use view ethics, at least in part, through the lens of capitalism. But first, there must be a thorough examination of ethical questions through examples of anthropology's own problematic past. There are numerous moral debates within anthropology over the conduct of colleagues that have transpired over the years. Such conduct includes espionage, questionable World War II operations, CIA involvement during the Cold War, the infamous project Camelot in the 1960s in Latin America, and the "Sanchez Affair" (when Oscar Lewis's *Children of Sanchez* in 1961 was translated into Spanish and the Mexican press expressed outrage). This "litany of shame" (Lucas 2009, 28) may focus on the AAA-centered ethics of informed consent, do no harm, transparency, etc. However, as Lucas posits, there is a greater degree of difficulty when the objects of one's research are not individuals, but whole groups or even society. How does one "obtain" consent from a "cultural way of life"? Another issue regarding transparency, do no harm, and informed consent is how can one study another when the very nature of "conducting research" involves a narrative public or commercial disclosure that "cannot but pose a threat to the privacy and dignity of the individuals studied," since this risk, no matter how diligent the researcher, is seldom fully disclosed (Lucas 2009, 28). Furthermore, the resulting claim of who should benefit – the advances of science and general human enlightenment, or the basic rights of human beings as a "culture" to which they belong – may result in an ethical stalemate, such is the case in the latest tension over Kennewick Man, contesting its preservation for scientific posterity or being returned to native Americans for burial (Rothstein 2006).

Instead of applying one ethical standard across all forms of anthropology, anthropologists in business would perhaps benefit from separate or amended ethical guidelines from academic anthropology, since practices in a capitalistic environment present different dynamics and challenges framed within a different ontology. Disclosure of one's aims and project goals are ethical in much research, for instance, but divulging brand names prior to discussions with subjects can taint research results. Transparency in corporate practices is also a shared ethic in business anthropology, but sharing corporate strategies is not expected or condoned. In fact, anthropologists in business typically sign non-disclosure agreements (NDAs) with their clients prior to initiating a project. This part of the ethical debate by non-anthropologists makes the relativity of business ethics situation driven and relativistic.

Marketing, as a subset of business anthropology, cannot avoid ethics, since market relations between companies and consumers plays a central role. Marketing is a moral activity in that it falls within the moral arena since "morality is integral to marketing" (Brenkert 2008, viii). This also means that there cannot be generalized moral formulas such as the AAA's provision to "do no harm," or, alternately, "do some good." For every marketing action there are moral consequences; since marketing is goal-directed and change-seeking, each action requires responsible thought. For example, in brand packaging, there are environmental implications; in products marketed to and for children, consideration should be given to potential ill effects of the product or its advertising. There are broader ethical questions about marketing as well. Does advertising encourage people to buy things they do not need? Does international marketing take advantage of developing country populations? Such criticisms are widespread, and some are valid. However, we suggest that ethical judgments should be applied to particular cases, an argument that we expand upon in our chapter devoted to advertising.

Nevertheless, there are broad ethical values and principles applicable to business anthropologists; for anthropologists in marketing, these include allowing consumers autonomy, freedom of choice, and truth in brand promises. Moreover, knowledge of how marketing and other business practices actually work is central for moral-ethical considerations. There will always be the possibility of philosophical contention and inappropriate actions because capitalism and business success depend upon active engagement, which is continuously goal-directed and "stuff happens." Sweeping generalizations are not helpful but case-by-case examples can guide practitioners.

Capitalism aims to modify behavior in a commercial milieu, and relations with consumers, suppliers, distributers, employees, and even competitors are "managed" for best outcomes. Seeking specific ends is not necessarily selfish and detrimental. Only if those ends override the interests of others are they problematic. As Adam Smith prescribed, self-interest works positively in capitalism, especially when it includes fulfillment of social values and norms, and where competition is closely aligned with codes of behavior. Ethics in business anthropology implies greater awareness of the operations, management, and interconnections of the entire field. In a similar fashion to the AAA, the American Marketing Association also admonishes firms from "doing harm to customers." Still, as Brenkert (2008) reminds us, this is only the starting point if we consider working within a goal-directed ontology. Marketing relationships must do more and work toward excellence. "Excellence in marketing is not compatible with making people or nature, all things considered, *worse off*. It requires making them *better off* not only in the short run," for example, as in any particular *singular* exchange that the AAA warns against, "but also in the long run, which applies not simply to this customer but also, as relevant, to future customers and generations" (Brenkert 2008, 54). Likewise, ethics in business anthropology does not prescribe any one kind of conduct or product to be produced and marketed in a certain way, since there are "multiple moral pathways" (Brenkert 2008, 54). As Miller (1997, 1998) notes, a better material and social life can be created by capitalism. In best-case scenarios, business anthropologists working in and for capitalistic firms can contribute to the production of goods and services that seek to improve the lives of people.

The Chapters That Follow

The chapters in this collection address a wide range of conceptual and practical engagement issues in the anthropology of business. We anticipate that they will stimulate thought and lively discussion among anthropologists, teachers of the next generation of business leaders, and students who seek guidance as they navigate today's complex global marketplace.

In Chapter 2, Elizabeth K. Briody and Tracy Meerwarth Pester discuss the 2012 AAA Code of Ethics from the perspective of their careers serving industry. Their experiences reveal a significant gap in how ethics are understood and practiced between a private sector setting and academic environments. They suggest that the AAA ethical guidelines require significant revisions, contending that without those revisions, the growing segment of AAA membership that engages in business will continue to disregard the AAA principles as inappropriate and discordant with what they do for a living.

In Chapter 3, John F. Sherry, Jr. explores several ethical entanglements that occur when anthropologists ply their trade in contemporary marketplaces. In particular, he examines dynamics in the personal, professional, and political domains in which these challenges are negotiated. His commentary is grounded in the disciplines of marketing and consumer research, which comprise the field he has practiced in as a scholar and consultant for the past three decades.

In Chapter 4, Allen Batteau and Bradley Trainor examine the dilemmas of moral reasoning at the intersections of disciplinary, professional, and institutional worlds. They note that anthropology as an academic discipline is a relative newcomer to the institutional world of business, and is only now confronting the ethical dilemmas commerce entails. They propose that moral development is a necessary part of institutional and professional development, and that ethical reasoning comes from working through difficult cases. They also argue that belonging to a community of ethical practice is a foundational part of being an ethical professional.

In Chapter 5, Julia Gluesing examines how business anthropologists who work for multinational enterprises (MNEs) grapple with ethical complexity. She writes that ethical challenges in MNEs arise from the predominant neoliberal viewpoint in such organizations, the dynamics of ethics in the face of unpredictable events, the embeddedness of ethics in culture, and the cross-boundary and intercultural nature of multi-stakeholder environments. Using a research project case, Gluesing discusses some ethical conundrums that can emanate from MNE work and how resolutions to these issues can be obtained. She also addresses the broader role of ethics in the future of business and organizational anthropology.

In Chapter 6, Christine Miller looks at how some designers have adapted anthropology's traditional fieldwork methods for private and public sector projects. She considers if and how ethical concerns engrained in anthropologists through their education and fieldwork training carry over to methods and ethical issues within the field of design. Through secondary sources and conversations with practicing designers, Miller provides insights on paradigmatic shifts within design over time and how these changes have influenced design research and practice, specifically in relation to ethics.

In Chapter 7 on advertising ethics we explore the criticisms and benefits of advertising from historical and cross-cultural perspectives. We then look closely at how anthropologists who work in advertising should reflect upon and how they might navigate ethical conundrums. We concur with Batteau and Trainor that general ethical mandates are unworkable in commerce. Anthropologists in advertising must sometimes make difficult professional choices, on occasion rationalizing the value of their work in a commercial context, while doing no harm to the subjects they study, or to culture at large.

In Chapter 8, Jo Aiken, Victoria Schlieder, and Christina Wasson examine how ethics were learned in a design anthropology class, noting that regardless of how clearly ethical codes are written, researchers can encounter gray areas in the field. They focus on a project for Motorola that confronted some students with unexpected and ethically ambiguous circumstances, looking closely at one study participant who may have been intoxicated, analyzing this as an "extreme case" that brought ethical dilemmas into sharp focus. The chapter concludes with suggestions for navigating ethical gray areas.

This volume closes in Chapter 9 with a pedagogical perspective, as Dawn Lerman explores the moral imperative of business schools within the context of the increasingly central role that commerce and consumption play within society. She argues for a more human-centered approach in business education, one that infuses an understanding of people, a respect for their diversity, and a commitment to incorporating dignity into the fabric of business education. This is a view that we believe anthropologists in business and, we imagine, all anthropologists, could endorse.

An Ethical Way Forward

Batteau and Trainor (2014) explored the ethics of anthropology's culture contact through time and distance, and how such contacts with the other relate to disparities and shifts of power. New economies, new territories, and new practices created emergent relations and new forms of power, all of which led to dilemmas, morals, and new thinking on how ethical conduct, and ethics as a construct, should be defined. For anthropologists working in industry, corporate encounters today necessitate an ethical response to such disparities in ever more complex situations. From this perspective, and others that the chapters in this volume richly illustrate, anthropology adds a unique sensibility to the ethics of business practice. For that reason, we anticipate that this volume will be an impetus for continuing reflection and better informed action on how to engage in ethical business anthropology. We hope that the cases, analyses, and arguments will be thought-provoking for practitioners at all career stages and be used by schools that teach business anthropology and related subjects. A limitation of this collection is that the chapters discuss matters only within the sphere of the scholar-practitioners who wrote them, and they reflect a US territorial focus. A more general review of broader business ethics (for example, Shaw 2005) reveals a far wider array of ethical topics, and other anthropological resources, including many cited earlier, cover broader geographical ground.

Applied anthropology makes a difference, delivering positive engagement with the world. Business anthropology is a positive force as well with, perhaps, more ethical conundrums. If the chapters included in this volume help practitioners navigate their behavior and convey the ethics of our work to our discipline, anthropology, business, and anthropologists in business will benefit.

Notes

1 Ethical perspectives include espionage and clandestine research (Boas 1919; Horowitz 1967; Beals 1969; Fluehr-Lobban 2003), cultural relativism and intervention (Redfield 1953; Herskovits 1973), informed consent and beneficence (Cassell and Wax 1980; Fluehr-Lobban 1994), IRB process (Sundar 2006), national and international ethical practice (Whiteford and Trotter 2008), ethics of military anthropology (Lucas 2009), national security environments (Albro et al. 2011), fieldwork (MacClancy and Fuentes 2013), ethical production of knowledge (Josephides 2015), and principles of professional responsibilities (Plemmons and Barker 2016). Ethical discussions also appear in Denny and Sunderland (2014), Jordan (2013), Ladner (2014), Malefyt and Morais (2012), and Nolan (2013); Urban and Koh discuss ethics in a review of ethnography on corporations (2013, 152); Jordan's statement of ethical principles (2012, 21) and in Ethnographic Praxis in Industry Conference (EPIC) posts such as Hammershøy and Madsen (2012), Treitler and Romagosa (2009), Batteau and Morais (2015). Ethical considerations appear on consumer research (Sunderland and Denny 2007), corporate studies (Cefkin 2009), and netnography (Kozinets 2010).
2 linkedin.com/grp/post/3957220597064303129509487?goback=%2Egmp_3957220.
3 These concerns led to a session, "Business Anthropology Ethics," at the 2012 meeting of the American Anthropological Association and later published (Morais and Malefyt 2014).

References

Albro, Robert, George Marcus, Laura A. McNamara, and Monica Schoch-Sspana, eds. 2011. *Anthropologists in the SecurityScape: Ethics, Practice, and Professional Identity.* Walnut Creek, CA: Left Coast Press.
Appadurai, Arjun. 2015. *Banking on Words: The Failure of Language in the Age of Derivative Finance.* Chicago: University of Chicago Press.
Baba, Marietta L. 2006. Anthropology and Business. In *Encyclopedia of Anthropology*, H. J. Birx, ed., 83–117. Thousand Oaks, CA: Sage Publications.
———. 2012. Anthropology and Business: Influence and Interests. *Journal of Business Anthropology* 1: 20–71.
Batteau, Allen W. and Robert J. Morais. 2015. *Standards of Practice for Ethnography in Industry.* EPIC Perspectives.
Batteau, Allen W. and Bradley J. Trainor. 2014. The Ethical Epistemes of Anthropology and Economics. *Journal of Business Anthropology* 1: 96–115.

Beals, Ralph R. 1969. *Politics of Social Research: An Inquiry into the Ethics and Responsibilities of Social Scientists*. Chicago: Aldine.

Bennett, Jane. 2001. *The Enchantment of Modern Life*. Princeton: Princeton University Press.

Bessant, J. R. and J. Tidd. 2007. *Innovation and Entrepreneurship*. Chichester: John Wiley & Sons.

Blomberg, Jeanette, Jean Giacomi, Andrea Mosher, and Pat Swenton-Wall. 1993. Ethnographic Field Methods and their Relation to Design. In *Participatory Design: Principles and Practices*, Douglas Schuler and Aki Namioki, eds., 123–155. Hillsdale, NJ: Lawrence Erlbaum Associates.

Boas, Franz. 1919. Correspondence: Scientists as Spies. *The Nation* 109, 284.

Bohren, Lenora and Linda Whiteford. 2013. Ethics and Practicing Anthropology – Pragmatic, Practical and Principled. In *A Handbook of Practicing Anthropology*, R. W. Nolan, ed., 291–302. Malden, MA: Wiley-Blackwell.

Borofsky, Robert. 2016. Maybe "Doing No Harm" is Not the Best Way to Help Those Who Helped You. *Anthropology News* 57, 1–2: 29.

Bourdieu, Pierre. 1993. *The Field of Cultural Production*. New York: Columbia University Press.

Brenkert, George. 2008. *Marketing Ethics*. Malden, MA: Blackwell Publishing.

Briody, Elizabeth K. and Tracy Meerwarth Pester. 2015. "Do Some Good" and Other Lessons from Practice for a New AAA Code of Ethics. American Anthropological Association Ethics Blog.

Çalışkan, Koray and Michel Callon. 2009. Economization, Part 1: Shifting Attention from the Economy towards Processes of Economization. *Economy and Society* 38, 2: 369–398.

Callon, Michel, Cécile Méadel, and Vololona Rabeharisoa. 2002. The Economy of Qualities. *Economy and Society* 31, 2: 194–217.

Carrier, James and Peter Luetchford. 2012. *Ethical Consumption: Social Value and Economic Practice*. New York: Berghahn.

Cassell, Joan and Murray L. Wax, eds. 1980. Ethical Problems of Fieldwork. *Social Problems* 27: 259–378.

Cassidy, J. 2002. *DOT.CON: The Greatest Story Ever Sold*. London: Penguin.

Cefkin, Melissa, ed. 2010. *Ethnography and the Corporate Encounter: Reflections on Research in and of Corporations*. New York: Berghahn.

Deane, Phyllis. 1996. Capitalism. In *The Social Science Encyclopedia*, 2nd edn, Adam Kuper and Jessica Kuper, eds., 71–73. London: Routledge.

Deleuze, Gilles and Felix Guattari. 1987. *A Thousand Plateaus: Capitalism and Schizophrenia*. Minnesota: University of Minnesota Press.

Denny, Rita M. and Patricia L. Sunderland, eds. 2014. *Handbook of Anthropology in Business*. Walnut Creek, CA: Left Coast Press.

Ehn, P. 1988. *Work-Oriented Design of Computer Artifacts*. Stockholm: Arbetslivscentrum.

Elliot, Stuart. 2013. Selling Products by Selling Shared Values. *New York Times*, Business Section.

Faier, Lieba and Lisa Rofel. 2014. Ethnographies of Encounter. *Annual Review of Anthropology* 43: 363–377.

Fluehr-Lobban, Carolyn. 1994. Informed Consent in Anthropological Research: We Are Not Exempt. *Human Organization* 53, 1: 1–10.

Fluehr-Lobban, Carolyn, ed. 2003. *Ethics and the Profession of Anthropology: Dialogue for Ethical Conscious Practice*. Walnut Creek, CA: Altamira Press.

Foster, R. 2008. *Coca-Globalization: Following Soft Drinks from New York to New Guinea*. New York: Palgrave Macmillan.

Gadrey, J. 2003. *New Economy, New Myth*. London: Routledge.

Geertz, C. 1973. *The Interpretation of Cultures: Selected Essays.* New York: Basic Books.

Gladwell, Malcolm. 2005. *Blink: The Power of Thinking Without Thinking.* New York: Back Bay Books.

Graeber, David. 2011. Consumption. *Current Anthropology* 52, 4: 489–511.

Greenwood, Susan. 2009. *The Anthropology of Magic.* Oxford: Berg.

Hammershøy, Laura and Thomas Ulrik Madsen. 2012. *Ethics in Business Anthropology.* Ethnographic Praxis in Industry Conference Proceedings, 67–73.

Herskovits, Melville J. 1973. *Cultural Relativism: Perspectives in Cultural Pluralism.* New York: Vintage.

Hollender, Jeffrey and Bill Breen. 2010. *The Responsibility Revolution: How the Next Generation of Businesses Will Win.* New York: John Wiley & Sons.

Holmes, Douglas R. 2014. *Economy of Words: Communicative Imperatives in Central Banks.* Chicago and London: University of Chicago Press.

Horowitz, I. L. 1967. The Search for a Development Ideal: Alternative Models and Their Implications. *Sociological Quarterly* 8: 427–436.

Horst, H. A. and D. Miller (eds.). 2012. *Digital Anthropology.* London: Berg.

Ingold, Tim. 2013. *Making: Anthropology, Archaeology, Art and Architecture.* New York: Routledge.

Ingold, Tim and Elizabeth Hallam. 2007. Creativity and Cultural Improvisation: An Introduction. In *Creativity and Cultural Improvisation*, Elizabeth Hallam and Tim Ingold, eds., 1–24. Oxford: Berg.

Jordan, Ann. 2012. The Importance of Business Anthropology: Its Unique Contributions. *International Journal of Business Anthropology* 1: 15–25.

———. 2013. *Business Anthropology*, 2nd edn. Prospect Heights: Waveland Press.

Josephides, Lisette, ed. 2015. *Knowledge and Ethics in Anthropology: Obligations and Requirements.* Oxford: Bloomsbury.

Kelsey, Anne. 2012. Anthropologists Approve Comprehensive Overhaul of Ethics Code. www.americananthro.org/StayInformed/NewsDetail.aspx?ItemNumber=13054.

Kotler, P. and G. Armstrong. 2016. *Principles of Marketing.* Boston: Pearson.

Kozinets, Robert V. 2010. *Netnography: Doing Ethnographic Research Online.* London: Sage.

Ladner, Sam. 2014. *Practical Ethnography: A Guide to Doing Ethnography in the Private Sector.* Walnut Creek, CA: Left Coast Press.

Latour, Bruno. 2005. *Reassembling the Social: An Introduction to Actor-Network-Theory.* Oxford: Oxford University Press.

Lucas, G. R. 2009. *Anthropologists in Arms: The Ethics of Military Anthropology.* Lanham: Rowman & Littlefield.

MacClancy, Jeremy and Agustin Fuentes, eds. 2013. *Ethics in the Field: Contemporary Challenges.* Oxford: Berghahn.

Malefyt, Timothy de Waal. 2012. Writing Advertising: The Production of Relationships in Historical Review. *Journal of Business Anthropology* 1, 2: 218–239.

———. 2015. Relationship Advertising: How Advertising Can Enhance Social Bonds. *Journal of Business Research* 68: 2494–2502.

———. Forthcoming. Marketing. In *The International Encyclopedia of Anthropology.* London: Wiley-Blackwell.

Malefyt, Timothy de Waal and Robert J. Morais. 2010. Creativity, Brands, and the Ritual Process: Confrontation and Resolution in Advertising Agencies. *Culture and Organization* 16, 4: 333–347.

———. 2012. *Advertising and Anthropology: Ethnographic Practice and Cultural Perspectives.* Oxford: Berg.

Malinowski, Bronislaw. 1954. *Magic, Science and Religion, and Other Essays.* New York: Anchor.

Maslowskaa, Ewa, Edward C. Malthouse, and Tom Collingera. 2016. The Customer Engagement Ecosystem. *Journal of Marketing Management* 32, 5–6: 1–33.

Mauss, Marcel. 1972. *A General Theory of Magic*. Trans. Robert Brain. London: Routledge & Kegan Paul.

McDonough, William and Michael Braungart. 2002. *Cradle to Cradle*. New York: North Point Press.

Miller, Daniel. 1997. *Capitalism: An Ethnographic Approach*. Oxford: Berg.

———. 1998. *A Theory of Shopping*. London: Routledge.

———. 2007. What is a Relationship: Is Kinship Negotiated Experience. *Ethnos* 72, 4: 535–554.

Miyazki, H. 2003. The Temporalities of the Market. *American Anthropologist* 105, 2: 255–265.

Moeran, Brian. 2015. *The Magic of Fashion: Ritual, Commodity, Glamour*. Walnut Creek, CA: Left Coast Press.

Moeran, Brian and Timothy de Waal Malefyt. 2016. *Performing Magical Capitalism*. EPIC Perspectives. www.epicpeople.org/performing-magical-capitalism/ (accessed February 13, 2017).

Morais, Robert J. and Timothy de Waal Malefyt, eds. 2014. Special Issue #1: Ethics. *Journal of Business Anthropology*.

Murphy, Patrick E. and John F. Sherry, eds. 2014. *Marketing and the Common Good: Essays from Notre Dame on Societal Impact*. Oxford: Routledge.

Nader, Laura. 1974. Up the Anthropologist: Perspectives Gained by Studying Up. In *Reinventing Anthropology*, D. Hymes, ed., 284–311. New York: Vintage Books.

Nolan, Riall, ed. 2013. *A Handbook of Practicing Anthropology*. Malden: Wiley-Blackwell.

Peterson, Mark. 2012. *Sustainable Enterprise: A Macromarketing Approach*. New York: Sage.

Plemmons, Dena and Alex W. Barker, eds. 2016. *Anthropological Ethics in Context: An Ongoing Dialog*. Walnut Creek, CA: Left Coast Press.

Redfield, Robert. 1953. *The Primitive World and Its Transformations*. Ithaca: Cornell University Press.

Rothstein, Edward. 2006. Protection for Indian Patrimony that Leads to a Paradox. *New York Times*. www.nytimes.com/2006/03/29/arts/artsspecial/29rothstein.html (accessed March 29, 2016).

Savitz, Andrew and Karl Weber. 2007. The Sustainability Sweet Spot: How to Achieve Long Term Business Success. *Environmental Quality Management* 17–28.

Shaw, William H. 2005. *Business Ethics*, 5th edn. Belmont, CA: Wadsworth.

Sherry, John F. Jr. 2008. The Ethnographer's Apprentice: Trying Consumer Culture from the Outside. *Journal of Business Ethics* 80: 85–95.

Sinatti, Giulia. 2015. *Anthropologist? You're Hired!* http://standplaatswereld.nl/2015/12/03/anthropologist-youre-hired/ (accessed February 23, 2017).

Smith, N. Craig. 2003. Corporate Social Responsibility: Not Whether, but How? *California Management Review* 45, 4: 52–76.

Strathern, Marilyn. 1987. The Limits of Auto-Anthropology. In *Anthropology at Home*, A. Jackson, ed., 16–37. London: Tavistock Publishers.

Sundar, N. 2006. Missing the Ethical Wood for the Bureaucratic Trees. *American Ethnologist* 33: 535–537.

Sunderland, Patricia L. and Rita M. Denny. 2007. *Doing Anthropology in Consumer Research*. Walnut Creek, CA: Left Coast Press.

Thrift, Nigel. 1997. The Rise of Soft Capitalism. In *Cultural Values*, 1(1): 29–57.

———. 2005. *Knowing Capitalism*. London: Sage.

———. 2006. Re-Inventing Invention: New Tendencies in Capitalist Commodification. *Economy and Society* 35, 2: 279–306.

Tidd, J. and J. Bessant. 2009. *Managing Innovation: Integrating Technological, Market, and Organizational Change.* Chichester: John Wiley & Sons.

Treitler, Inga and Frank Romagosa. 2009. *Ethnographer Diasporas and Emergent Communities of Practice: The Place for a 21st Century Ethics in Business Ethnography Today.* Ethnographic Praxis in Industry Conference Proceedings.

Tsing, A. 2005. *Friction: An Ethnography of Global Connection.* Princeton: Princeton University Press.

Urban, Greg and Kyung-Nan Koh. 2013. Ethnographic Research on Modern Business Corporations. *Annual Review of Anthropology* 42: 139–158.

Von Hippel, Eric. 2005. *Democratizing Innovation.* Cambridge, MA: MIT Press.

Wasson, Christina. 2000. Ethnography in the Field of Design. *Human Organization* 59, 4: 377–388.

Wax, Murray and Rosalie Wax. 1963. The Notion of Magic. *Current Anthropology* 4, 5: 495–518.

Whiteford, Linda and Robert T. Trotter II. 2008. *Ethics for Anthropological Research and Practice.* Long Grove, IL: Waveland Press.

Zaloom, Caitlin. 2006. *Out of the Pits: Traders and Technology from Chicago to London.* Chicago: University of Chicago Press.

2

REDESIGNING ANTHROPOLOGY'S ETHICAL PRINCIPLES TO ALIGN WITH ANTHROPOLOGICAL PRACTICE

Elizabeth K. Briody and Tracy Meerwarth Pester

Introduction

Ethics is a contested topic within the American Anthropological Association (AAA) and has been for decades. The connection of ethics to the work anthropologists do is one important reason. Thirty years ago, the small group of practicing or professional anthropologists was criticized for the positions it held (outside academia) and the job functions that it performed (many of which did not involve research). Because practitioners did not fit the mold of their academic colleagues, they often encountered disparagement and exclusion whether intentional or not. At times members of this group were even considered unethical for working in the private sector.

Fast forward to today, where that small group has since blossomed into a *force majeure*. Increasing numbers of graduating students, especially M.A. graduates, are working in the private, non-profit, and government sectors and many professors are engaged in consulting with organizations and communities. The disciplinary split between theory and practice, and academic and professional anthropologists, now appears on the mend. The labeling of who is, or is not "ethical," seems to have dissipated and in its place has emerged a healthy engagement across that once rigid boundary line. Moreover, efforts to involve practitioners in AAA governance have been largely successful; many serve in AAA and section committee leadership positions. Nevertheless, it takes time for organizations and institutions to change. Much more needs to be done to acknowledge and celebrate practice as a growing and contributing segment of the field.

We examine the intersection of anthropological practice and AAA ethical principles based on our work in the private sector at General Motors (GM). We define *anthropological practice* as work in which anthropological skills and knowledge is used to identify and solve human problems; it is often viewed as a contrast to work in college/university teaching and/or research positions. Our chapter is a friendly test of the 2012 AAA Principles of Professional Responsibility (PPR) from a practitioner standpoint, and an opportunity to explore its boundaries. (The AAA website houses the AAA Statement on Ethics under which is subsumed the PPR. The AAA website alternately uses the terminology AAA Code of Ethics [www.american-anthro.org/ParticipateAndAdvocate/Content.aspx?ItemNumber=1895, accessed September 2, 2016].)

Our goal is to assess the PPR, discovering where the fit works well for practitioners, and where there are weaknesses or gaps. Because we were *researchers* at GM R&D, an industrial research laboratory, there was alignment with the AAA ethical principles. (Others engaged in anthropological practice should examine these principles based on their own work roles, which may not include research.)

We begin by discussing ethics and practice generally. Next, we describe the GM code of conduct and the AAA PPR. Third, we discuss four of the projects on which we worked while employed at GM. We examine these projects in relation to two different ethical systems – one through our employer and one through our professional association. Fourth, we suggest new avenues for the next iteration of the AAA statement of ethics. Finally, we outline some strategies for strengthening collaboration and understanding between practitioners and their academic counterparts. In that process, we propose realigning anthropology's focus to be more holistic and inclusive of *all* kinds of anthropological work.

Ethics as Process

AAA Past President Monica Heller writes: "our ideas about something (anthropological ethics, in this case) are always developed in interaction with other people and in connection to our experiences" (Heller 2016, 231). The resulting ethics statement "does not get fixed forever in a unified interpretive process" since it is a "living document" (Heller 2016, 232). Barker and Plemmons (2016, 212) similarly indicate that the PPR is "explicitly intended to be dynamic and subject to regular reconsideration and revisions." Indeed, the AAA has been engaged in specifying, and subsequently revising, its code of ethics at least since 1967. Different now is that it is no longer referred to as a code but rather a statement of ethics. The value in a set of principles or guidelines is that they "help anthropologists think and act when presented with ethical dilemmas" (Dominguez 2016, 20).

Many anthropology associations (e.g., Society for Applied Anthropology, Society for American Archaeology) – have developed ethical statements or standards of conduct (Whiteford and Trotter 2008) to assist their members. Ethical guidelines are designed to aid members in their work. Members may consult such guidelines to discern and discuss an issue, decide on a course of action, teach, or make a judgment about an ethical situation. Recent blog posts (e.g., http://ethics.americananthro.org//) and publications highlight ethical dilemmas and help to sharpen our understanding of the choices faced (LeCompte and Schensul 2015; Plemmons and Barker 2016).

Anthropological Practice

An important dimension of anthropology's coming of age is the rise and salience of anthropological practice. The National Association for the Practice of Anthropology (NAPA), a section of the AAA, describes the role of *practicing or professional anthropologists*:

> to understand and help people around the world … often by working in tandem with community leaders, non-profit institutions, companies, governments and other stakeholders, to understand, create, implement, and evaluate programs, products, services, policies, laws, and organizations.
>
> *(http://practicinganthropology.org/practicing-anthro/, accessed August 20, 2016)*

Results from AAA's 2016 member survey indicate that 19% of employed respondents work outside of higher education (Ginsberg 2016, 1) in non-profit organizations (21%), government agencies (20%), private for-profit firms (17%), non-academic research (14%), or other (7%) or are self-employed (20%) (Ginsberg 2016, 3–4). While two-thirds of these respondents had Ph.D.s, most practitioners exit the university today with a master's degree (Fiske et al. 2010). The Consortium of Practicing and Applied Anthropology (https://copaainfo.org/programs/) now counts 36 academic departments as members (Toni Copeland, personal communication, August 21, 2016).

Coping with Change

Yet, these changes have not come without a cost. Certainly academia faces important challenges with fewer and fewer full-time, tenure-track faculty positions in anthropology. Additionally, many programs have not responded to student requests for practical career skills and exposure to applied work – in part because faculty often have "little experience or interest in applied work" (Briody and Nolan 2013, 376). This pattern carries over into "discussion of the ethics of practice [which] tends to be hampered by the relative lack of understanding of and experience with what practitioners actually do on a daily basis" (Nolan 2013, 3).

Practitioners also have borne some costs – involving ethics. One of us (Briody) graduated in 1985 with a Ph.D. and began to present results of her research at anthropology conferences and in university settings. Some attendees were curious about what an anthropologist did at GM – a question that arose repeatedly during her GM career from 1985 to 2009. Others either disparaged or voiced inaccurate assumptions about her work. She faced various allegations of unethical behavior as in these suggestive examples:

- *Student question:* "How can you work at a corporation (GM) that destroys the environment?"
- *Professor's assertion:* "You have to publish what *they* (GM) tell you to publish."

She quickly absorbed a view held by many academically-based anthropologists and their students at that time that private sector work was tainted. Practitioner research did not align with the principles of academic freedom. It was problem-oriented rather than theoretically driven (Nolan 2013, 394), and therefore not considered as scholarship-worthy. And, those studying corporate culture were reminded that they often overlooked a corporation's tendency to give "primacy to profits regardless of human costs" (Nash and Kirsch 1994). Cassell and Jacobs (1987, 1) suggest one explanation of this phenomenon: "on occasion, the concept of 'ethics' is used as a weapon: my beliefs differ from yours, therefore *you* are unethical."

A lot has changed since the start of the 21st century when one of us (Meerwarth Pester) began her career, working at GM from 2000 to 2007. In many locations near applied programs, the lines between academics and practitioners are blurring and anthropology's local culture has evolved to become more inclusive. The number of new graduates, shifting employment patterns, and availability of more applied anthropology programs illustrate the transition of an academically based discipline to a mixed model composed of academic and professional anthropologists. The convergence of these three factors has put pressure on the former to reach out beyond the classroom to connect their students with the different worlds of work. Additionally, many practitioners have been enticed to reach into the classroom to offer their expertise and advice about how to apply anthropology in different work settings. All of this is very good news, given that the U.S. Bureau of Labor Statistics expects that employment for both anthropologists and archaeologists will increase by 21% between 2010 and 2020, a faster rate than the average for all occupations (www.bls.gov/ooh/life-physical-and-social-science/anthropologists-and-archeologists.htm).

Yet, much more needs to be done to make anthropology a welcoming place for those engaged in a myriad of job functions that apply their knowledge and skills in innovative ways. We argue that the time for ignorance is over:

> A faculty career that begins with a PhD advisor who guides the student into the profession, leading first to a postdoc or tenure-track assistant professor position, and then tenure in a smooth and linear way is a mythical model that does not offer practical guidance for the real career paths of anthropology PhDs.
>
> *(Rudd et al. 2008, 25)*

Graduate programs that do not help "prepare students for a range of occupational sectors are behaving irresponsibly" (Bennett and Fiske 2013, 313). Moreover, the time for disrespect – that only those "not good enough" for an academic appointment seek practice work (Nolan 2013, 394; Bartlo 2012, 24) – is over. Some anthropologists have a strong preference for practice over academic work, and are good at it. We see that anthropology has been embroiled in ethical issues with itself, with many resisting this wave of change within the field. Denigrating practitioners' work is neither professional nor collegial. Students and professors would benefit from a deeper knowledge of the ethics of practice, along with exposure to alternative models of anthropological work.

Ethics at Work

Practitioners have complex relationships with their work organizations involving peers and those in their chain of command, and often, external publics such as suppliers, customers, partners, regulatory agencies, policymaking bodies, and the media. Their job responsibilities not only require attention to the rules, processes, values, and expectations for conduct as specified by their employer, but also those of other organizational entities or communities with which they interface. "Dual-identity professionals," such as practitioners working for a corporation, must deal with multiple ethical codes in their work; indeed, the work of practitioners is "inextricable from a variety of other goals and professional contexts" (Albro 2009, 17). Another difficulty from a practitioner standpoint has been that the variation and complexity of anthropological work and careers continue to evolve without being fully connected with or captured by past AAA ethical codes (Tashima et al. 2008). We now describe the two ethical codes pertinent to our work as practitioners.

GM's Code of Conduct

Many organizations specify in writing a code of conduct for employees. Typically the code of conduct is linked thematically with the organization's values and sometimes with the mission and vision. GM has a corporate code of conduct called *Winning with Integrity*. It consists of four broad categories (see Figure 2.1).

This code of conduct pertains first to the behavior of individual employees who are expected to be aware of and understand corporate rules generally, and to act "with integrity." However, it extends beyond individual choice to policies, procedures, and expectations evident within departmental, unit, and corporate arenas. Fair treatment and respect, equal employment opportunity, and accuracy of GM information and use of GM property are important aspects of workplace integrity. Safety as well as protection and use of GM information and resources are other dimensions of workplace integrity that matter enormously at GM. Avoiding conflicts of interest, insider trading, and improper payments or gifts to or from government officials globally are among the markers of integrity in the market place. Supporting GM's environmental principles is one of the key facts of integrity toward the environment.

AAA's Principles of Professional Responsibility

The preamble to the current version of the AAA's Statement of Ethics frames anthropological work in terms of both research and practice. It also points to goals such as knowledge dissemination and the use of knowledge for solving human problems. Seven principles "intended to foster discussion, guide anthropologists in making responsible decisions, and educate" are described (see Figure 2.2), and supplementary resources and reference documents provided.

1. Personal integrity
   - Understanding the rules
   - Acting with integrity when the rules seem unclear
2. Integrity in the workplace
   - Fair treatment and respect
   - Equal employment opportunity
   - Speak up for safety
   - Conflicts of interest
   - Protection and use of GM information and resources
3. Integrity in the marketplace
   - Giving to and receiving from third parties (including government officials)
   - Fair competition
   - Insider trading
   - Export compliance
4. Integrity toward the environment
   - GM environmental principles
   - Dangerous goods in transportation

FIGURE 2.1 GM Winning with Integrity, GM's Code of Conduct (January 2016).

Source: www.gm.com/content/dam/gm/en_us/english/Group4/InvestorsPDF Documents/WWI.pdf, accessed August 21, 2016.

1. Do no harm
2. Be open and honest regarding your work
3. Obtain informed consent and necessary permissions
4. Weigh competing ethical obligations due collaborators and affected parties
5. Make your results accessible
6. Protect and preserve your records
7. Maintain respectful and ethical professional relationships.

FIGURE 2.2 AAA Principles of Professional Responsibility (November 1, 2012).

Source: http://ethics.americananthro.org/category/statement/, accessed August 20, 2016.

The PPR emphasizes a primary ethical obligation to avoid harm and weigh the potential consequences of anthropological research. It supports transparency regarding the goals, methods, and dissemination of the work, as well as informed consent. It describes anthropologists' obligation to figure out the appropriate balance when trying to reconcile different ethical standards held by study participants, colleagues, students, funders, and employers. Protecting and preserving one's data is considered an ethical responsibility. Professional relationships should be respectful such as when mentoring students, supervising staff, or working with clients, and ethical in terms of scientific and scholarly conduct.

Aligning GM Projects with Two Different Ethics Statements

In this section we summarize four of our applied research projects. We examine our actions on these projects in light of selected principles found in the AAA's 2012 PPR and GM's 2016 Winning with Integrity code of conduct. We assess the usefulness of these principles in guiding our work.

Project 1: Decision Paralysis on a GM Global Vehicle Program

GM was seeking ways of becoming a more competitive global firm. It was trying to develop global architectures for vehicles, share components, and reduce costs. It was believed that economies of scale would result because there would be less engineering and fewer expensive dies used in making parts. This project involved an examination of the work and interactions among three GM engineering organizations charged with developing a car that could be sold in several global markets.

Anthropological Role

Briody's role involved conducting a study and offering consulting advice on this innovative approach to product development. She followed key guidelines to foster trust and rapport with members of the global vehicle program and worked with them on problem solving throughout all project phases:

- Maintaining study participant confidentiality.
- Evaluating data as neutrally and objectively as possible.
- Raising awareness of the findings through discussions, presentations, and internal reports.
- Offering recommendations to improve decision making and governance.
- Collaborating with program leaders on possible mitigation strategies in workshops.

Cultural Issues

As the paradigm for global vehicle work emerged, a new corporate emphasis on collaboration and partnership integration was introduced which ran counter to the autonomous culture in place in the three engineering units. Little agreement across organizational boundaries was reached on the multitude of decisions that were supposed to be made; unit work practices, assumptions, goals, and expectations were so different. Moreover, the program manager did not have the necessary authority to make the hard calls when disagreements arose. As a result, no one was able to work collaboratively and productively across organizational boundaries on a consistent basis – despite valiant efforts – because employee allegiances were to their home units. The home units paid their salaries and determined their career path. Consequently, decision paralysis set in, characterized by such factors as the amount of conflict, delays, rework, cost in labor hours, lack of an agreed-upon way of making decisions, and intervention in program decisions by corporate leaders.

Outcomes

When the program ultimately failed, with a loss of 2.2 million cars, careers were damaged – particularly of those in senior positions. Some retired, some left the firm, and some stayed but no longer advanced up the career ladder. However, the program manager role and the structure of global product programs changed significantly after our discussions with corporate leaders, internal presentations, and publication of technical reports. On later vehicle programs, program managers had increased authority over decision making and resources. Reporting relationships were streamlined when vehicle operations became global, leading to improved program effectiveness and efficiency.

Ethics

AAA Principle 7 (Maintaining Respectful and Ethical Professional Relationships) and GM Principle 2 (Integrity in the Workplace – Fair Treatment and Respect) were consistent with the behavior and approach Briody tried to exhibit toward study participants who were also GM colleagues (see Table 2.1).

AAA Principle 1 (Do No Harm) did not provide sufficient guidance for this project (see Table 2.1). Some "harm" came to those vehicle program leaders who were put in an untenable situation without the proper organizational structure and support. Indeed, the study made explicit the structural, ideological, and behavioral weaknesses contributing to the program's failure. AAA Principle 1 should acknowledge that harm – job loss, for example – can and does happen, despite anthropologists' best intentions and attention to best practices. Anthropologists may not be able to change belief systems about perceptions of failure, including those who are the scapegoats. However, they may be able to temper such beliefs by directing attention to the actual culprit – in this case, the lack of alignment between organizational goals and structure. Had that alignment existed, and the appropriate incentives been established, those working on this vehicle program would have at least had a shot at being successful.

Project 2: Productivity Issues Due to GM R&D Workspace

GM was planning to renovate parts of its Warren, Michigan R&D facility to ensure that its offices, laboratory spaces, and equipment were updated. Three constraints were expected to affect the renovation. First, a cap on costs would limit how much remodeling could be done. Second, the R&D complex would be subject to the

TABLE 2.1 Exploration of Ethical Principles by Ethics Code and GM Projects

	Principles Meeting or Exceeding Practitioner Expectations	Principles Falling Short of Practitioner Expectations
1. Decision Paralysis on a GM Global Vehicle Program	• AAA 7 • GM 2	• AAA 1
2. Productivity Issues due to GM R&D Workspace	• AAA 7 • GM 1 • GM 2	• AAA 1 • AAA 2 • AAA 4 • GM 1
3. Blaming Behavior in a GM Truck Plant	• AAA 2 • GM 1	• AAA 1 • AAA 3
4. Collaboration as GM's Ideal Plant Culture	• AAA 2 • AAA 5 • GM 1	• AAA 1 • AAA 2

rules and regulations of the National Register of Historic Places because of its historic designation. A third constraint, leadership beliefs, also played a role in the planning. The VP appointed a group to conduct a literature review of researcher workspace. That group concluded that individual offices were the most suitable for researcher workspace.

Anthropological Role

The VP's direct report, the senior executive in charge of R&D, called in GM's anthropologists. The assignment involved conducting two sequential field studies to identify the most appropriate workspace for GM's researchers in the United States and worldwide. In the exploratory study, our team of six anthropologists explored many aspects of R&D researcher work through observations, interviews, photographs, and validation sessions (presentations with discussion) on the preliminary findings. In the confirmatory study, we included work diaries, photographs, video footage, and large-forum discussions with interns. Researchers working at R&D were aware the study was going on and typically were willing to participate. Establishing rapport was easy because we worked in the same complex and knew each other – at least by sight. The potential to affect how R&D researchers did their work made explaining the study straightforward.

Cultural Issues

All three studies demonstrated both the overwhelming preference among researchers for private offices and the detrimental effects of cubicles on their productivity. However, the executives preferred cubicles for their "look and feel" and cubicles were far cheaper than offices per square foot. The VP, who had considerable influence over the renovation budget, repeatedly expressed his preference for cubicles. He believed cubicles encouraged researcher collaboration, despite our evidence to the contrary. It was at the VP's request that the three successive studies were carried out because, one R&D colleague joked to us, "He didn't like the answers he was getting."

Outcomes

The results of our first study, consistent with the early literature study, revealed that individual offices were the appropriate workspace for researchers. This study yielded a cultural model of R&D workspace that underscored researcher values of productivity and pragmatism. The second anthropological study produced findings consistent with the first, even controlling for research site – Warren and Bangalore – and cohort differences. As the conclusions of each successive study were released, the VP expressed increasing annoyance and dissatisfaction. Our relationship with the VP was affected; his behavior repeatedly indicated an inability to move beyond his initial preference for cubicles. None of us wanted to be at odds with a senior leader, much less someone in our own chain of command. Ultimately, we ended up working solely with the senior executive and his staff who reported to the VP. These individuals were convinced of the validity and reliability of our studies. Their interventions based on our work led to the construction of single offices in the newly renovated area of the Warren complex. The executive at the Bangalore R&D site used our data to justify building individual offices as his site was expanding.

Ethics

Our actions were consistent with GM Principle 1 (Acting with Integrity When the Rules Seem Unclear) and GM Principle 2 (Integrity in the Workplace – Accuracy of GM Information) as evident in Table 2.1. We recognized the conflict with our VP and understood the potential difficulties of arguing for a position he did not support. However, we chose to present what we had learned as accurately as possible, thereby upholding GM's code of conduct. We also attended to AAA Principle 7 (Maintaining Respectful and Ethical Professional Relationships) even though our relationship with the VP was strained.

Table 2.1 also shows that we followed AAA Principle 2 (Be Open and Honest Regarding Your Work) and AAA Principle 4 (Balance Competing Ethical Obligations due Collaborators and Affected Parties) to the extent possible. However, both principles fell short of our expectations. No acknowledgment of the risks anthropologists may face (e.g., with a sponsor) was included. We found the portrayal of the two principles imbalanced. Disagreeing with a VP has a cost: it could have been, and some believe it was, a career-limiting move for our team. It would have been helpful to have some "reality check" as part of the principle on how sponsors, study participants, or other key stakeholders might respond. AAA Principle 4 also references AAA Principle 1 when it states: "Anthropologists must often make difficult decisions among competing ethical obligations while recognizing their obligation to do no harm." Our team was brought in to advise GM management on a multi-million dollar renovation. Our work was far more than doing no harm; it was about taking a stand based on the evidence. Finally, GM Principle 1 (Personal Integrity – Acting with Integrity When the Rules Seem Unclear), like AAA Principle 4, also offers no guidance in negotiating the muddy waters of power and hierarchy.

Project 3: Blaming Behavior in GM Truck Plant

One of us (Briody) requested an opportunity to conduct a plant cultural study. The study occurred at a time when the U.S. quality movement was in full swing and vehicle quality was becoming an increasingly important marketplace differentiator. Managers in the truck plant were trained in a quality program. Plant publications contained interviews with plant leaders on quality. Signs emphasizing quality, along with plant audit scores, were posted. Team-based problem solving on quality issues was inaugurated. Thus, quality became the stated plant goal.

Anthropological Role

Fieldwork began with no preconceived notions of what cultural themes or patterns would be found. Briody's mentor introduced her to many employees who served as a foundation for her network. Establishing rapport, building trust, and maintaining confidentiality were relatively easy. Her conversations with hourly employees and their supervisors in assembly, material handling, and repair occurred as people were working. She spent time at individual workstations along the assembly line, as well as on jitneys (as a passenger) used by material handlers to track down parts.

Cultural Issues

Briody's analysis of the ethnographic data revealed an endemic practice of blaming. Not only were plant employees seven times more likely to blame than praise each other, but also the blaming was patterned. Employees blamed those on the previous shift, not their own shift, and those upstream, but not downstream from them, or in their own work area. Employees also engaged in blame-avoidance behaviors, such as hoarding parts or trading parts, because they were fearful of being held accountable for parts that ran short. While employees repeatedly indicated they wanted to produce quality work, they were unable to do so because of the incessant demand to meet efficiency and production quotas.

Outcomes

Three unexpected reactions to the release of Briody's internal technical report occurred. First, the plant manager spurned the findings and recommendations during a meeting with her and her supervisor. Despite the fact that the plant manager had sponsored the project, assigned Briody a mentor, and interacted with her on multiple occasions, he avoided all discussion of product quality and stridently asserted his plant's strengths (in logistics related to vehicle delivery).

Second, a new plant manager at a nearby plant called Briody after receiving a copy of the report and asked if the plant was his plant. Briody explained that it was not. The plant manager spoke at length about the quality problems and blaming that were rampant in his plant. Briody insisted that the study was not done in his plant because he would have known about it. Nevertheless, he continued to declare that the study must have been done in his plant because the results were so accurate. Exasperated 30 minutes later, Briody told him, "It could not have been your plant because I don't do covert research." That remark seemed to mean something. He thanked her for her time and hung up.

A third unexpected and positive outcome was the study's review at a GM Board meeting. It raised the visibility of anthropology and definitively introduced the notion of culture into the highest ranks of the corporation.

Ethics

GM Principle 1 (Personal Integrity – Understanding the Rules) guided Briody's approach (see Table 2.1). The common practice included working through her own management to get permission to do the study, and then explaining to plant employees what she was doing in relatively simple terms:

- Introductions: "My name is Elizabeth and I work at the Tech Center in Warren."
- Project description: "I am trying to learn about the plant's culture – how this plant works."
- Confidentiality: "I won't attach your name to what you tell me."

Briody's approach was also consistent with AAA Principle 2 (Be Open and Honest Regarding Your Work) both in terms of how she approached study participants, and how she addressed the concerns of the new plant manager at a nearby plant.

On the other hand, Table 2.1 shows that AAA Principle 3 (Obtain Informed Consent and Necessary Permissions) was highly problematic because of its insistence on the range of topics to be covered, including:

> the research goals, methods, funding sources or sponsors, expected outcomes, anticipated impacts of the research, and the rights and responsibilities of research participants ... the possible impacts of participation, and [the fact that] confidentiality may be compromised or outcomes may differ from those anticipated.

The sheer number of plant employees, unrelenting work pace, and accepted plant practice of letting employees know a project was underway made satisfying the numerous formal requirements of informed consent impractical and countercultural. Providing the breadth and depth of information required in the principle would likely have been viewed with suspicion and rejection, thereby compromising the gathering of valid field data. We also believe it is disingenuous to state that it is the "quality of the consent, not its format, which is relevant" when there is a clear expectation to use a lengthy and formal consent process. In addition, AAA Principle 1 (Do No Harm) also comes into play. The larger goal behind any applied research project is not to be passive, but rather to engage, advise, propose change, and often, participate in the change process. Briody's report offered specific recommendations to help address, not just study, plant cultural issues.

Project 4: Collaboration as GM's Ideal Plant Culture

GM's automotive industry had lost ground to Asian competitors who first spearheaded quality improvements and then became skilled at reducing waste and cost, reducing lead time to market, and learning effectively from their mistakes. Despite dramatic improvements in product quality over the last few decades, the erosion of GM's customer base persisted, and GM's relationships with the UAW International Union continued to be contentious. The purpose of this project was to identify and implement an ideal work culture in GM's newest plant, and develop interventions to help spread that ideal culture to other GM manufacturing facilities in the United States.

Anthropological Role

Our six-member research team was involved in collecting ethnographic data in three assembly plants and one stamping plant. We sought out hourly, salaried, and executive employees and representatives of the UAW in various locations (e.g., workstations, offices, iteam/break rooms, cafeteria, union locals). The leadership team of GM's newest plant, composed of both GM and local UAW leaders repeatedly requested help from us, seeking insights, solutions, and best practices that could be put in place. During the project, we held 35 validation sessions during which attendees were asked to challenge, confirm, and/or expand upon our results. As the project moved into the application phase, GM manufacturing gained both active consultation and proactive action including the development of 10 tools (or interventions) to help in the establishment of an ideal plant culture in the new plant.

Cultural Issues

Strong, healthy collaborative relationships were the missing ingredient in helping GM to achieve its business goals. Employees indicated their hopes for the future by moving from the "old way" in which relationships were divisive and exclusionary and caused by a directive and authoritarian management style, to a new or ideal way that supported and valued employee expertise and problem-solving abilities. The leadership team, local UAW leaders, and senior GM manufacturing executives accepted the findings and recommendations. After the 10 tools had been tested in several plants, senior GM manufacturing leaders approached the UAW International with plans for a formal evaluation of the tools. Problems surfaced when the UAW International, and their representatives in selected plants, argued against adoption of the research results and tools because the work was not carried out under the umbrella of the GM management–UAW International structure.

Outcomes

The project became politicized because it was perceived as a management-only initiative. Moreover, the GM–UAW negotiations were approaching – a time when positions harden and cooperation can be elusive. However, the tools and the cultural model on which they were based successfully contributed to a "culture of collaboration" at the new GM plant at Lansing Delta Township in Michigan, which has gone on to become the best manufacturing facility in GM. The approach, change model, and tools have since been applied successfully in several projects in the health industry.

Ethics

AAA Principle 5 (Make Your Results Accessible) and AAA Principle 2 (Be Open and Honest Regarding Your Work) were helpful in guiding our project (see Table 2.1). Transparency about project goals occurred alongside rapport building. We also shared what we were learning as quickly as possible. Our validation sessions engaged plant and senior manufacturing leaders with us in dialogue about our results, recommendations, and interventions. Later, we were able to make the tools publicly available and publish the results in our AAA-award-winning book *Transforming Culture*. GM Principle 1 (Personal Integrity – Understanding the Rules) also played a role in our orientation to the project. Part of "Understanding the Rules" for any GM researcher includes the creation of an implementation component. The development, testing, and distribution of the tools fulfilled that purpose.

Two other AAA Principles fell short of our expectations (see Table 2.1). With respect to AAA Principle 2 (Be Open and Honest Regarding Your Work), all stakeholders may not be known *a priori* (e.g., at project launch, at a later stage), and some constituency may be powerful enough to derail the work. Despite being transparent throughout the project, our research team, GM plant management, GM senior manufacturing management, and the UAW locals were blindsided by the UAW International's reaction. This principle should recognize such situations can and do arise – particularly during the application phase of a project. Our criticism of AAA Principle 1 (Do No Harm) as outlined in Project 3 applies to Project 4 as well.

Our team was invited to help with the start-up of a new GM plant. Consequently, our role entailed far more than the "promotion of well-being, social critique or advocacy" because it involved active participation and decision making as both organizational insiders and consultants.

New Horizons on Anthropology's Ethics

We now turn our attention to the relevance and usefulness of the AAA PPR for anthropological practice. Filling in what practitioners would consider weaknesses or gaps would be extraordinarily helpful. We see three ways in which the 2012 PPR could expand to accommodate anthropological practice. The three concepts we are proposing, fundamental to applied research or anthropological practice, are intricately interwoven with one another. Without their inclusion, the AAA code does not adequately guide the work of the fastest growing segment of the field.

Recognize that Practitioners May Adhere to Multiple Ethics Codes

First, practitioners have dual or even multiple identities when it comes to ethics. We typically tried to use both the GM code of conduct and the PPR as our guides. While using multiple ethics codes often happens in the field in the "background" of practitioner work, not much has been written about the experience of this integration, its benefits, and challenges.

The specific AAA and GM principles had important value for us as practitioners. Separately, the two sets provided different perspectives on work and emphasized different domains. The AAA statement is heavily research-oriented as indicated in the 65 occurrences of the word "research" and its cognates (e.g., "research participants," "researcher"). The GM code is framed in terms of the concept of integrity regarding all aspects of employee behavior. It is particularly concerned with inappropriate actions of individuals, including those that are illegal and have a negative impact on corporate activities and image, and adherence to legislative and regulatory mandates.

We were fortunate to have two distinct ethical statements on which to rely. When we viewed them together, we understood them as examples of point–counterpoint. Each complemented the other with the potential to offer specific guidance that the other code did not have. When the codes sent different messages, we were able to make comparisons and use the differing aspects to inform our decisions. Hardest was when one or both statements sent no particular message and we had to sort the issues out without formal guidance.

We became adept at comparing the two ethics statements when discussing any ethical challenge and then reaching a decision. The AAA principles would be improved significantly by acknowledging that they may not stand alone, but rather alongside employer or other codes, and that all contribute to a more mindful practice. This kind of formal acknowledgment is perhaps best suited for the preamble.

Include Practice Prominently in the AAA PPR

Second, the PPR only minimally includes practice, and largely in the preamble. One indicator is that there is no mention of the word "application" and but one occurrence of the word "applied." This lack of attention to practice is remarkable both because of the demographic shifts to practice work and the ongoing interest expressed by students in practice careers and experiences, and because application can serve as a feedback loop to theory.

The PPR is not practice-friendly. It virtually ignores the kinds of issues with which practitioners grapple on a regular basis. The "stages of anthropological practice," for example, never extend beyond "dissemination of the results." There is no discussion of developing recommendations, working with stakeholders collaboratively, implementing interventions, or evaluating how well the interventions worked. This gap is problematic because during implementation, the focus is no longer on "research participants," but on stakeholders "who have greater impact and control over what is being done in their communities" (van Willigen and Kedia 2005, 349). Stakeholder buy-in is essential; without it, the implementation effort will surely fail. The PPR fails to recognize that application should be addressed as carefully and cogently as basic research.

Moreover, the current AAA statement shies away from change. There appears to be a reticence to influence or alter the culture of a particular group, organization, or community. Only four occurrences of the word "change" appear in the PPR and none of them refers to changes in the culture of the group involved. There is no discussion of the notions of "planned change," "organizational-culture change," "cultural transformation," or "community change" that are tied to applied research or practice work – even though applied research and action anthropology have been part of the discipline for decades. Indeed, change is part of practitioners' cultural model of the work they do. We conclude that change is not a priority within the PPR, even if it enhances or improves the current state. Similarly, specific interventions to address an issue or improve the effectiveness of an organization or community are neither fully comprehended nor valued within the statement.

This omission is surprising. An "interventionist ethic" is part of many anthropologists' "professional identity and sense of responsibility" (Katz 2012, 204). When employed in the public, private, or non-profit sectors, job performance is largely a function of problem solving to change something (e.g., work practices, policies). Practitioners are actively engaged in what might become some aspect of the future state. Deadlines are pending on delivering completed assignments and results, which will have an impact on decisions, strategy, direction, and a host of other factors that can make the former cultural processes and practices obsolete. Moreover, new and urgent issues arise that need to be tackled. Practitioners are part of ongoing change processes within an organization or community. They are also professionals whose work is designed to foster change. Professional anthropologists typically work on implementation of agreed-upon changes. (Other practitioners whose job functions do not include research, such as consultants, administrators, or cross-cultural trainers, also operate within a paradigm of change.) Consequently, they are not only in the throes of change, but leading it away from the status quo. AAA's PPR should provide guidelines for basic research, *and* applied research and practice in each ethical principle.

Do Some Good

Third, the current PPR is preoccupied with the concept of harm. We count nine occurrences of the word "harm" or its cognates (e.g., "harmful"). This overwhelming emphasis on "harm" without a corresponding emphasis on "help" is unexpectedly imbalanced. It does not reflect fully what practitioners do and how they approach their work.

Anthropology's new ethical horizon should move beyond the Do No Harm principle to Do Some Good. Professional anthropologists routinely evaluate their options between these two poles as they settle on a course of action. However, their sights are set 180 degrees away from deliberately and intentionally causing any injury or damage. Much of their inspiration springs from a desire to make a difference. They are working inside some cultural system – whether as employees, contractors, consultants, or even volunteers – and trying to make it better in some way. While we realize the preference of some anthropologists to "work as outside critic" (Rylko-Bauer et al. 2006, 183), practitioners accept the challenge of using their skills and knowledge to implement change and improve conditions for communities and organizations. Rogers (2013) recently came to this conclusion as well in his work for a pharmaceutical company on experimental therapies. The ethics of practice is not well served by being defined in the negative, but rather "requires an active positioning of insights rather than a passive protection and representation of subjects" (Madsen and Hammershoy 2012).

Practical Solutions for a Divided Field

We see anthropology as a divided rather than a united field in terms of the:

- careers anthropologists follow;
- perceptions of and relationships with anthropologists whose work is different from theirs;
- assessment of the usefulness and relevance of the current PPR.

Anthropology's identity, relevance, and impact would be better served with greater integration across the ideological boundaries of theory and practice, and with greater cohesion between academia and practice. Fortunately, many academic anthropologists engage in applied research, teach their students about the value of practice and alternative models of work, and help bridge the divide between an "external" and "critical" view from the academy, and the "internal" and "instrumental" view from practice (Rogers 2013). These applied academic anthropologists have worked tirelessly with practitioners in their classrooms, on projects, and on AAA and other committees to build connections and expand learning and career possibilities.

We know that there is more to be done to narrow the gap between practice and academia (Bennett and Fiske 2013; Nolan 2013), and to create greater integration and cohesion among anthropologists. Our focus on the intersection of ethics and applied research on four projects exposed some of the difficulties for professional anthropologists with the PPR. We propose three solutions. First, *the ethics under which practitioners work needs to be incorporated into the PPR.* An analysis of our four projects in the form of a "friendly test" of these principles has yielded some useful findings. Foremost among them is that practitioners are closely tied to problem solving, collaboration, and change. They engage in these activities as a routine part of their work. They hope to improve current conditions through their knowledge and expertise, and sometimes mitigate the consequences of difficult circumstances, like disaster relief, public health issues, or organizational failure. Explicitly recognizing the role of change agent is an essential addition to the PPR.

Second, we note that ethics training is not yet a mainstay of anthropological education (Trotter 2009). We believe that *the ethics of both research and practice should be part of the graduate and undergraduate curricula,* no matter what a student's career path is likely to be. It turns out that applied programs are much more likely to offer ethics training (Trotter 2009). An introduction to ethics through specific classes such as ethnography or pre-internship seminars, and scenario-based learning has become more prevalent. Such classes and the required internship or practicum expose students to multiple ethics codes when working with study participants; they also introduce students to stakeholder groups who may play a role in implementation, and to the job market generally. Ethical dilemmas from practice can be brought back into the classroom for discussion. An applied anthropology faculty designed one ethical problem-solving guide in response to student requests; students and others have used it successfully (Whiteford and Trotter 2008; Bohren and Whiteford 2013).

Third, anthropology needs to move beyond the Do No Harm principle. Of course it is important to think through, plan carefully, execute effectively, and evaluate objectively any project or effort in which one is involved. In that sense, the Do No Harm principle continues to be helpful and relevant. However, it is limiting because it does not encourage or motivate anthropologists to imagine the ways in which their work might make a positive contribution to organizations and communities. Indeed, the PPR currently can be interpreted as a justification for studying but not altering the status quo, rather than as a call to address issues of the human condition. Therefore, *we recommend adoption of a new principle: Do Some Good.* When used together, Do No Harm and Do Some Good complement and balance each other. Exposed to both principles, new cohorts of students will learn the value of careful preparation and of thinking and acting innovatively to find and implement solutions to cultural problems.

The Do Some Good principle could easily serve in an umbrella role for all other principles. In addition, problem solving with the intent to Do Some Good has the potential to inspire *all* anthropologists. It is already the case that academic anthropologists Do Some Good by educating their students, introducing them to professional conferences, and mentoring them through the grant writing and publication processes. The orientation to Do Some Good can and should be expanded. We ask how might our proposed solution be put into practice? How might anthropology take on more of the attributes of a profession that is outwardly focused without losing sight of its knowledge-generation, testing, and documentation functions?

We suggest increased bridge building between practice and academia. Certainly practitioner participation in academia via guest lectures and mentoring, and within the AAA through serving on committees and task forces, is a key component. Such participation raises awareness of anthropology's diversity and provides the potential for future contact. Bridge building also can enhance collegiality and understanding, and lead to collaborations. Practitioners could consider the following:

- Inviting an academically-based anthropologist to shadow you for a day, assuming various permissions have been satisfied.
- Organizing AAA workshops for professors on cutting-edge issues for practitioners.
- Seeking an academic partner to participate in a practice-oriented project.
- Initiating and co-authoring a journal article with an academic partner.

Academic anthropologists might consider the following:

- Using the classroom to explore ethical issues faced by practitioners, with a professional anthropologist guiding the discussion.
- Creating an alumni network to benefit student learning and the job search.
- Soliciting funds for practitioners to visit campus, give talks, and advise students.

Such strategies will help reduce the parochialism that continues to exist within the discipline about the value of practice – an ethical problem in itself. Such strategies will help strengthen collaboration between those anthropologists whose primary role is teaching and research, and those anthropologists who are employed as in the wider world of work beyond university settings. Such strategies have the potential to lead to problem solving on various anthropological initiatives, projects, or cooperative efforts, and therefore to Do Some Good for the broader community. We strongly believe that if these approaches are adopted, anthropology has a better chance of adapting to changing circumstances, remaining relevant, and being able to unify the field for the greater good.

References

Albro, Robert. 2009. Ethics and dual-identity professionals: Addressing anthropology in the public sector. *Anthropology News* 50, 6: 17–18.
American Anthropological Association. Ethic Blog. "Multispecies Ethics." http://ethics. americananthro.org// (accessed August 21, 2016).

American Anthropological Association. Ethic Blog. "Principles of Professional Responsibility." http://ethics.americananthro.org/category/statement/ (accessed August 20, 2016).

Barker, Alex W. and Dena Plemmons. 2016. What's different? In *Anthropological ethics in context: An ongoing dialogue*. Dena Plemmons and Alex W. Barker, eds. Walnut Creek, CA: Left Coast Press, 207–212.

Bartlo, Wendy D. 2012. Crossing boundaries: The future of anthropology graduates and the non-academic job market. *Anthropology News* 53, 2: 24–25.

Bennett, Linda A. and Shirley J. Fiske. 2013. The academic-practitioner relationship. In *A handbook of practicing anthropology*. Riall W. Nolan, ed. Malden, MA: Wiley-Blackwell, 303–316.

Bohren, Lenora and Linda Whiteford. 2013. Ethics and practicing anthropology: Pragmatic, practical, and principled. In *A handbook of practicing anthropology*. Riall W. Nolan, ed. Malden, MA: Wiley-Blackwell, 291–302.

Briody, Elizabeth K. and Riall W. Nolan. 2013. High-performing applied programs. In *A handbook of practicing anthropology*. Riall W. Nolan, ed. Malden, MA: Wiley-Blackwell, 372–387.

Bureau of Labor Statistics, U.S. Department of Labor. 2012–13 ed. Occupational outlook handbook. Anthropologists and archeologists. www.bls.gov/ooh/life-physical-and-social-science/anthropologists-and-archeologists.htm (accessed April 27, 2013).

Cassell, Joan and Sue Ellen Jacobs, eds. 1987. *Handbook on ethical issues in anthropology*. Special publication No. 23, Washington, DC: American Anthropological Association.

Consortium of Practicing and Applied Anthropology. Member Departments. https://copaainfo.org/programs/ (accessed August 21, 2016).

Dominguez, Virginia R. 2016. Introduction: Ethics, work, and life – Individual struggles and professional "comfort zones" in anthropology. In *Anthropological ethics in context: An ongoing dialogue*. Dena Plemmons and Alex W. Barker, eds. Walnut Creek, CA: Left Coast Press, 9–21.

Fiske, Shirley J., Linda A. Bennett, Patricia Ensworth, Terry Redding, and Keri Brondo. 2010. *The changing face of anthropology: Anthropology masters reflect on education, careers, and professional organizations*. Arlington, VA: American Anthropological Association.

General Motors. *Winning with integrity*. www.gm.com/content/dam/gm/en_us/english/Group4/InvestorsPDFDocuments/WWI.pdf (accessed August 20, 2016).

Ginsberg, Daniel. 2016. *AAA members outside the academy: 2016 membership survey #2*. Arlington, VA: American Anthropological Association.

Heller, Monica. 2016. Ethics as institutional process. In *Anthropological ethics in context: An ongoing dialogue*. Dena Plemmons and Alex W. Barker, eds. Walnut Creek, CA: Left Coast Press, 231–235.

Katz, Solomon H. 2012. Action anthropology: Its past, present, and future. In *Action anthropology and Sol Tax in 2012: The final word?* Darby C. Stapp, ed. Richland, WA: Northwest Anthropology LLC, 183–224.

LeCompte, Margaret D. and Jean J. Schensul. 2015. *Ethics in ethnography: A mixed methods approach*. Ethnographer's Toolkit, book 6. Lanham, MD: AltaMira Press.

Madsen, Thomas U. and Laura Hammershoy. 2012. Ethical dilemmas in business anthropology revisited: How a phenomenological approach to the practice of ethnography can shed new light on the topic of ethics. *Ethnographic Praxis in Industry Conference (EPIC) podcast* Savannah, GA, October 14–17.

Nash, June and Max Kirsch. 1994. Corporate culture and social responsibility: The case of toxic wastes in a New England community. In *Anthropological perspectives on organizational culture*. Tomoko Hamada and Willis E. Sibley, eds. Lanham, MD: University Press of America, 357–371.

National Association For The Practice of Anthropology. Ethical Guidelines. "Background." practicinganthropology.org/about/ethical-guidelines/ (accessed February 4, 2014).

National Association For The Practice of Anthropology. practicinganthropology.org/practicing-anthro/ (accessed April 26, 2013).

National Science Foundation. Survey of earned doctorates. Doctorate recipients by major field of study: Selected years, 1981–2011. www.nsf.gov/statistics/sed/2011/pdf/tab12.pdf (accessed April 27, 2013).

Nolan, Riall W., ed. 2013. *A handbook of practicing anthropology*. Malden, MA: Wiley-Blackwell.

Plemmons, Dena and Alex W. Barker, eds. 2016. *Anthropological ethics in context: An ongoing dialogue*. Walnut Creek, CA: Left Coast Press.

Rogers, Mark. 2013. *How do you sleep at night? Business anthropology roundtable*. Annual Meeting of the Society for Applied Anthropology, Denver, CO, March 19–23.

Rudd, Elizabeth, Emory Morrison, Joseph Picciano, and Maresi Nerad. 2008. *Social science PhDs five+ years out: Anthropology report*. Center for Innovation and Research in Graduate Education, University of Washington, Seattle, WA, February 14.

Rylko-Bauer, Barbara, Merrill Singer, and John van Willigen. 2006. Reclaiming applied anthropology: Its past, present, and future. *American Anthropologist* 108, 1: 178–190.

Tashima, Niel, Cathleen Crain, Elizabeth Tunstall, Kendall Thu, and Paul Durrenberger. 2008. Ethics and the anthropological profession in the 21st century. *Anthropology News* 49, 8: 17.

Trotter, Robert T., II. 2009. Formalizing ethics training in anthropology: An extension of methods education. *Anthropology News* 50, 6: 32–33.

Van Willigen, John and Satish Kedia. 2005. Emerging trends in applied anthropology. In *Applied anthropology: Domains of application*. S. Kedia and J. van Willigen, eds. Westport, CT: Praeger, 341–352.

Whiteford, Linda M. and Robert T. Trotter, II. 2008. *Ethics for anthropological research and practice*. Long Grove, IL: Waveland Press, Inc.

3

SUCH BITTER BUSINESS

Reconciling Ethical Domains in Practice

John F. Sherry, Jr.

> 'Tis now the very witching time of night,
> When churchyards yawn and hell itself breathes out
> Contagion to this world: now could I drink hot blood,
> And do such bitter business as the day
> Would quake to look on.
>
> *Hamlet* Act 3, Scene 2

Positioning

I take my ambivalent title from Hamlet's meditation on the improprieties that dark disinhibition affords us all. Embittered by an institutional expectation that we be defensively virtuous in pursuing an enterprise assumed to be inevitably immiserating, business anthropologists must resist a world-weariness in pursuing their vocation. That we somehow must be less principled in nature or more ethically accountable by charter than our mainstream brethren and sistren is the needle by which we are pricked when they are giving us the business. We spend a disproportionate amount of hard-won writing time in justifying practice to our orthodox colleagues. The thought that we might actively negotiate ethical considerations on a regular basis with our various stakeholders likely troubles few critics. I explore a few of these considerations in this chapter.

I write from the perspective of a professional anthropologist who has spent an entire career in the fields of marketing and consumer research, both as a business school professor and independent consultant. Throughout my career, I have written a dozen essays on ethics (e.g., Sherry 1987, 2000, 2001, 2008, 2014a, 2014b), explored ethical frameworks in all the courses I have taught, negotiated ethics in my own research and practice, and even served on an early NAPA committee seeking to advise the AAA on the revision of its code of ethics. This fascination with ethics arose obliquely from my professional training and less from personal inclination, and mostly as a result of my ambivalent relationship with the forces of consumer culture.

A recent example may be instructive. A year or so ago, standing over the copy machine in a rush to collate last-minute material in time for class, I heard this cheerful greeting over my shoulder: "Hey, I just read about a group of anthropologists even more despised than you!" My colleague, an accounting professor and joking relationship partner privy to discussions of the turbulent history between my home and host disciplines, glossed his account of the Human Terrain System Project (HTSP) in the following manner: "Looks like they [the discipline] hate military advisors more than marketers!" "Yeah, my stock is rising," I opined on my way out the door. "You of all people know its accrual world." In no other subdiscipline of anthropology is ethics presumed to be as integral as in our own.

My apprentice and journeyman years were shaped by an institutional climate that was actively hostile to business. I think it is safe to say that, in that era, the only reason one might study contemporary commerce would be to subvert it; the thought that one might improve it would be heretical. And yet, its meaning systems and material flows were such a formative but unexamined part of our lives that such pervasively un-reflexive criticism proved increasingly disingenuous. Similarly, the challenge faced by anthropology in entering the lists of entrenched disciplines inquiring into business and advising managers was no less fraught. Our bones-and-stones image and centripetal energy did not comport with the psycho-statistical and econometric orientation of the prevailing climate. Not yet the ethnopreneurs or entreprenographers of the buyosphere, we crossed (and re-crossed) that metaphorical land bridge with a generalized toolkit and a sense that we were doing something of which our elders disapproved and of which our hosts were skeptical.

Having (immorally, in my estimation) overproduced PhDs for a glutted academic market for so many years, having failed for so long to develop curricula that would prepare doctoral students professionally and psychologically for the commercial market the preponderance of them would be obliged to enter, and having come so late in the game to embrace the sphere of business broadly construed as a legitimate field of scholarly inquiry, our discipline finds itself at an interesting ethical juncture. Can the profession sanction if not celebrate a business anthropology in the wake of the rise of a vast network of local practitioner organizations, the success of EPIC in mobilizing alternative vocational identities, the growing interest of other disciplines in interpreting and exploiting the world of commerce, and the emergence of other controversies (e.g., the HSTP in anthropology, the research misconduct epidemic in psychology that threatens to metastasize to other fields, etc.)? Should those of us in this discontinuous but hardy juggernaut-in-the-making subdiscipline who have felt estranged or existentially homeless accommodate or resist prospective rapprochement?

In this chapter, I explore some of the ethical entanglements that occur when anthropologists ply their trade in contemporary marketplaces. In particular, I examine dynamics in the personal, professional, and political domains in which these challenges are negotiated. I ground my commentary in the disciplines of marketing and consumer research.

Professing

Professing for me is a fusion of paideia and praxis that addresses both ethical problem-solving and ethical problem-finding. The two are often intimately intertwined, and their parameters occasionally difficult to specify until one is deeply immersed in an emergent challenge. We suspect there are moral implications to our work, but may be unable to discern them effectively until that work is well underway.

Because I am a full-time academic in a professional school, I have a number of stakeholder obligations that differ from my counterparts both in mainstream anthropology departments and in positions as practitioners. While I straddle these worlds, I also combine them in a fairly distinctive way. I explore the intersections and disjunctures in more detail in the following sections of this chapter, but identify a few of them upfront to help orient the reader to the larger argument.

My pedagogy has always had an engaged or activist component in several senses. First of all, I have served as a culture broker of sorts, encouraging synergistic cross-communication between my home and host disciplines, and seeking reformation of each in the process. I view this to be in part an ethical undertaking that encourages the disciplines to exploit unrealized potential. Second, I have sought to speed the adoption of my home discipline orientation by business people actively shaping the world of commerce. I view this to be in part an ethical undertaking that improves the efficacy of the stakeholder ecology determining in large measure our quality of life. Finally, I have interacted with the business community in a number of ways – internship, consultations, workshops, presentations, curricular and program collaborations, etc. – that has helped enhance the relevance of what I do as an applied anthropologist. I view this to be in part an ethical undertaking that sharpens my own craft and broadens the range of challenges to which it may be applied.

Researching

Even more than inquiring deeply into an issue and contributing to a larger scholarly conversation intended to enhance our general understanding of cultural phenomena, I think of the research we do primarily as hedonic consumption. It is a playful effort that brings us much joy, even if the topic of investigation is somber or its ramifications dire. The meanings revealed in the interpretations we co-create with our informants are not merely edifying, they are thrilling. This hedonic charge might even be more galvanizing for practitioners whose insights are translated into breakthrough brand strategies, creative new products or services, compelling advertising campaigns, improved customer journeys through more engagingly designed servicescapes, practical and humane organizational restructurings, cogent expert witness testimony in product liability trials, or any of the countless other managerial or civic interventions that anthropological or ethnographic perspectives enable.

The research I conduct as a humanistic social scientist into contemporary marketing and consumer behavior is as "pure" as mainstream ethnological inquiry insofar as I seek to understand a focal phenomenon as holistically as I can, and report my findings in scholarly outlets for colleagues to assess, refute, or extend. Such work may be applied, like all other, by individuals whose intentions are unknown to or unendorsed by me, as it is part of the public record. My research differs from the mainstream insofar as the journals of my host discipline may encourage or demand that I reflect upon the managerial, public policy, or societal implications of my findings. That gives me an opportunity to consider the most benign, prosocial applications I can imagine, and offer them to the reader for reflection, as well as alert readers to potential misguided applications. That is one way to influence the ethical use of research findings.

Another way is to leverage the reflexive component of anthropology's interpretive turn by applying a critical lens to my host discipline. By subjecting the ontology, epistemology, axiology, and praxis of the host to the kind of ongoing rigorous scrutiny that only (or primarily) an "outsider" perspective can mount, researchers from my consumer culture theory (CCT) tradition are helping to foster more reflective contemplation and lobby, where appropriate, for reformation of the discipline (Cayla and Zwick 2011). This meticulous close reading honors our ethical obligation to refine and improve inquiry at the same time we hold ourselves accountable for assessing – as well as enhancing or mitigating – its societal impact.

Consulting

Consulting is hedged about with practical and moral ambivalence, as a quick check of the myriad web pages devoted to jokes about consultants readily confirms (see, for example, www.weitzenegger.de/en/to/jokes.html). It is not just mainstream anthropology that is suspicious of the enterprise; even willing clients harbor doubts.

In consulting, field work is frequently compressed compared to conventional practice. Depending upon the ambition of a client, immersion can range from simple site visits through durations that the field has legitimized as either "rapid appraisal" or "diagnostic," to longer-term engagements. Some ethnographic consultants may be on retainer to conduct ongoing periodic inquiry for a client, and some have made the transition to full-time in-house employees. Field work may encompass multiple venues (beyond immediate user experience itself) or be multi-sited in nature.

As a consultant, my proposals always reflect my best good faith estimate of the amount of time a respectable inquiry will take. Sometimes the estimate is accepted without question, sometimes it is reduced through negotiation, and, on occasion, it is even extended, given either insightful pre-launch discussion or interesting mid-study results. [I have been known to lose a bid as well.] While practitioners don't often have the same luxury of time as their academic counterparts, we do have an ethical sense of what can be accomplished in a particular time frame.

Another way a consultant negotiates his or her ethical obligations is by being selective in the kinds of assignments that are accepted, such that engagements are consistent with one's own system of values. For example, declining opportunities afforded by industries one considers inherently dangerous (a slippery slope for sure, but a common heuristic nonetheless) is an option. Or accepting an assignment granting entrée to a domain otherwise difficult or impossible to access in the hope that it will eventually result in a more comprehensive and holistic investigation of a phenomenon through which one can network once one is "off the clock." Or referring an inquiry to a colleague who has more expertise in the area, allowing that one's own start-up cost (versus "fresh eyes" as a newcomer) would likely provide less insight, and therefore less value, to a prospective client.

While the proprietary nature of consulting agreements usually (but not always) precludes publication of results beyond the firm and its designated clients, the lessons learned can often be translated into compelling material that facilitates learning in the classroom. The work itself, suitably disguised, often serves as a rite of passage that increases the credibility of the teacher and demonstrates the relevance of the approach to otherwise skeptical apprentices. Work resulting in a tangible outcome (a new product, a new ad, a new merchandising strategy, etc.) may be regarded as de facto publication whose efficacy may be critically examined in the public sphere.

As with academic research, the goal of consulting is to help the client understand the lived experience of stakeholders. The difference is that such understanding is then devoted to creating or refining an offering that more nearly satisfies the actual want of the stakeholder, an outcome that may go begging if the client is reliant upon the standard marketing research toolkit. Because ethnographic research arguably "gets closer" to the consumer, for example, it can inform interventions in a more humane and effective fashion than might otherwise be possible. It is an ethical complement or alternative to traditional marketing practice that is more faithful to consumer experience.

Teaching

I have been fortunate enough to pursue most of my career in the marketing departments of two elite private universities with top-ranked business programs, one at the graduate level and one at the undergraduate level. I have helped prepare three generations of managers to enter or re-enter the workforce. In each of the courses I have taught, in addition to anthropological and ethnographic perspectives of their vocation, I have also treated the ethical implications those perspectives have for the personal, organizational, social, and cultural spheres my students inhabit. The same goes for doctoral students, whose training has begun with IRB compliance procedures and culminated in the reflexive analysis driving the ascendance of critical marketing (Saran et al. 2007; Tadajewski and Brownlie 2008).

Thanks in part to their privileged education (and the tireless efforts of my colleagues) my students have gone on to become influential corporate decision makers and disciplinary thought leaders of heightened ethical sensitivity. They understand that they are behavioral architects shaping the quality of life in society, believe that marketing is among the most powerful forces of cultural stability and change at work around the globe, and accept that every marketing decision has a moral dimension. They see themselves as moral agents, not merely business agents. They also understand their complicity as consumers in the struggle to realize the common good, as they ponder the mechanics of enlightened consumption. To the extent that marketing is a utopian vision, their ability to perceive the unanticipated and unintended dystopian consequences of enacting that vision from the perspectives of as many stakeholders as possible is both a commercial and civic virtue.

While ethical behavior is a theme that runs throughout these courses, I usually prime discussion early on with brief explorations of ethical challenges of the day, move to a consideration of classic ethical lapses and achievements, and arrive at a habit of mind that seeks out opportunities for proactive ethical action. I typically set legal standards and professional codes – in this case, the American Marketing Association's (https://archive.ama.org/archive/AboutAMA/Pages/Statement%20 of%20Ethics.aspx) Statement of Ethics – as the lowest bar an ethical manager is expected to clear. [I assume home-discipline instructors would cite the National Association for the Practice of Anthropology guidelines (http://practicinganthropology.org/about/ethical-guidelines/) instead.] I employ a particular model of ethical theory (Hunt and Vitell 1986, 1993) that helps students identify micro, meso, and macro dimensions of perceived ethical challenges as well as their perceived alternatives and consequences. Most students are able to contribute compelling examples from their personal experience, with complexity generally increasing with managerial seniority. This initial screening leads to discussion of the deontological and teleological evaluations that inform the ethical judgment that shapes managerial interventions.

Again, after preliminarily probing students' understanding of duty- and consequence-based ethics, I find it helpful to experiment with specific approaches of each type to stimulate reflection and insight. In considering deontological evaluation, I often contrast an approach with which my current students are familiar – Catholic Social Teaching (Laczniak et al. 2013) – with one that is less familiar to them – the Buddhist Noble Eightfold Path (Mick 2013). I explore teleological evaluation using ecological dynamics (Hardin 1985) to give students a wide-angled view of the ramifying consequences of their decisions as consumers and managers. This inevitably leads us to discussions of sustainability and triple-bottom-line accountability (Mish and Scammon 2010), and from there to the interplay of evaluative frameworks. I frequently use Donaldson's (1989) model to explore the nature and range of human rights and correlative corporate duties to help students envision the parameters of an enlightened firm. In one course in particular, I challenge my students to take a cosmic perspective of ethics by positing a kalogenic universe (Henning 2005) and asking them to imagine its moral consequences, but that is a topic best deferred to another chapter.

While such training cannot ensure the production of virtuous consumers and managers, it can complexify and deeply enrich the input into perceptions and decisions that might otherwise present themselves as merely economic (or, worse, habitual) in character. Since this is precisely what anthropological and ethnographic inquiry aspire to achieve, ethical scrutiny is an apposite handmaiden. This pairing is no less relevant in any of our home discipline's field pursuits, I believe, and yet, as new to the curriculum as formalized methods training itself arguably is, instruction in ethics is in an embryonic stage. Our applied fields are the most likely contributors to and leaders of a reformation in this state of affairs.

> And appetite, an universal wolf,
> So doubly seconded with will and power,
> Must make perforce a universal prey,
> And last eat up himself.
> (*Troilus and Cressida, Act 1, Scene 3*)

Personalizing

Let me return to my confession of an ambivalent attitude toward consumer culture with which I began this chapter. On the one hand, as an anthropologist, I have critically observed and deeply felt the dystopian consequences of this culture, which I have grossly apportioned to two buckets: distraction and destruction (Sherry 2000). In the former case, the zeitgeist coaxes us to divert attention and effort from gravitas to levitas, leading us to neglect what is truly important in favor of frivolous pursuits. In the latter case, the deadly dialectic of creative destruction and destructive creation renders our existence hazardous, with ecocide, ethnocide, and egocide being inevitable consequences.

On the other hand, as a human being (who, let's face it, is still an anthropologist), I am entranced by material culture and its immaterial intimations. The stuff and services (hereafter stuff) of the marketplace are auratic occasions of immanence and transcendence beyond the enduring delight they may produce. We've co-evolved with stuff, projecting into it and introjecting it, animating it with narrative in our quests for meaning (Belk 1988; Sherry 2005). We continue to refine and perfect its functional, behavioral, aesthetic, and ecological (Levy and Czepiel 1974; Sherry 2001) qualities. The bulk of the CCT literature is devoted to understanding this multi-dimensional experience. For better and for worse, Stuff "Я" Us.

In deference to F. Scott Fitzgerald, I hope that the ability to entertain these two opposed ideas simultaneously in mind, and use their countervailing energies to achieve a prosocial outcome is the test of a first-rate business anthropologist, and not merely a sign of self-deceptive compartmentalization. Elsewhere (Sherry 2014a) I have argued that the darkside costs of consumer culture can be mitigated if not eliminated entirely by anthropologically informed marketing strategy. Even the foremost architect of modern marketing recognizes the need for redressive action (Kotler 2015; see also http://fixcapitalism.com/), as have others of his guild (Chang 2011), and is sensitive to this argument. Given the variations of capitalism at work in the world today and the totalizing force of its grip on our economic imagination, it seems clear to me that anthropological tinkering is not merely feasible, but ethically imperative.

The same is true as far as corporations are concerned. The nature of the firm in terms of structure and function, priorities and goals, and local and global impact is in flux. I expect this flux to accelerate, especially as officers (and student-officers-in-training) have increasing access to ethnographic research on organizations and consumers, and employ greater numbers of business anthropologists. The monolithic view of firms as nefarious is not ethnologically viable, and hinders our further efforts at prosocial engineering. Recent experiments in corporate social responsibility, cause-related marketing, and triple bottom line accounting, among others, suggest that firms can become effective contributors to the common good. Perhaps more guidance from anthropologists will help.

Concluding

The late Theodore Hesburgh, President Emeritus of the University of Notre Dame, was fond of observing that it is easier to exemplify values than to teach them (O'Brien 1998). Of the companies I have worked with over the years, two in particular stand out for their determination both to walk the walk as well as talk the talk. Each has been an early adopter and regular deployer of anthropological perspectives and methods. Each has expected its employees to embody and enact the ethical principles of the enterprise. Each has produced a public account of its efforts in the hope that proprietary experience might induce common enlightenment and engender ethical behavior.

The first company, IDEO (www.ideo.com/), is a design and innovation consulting firm that delivers breakthrough interventions across industries and sectors, tackling challenging social marketing problems as well as traditional commercial ones. It also stages open platforms for community engagement in many aspects of the design process. Among the books IDEO officers have written on the firm's methods and procedures (e.g., Kelley 2005; Brown 2009; Kelley and Kelley 2013) is a treatment of research ethics (Suri 2015) that includes reflexive commentary on the adumbrated principles.

The second company, Motorola (www.motorola.com/us/home), a global mobile communications firm that has been foundational and episodically catalytic in its industry, has grappled innovatively with issues of cross-cultural diversity and sustainability practices in recent decades. Through its Mobility Foundation, it also fosters community engagement across a range of stakeholders. The company has published a fascinating interdisciplinary collection of cases and commentaries on the ethical challenges it has faced around the world (Moorthy et al. 1998).

By so publicly proclaiming the ethical principles and procedures by which they intend to conduct business, these firms not only set a moral standard for themselves to attain and for others to emulate, but also they benefit from the criticism that any breach or lapse might occasion, the shortfalls yielding insights for improving code enforcement and refining judgment. Anthropological understanding of the lived experience of these standards, and of their antecedents and consequences, can assist in the honing of ethical guidelines and practices.

To contribute to the research conversation on consumption experience across stakeholders, to collaborate in the training of enlightened managers and consumers, and to partner with creative specialists on innovative projects, are among the joys of my profession. To help create a foundational field that Levy (1976) has christened "marcology" that is deeply informed by cultural ecology (Sherry 2008) and that helps decision-makers sensitively, sustainably, and ethically address stakeholder wants is an aspiration I pursue. To banter with colleagues across (sub)disciplinary boundaries about the ethics of enterprise ethnography is one of the costs of doing such business. The literature burgeons, unconsulted it seems beyond our hothouse, but the present volume may portend a change, collecting wisdom between convenient covers as it does. Business anthropologists have a solid set of ethical guidelines that is continually being revised to address emergent challenges. We strive to transmute bitter business to better business.

References

Belk, Russell. 1988. Possessions and the Extended Self. *Journal of Consumer Research* 15, 2: 139–168.

Brown, Tim. 2009. *Change by Design: How Design Thinking Transforms Organizations and Inspires Innovation.* New York: Harper Business.

Cayla, Julien and Detlev Zwick. 2011. *Inside Marketing: Cultures, Ideologies and Practices.* London: Oxford University Press.

Chang, Ha-Joon. 2011. *23 Things They Don't Tell You About Capitalism.* New York: Bloomsbury.

Donaldson, Thomas. 1989. *The Ethics of International Business.* New York: Oxford University Press.

Hardin, Garrett. 1985. *Filters Against Folly.* New York: Viking.

Henning, Brian. 2005. *The Ethics of Creativity: Beauty, Morality and Nature in a Processive Cosmos.* Pittsburgh: University of Pittsburgh Press.

Hunt, Shelby and Scott Vitell. 1986. A General Theory of Marketing Ethics. *Journal of Macromarketing* 6, 1: 5–16.

———. 1993. The General Theory of Marketing Ethics: A Retrospective and Revision. In *Ethics in Marketing*, N. Craig Smith and John Quelch, eds., 775–784. Homewood, IL: Irwin.

Kelley, Tom. 2005. *The Ten Faces of Innovation.* New York: Currency Doubleday.

Kelley, Tom and David Kelley. 2013. *Creative Confidence.* New York: Crown Business.

Kotler, Philip. 2015. *Confronting Capitalism: Real Solutions for a Troubled Economic System.* New York: AMACOM.

Laczniak, Gene, Thomas Klein, and Patrick Murphy. 2013. Caritas in Veritate: Updating Catholic Social Teaching for Macromarketing and Business Strategy. *Journal of Macromarketing* 30, 3: 293–296.

Levy, Sidney. 1976. Marcology 101, or the Domain of Marketing. In *Marketing 1776–1976 and Beyond*, Kenneth Bernhardt, ed., 577–581. Chicago: American Marketing Association.

Levy, Sidney and John Czepiel. 1974. Marketing and Aesthetics. In *Combined Proceedings of the American Marketing Association*, Series 36, R. C. Curhan, ed., 386–391. Chicago: American Marketing Association.

Mick, David. 2013. *Recovering from the Occident: Buddhism and Its Implications for Consumer Research.* Working paper, McIntire School of Commerce at the University of Virginia, Charlottesville, Virginia.

Mish, Jenny and Debra L. Scammon. 2010. Principle-Based Stakeholder Marketing: Insights from Private Triple-Bottom-Line Firms. *Journal of Public Policy & Marketing* 29, 1: 12–26.

Moorthy, R. S., Richard DeGeorge, Thomas Donaldson, William Ellos, Robert Solomon, and Robert Textor. 1998. *Uncompromising Integrity: Motorola's Global Challenge*. Schaumburg, IL: Motorola University Press.

O'Brien, Michael. 1998. *Hesburgh: A Biography*. Washington, DC: Catholic University of America Press.

Saran, Michael, Pauline Maclaran, Christina Golding, Richard Elliott, Avi Shankar, and Miriam Catterall, eds. 2007. *Critical Marketing: Defining the Field*. New York: Elsevier.

Sherry, John F. Jr. 1987. Cultural Propriety in a Global Marketplace. In *Philosophical and Radical Thought in Marketing*, A. Firat, N. Dholakia, and R. Bagozzi, eds., 179–91. Lexington, MA: Lexington Books.

———. 2000. Distraction, Destruction, Deliverance: The Presence of Mindscape in Marketing's New Millennium. *Marketing Intelligence and Planning* 18, 6–7: 328–336.

———. 2001. Sometimes Leaven with Levin: A Tribute to Sidney J. Levy on the Occasion of His Receiving the Converse Award. In *The Fifteenth Paul D. Converse Symposium*, Abbie Griffin and James Ness, eds., 54–63. Chicago: American Marketing Association.

———. 2005. Brand Meaning. In *Kellogg on Branding*, T. Calkins and A. Tybout, eds., 40–69. New York: John Wiley.

———. 2008. The Ethnographer's Apprentice: Trying Consumer Culture from the Outside In. *Journal of Business Ethics* 80: 85–95.

———. 2014a. Slouching Toward Utopia: When Marketing *Is* Society. In *Marketing and the Common Good: Essays on Societal Impact from Notre Dame*, Patrick Murphy and John F. Sherry, Jr., eds., 43–60. New York: Routledge.

———. 2014b. Can We Get There from Here? Charting the Contours of the Common Good. In *Marketing and the Common Good: Essays on Societal Impact from Notre Dame*, Patrick Murphy and John F. Sherry, Jr., eds., 309–315. New York: Routledge.

Suri, Jane. 2015. *The Little Book of Design Research Ethics*. Palo Alto, CA: IDEO.

Tadajewski, Mark and Douglas Brownlie. 2008. *Critical Marketing: Issues in Contemporary Marketing*. Chichester: John Wiley.

4

THE ETHICS OF THE PROFESSION OF BUSINESS ANTHROPOLOGY

Allen W. Batteau and Bradley J. Trainor

In recent years, Business Anthropology has grown into a practical and scholarly pursuit in the mainstream of anthropological inquiry and employment. Titles such as Karen Ho's *Liquidated* (2009), Caitlin Zaloom's *Out of the Pits* (2006), Daniel Miller's *Capitalism: An Ethnographic Approach* (1997), and Sunderland and Denny's *Doing Anthropology in Consumer Research* (2007) attest to the increasing prominence of business inquiry and application within anthropology. Yet, along the way the discourse of ethics in Business Anthropology has not kept pace, and the available resources, including the AAA Code of Ethics, the SfAA Code of Ethics, and the NAPA Principles of Practice offer such broad generalities as to be difficult to apply in many typical business engagements. In contrast to the seeming simplicity of indigenous village societies on which the academic discipline of social anthropology first cut its teeth, the worlds of government, business, and other powerful, multi-national institutional configurations present the professional anthropologist with a dizzying array of normative conflicts that the discipline has only begun to address.[1]

In this chapter we propose to develop a framework for ethical reasoning within Business Anthropology. After illustrating some challenges commonly encountered in fieldwork, we focus on the heart of the matter, the challenges of ethical reasoning and moral agency in complex institutional environments. We then review several cases drawn from anthropological literature of ethical dilemmas in the business world, as an empirical foundation for our central argument: Moral development is a necessary part of institutional and professional development; codes are a useful but limited resource; and training in ethical reasoning comes not from memorizing codes but from working through difficult cases. Thus the challenge for Business and other applied Anthropologists is to build communities of ethical practice, in which ethical reasoning is foundational, and not simply an item on a proposal checklist.

Fieldwork and Ethical Challenges

A software company is commissioned by a research institute to conduct a study of gear manufacturing processes; the research institute is bidding for a federal contract to establish a model automated gear manufacturing laboratory, and they need a formal description of the gear manufacturing process from both engineering and managerial perspectives. An ethnographer employed by the software company (Batteau) is instructed on Friday to depart in two days for the location of a cooperating factory, a community-based gear manufacturer, where for the next two weeks he will use his field skills to capture both the formal and the informal aspects of operating and managing a gear factory. The cooperating factory provided the ethnographer with a private office with a desk, and a liaison to set up interviews (a former president of the company who knew all of the employees). Being community-based, many at the factory were neighbors or friends outside of work, and relationships at the site were complicated by these multiple intersections. The interviews concerned primarily the management processes, and interfaces among multiple functions within the factory including engineering, sales, and manufacturing. The fieldwork was conducted in the office (although there was also a factory tour), with the liaison bringing in informants as requested by the ethnographer. Field notes were written up every evening in a nearby motel.

Over the two weeks' experience, no dramatic illegal or unethical practices were observed or reported, although there were sufficient incongruities in the data that could have been the basis for a more intensive, academic inquiry: Accounts of order management processes, from sales and from engineering, were flat-out contradictory, and there were some suggestions of sharp dealing from sales personnel. These presented the ethnographer with an interesting dilemma: Should he (a) try to get to the bottom of the matter by determining which was true or false, (b) arbitrate or mediate their different viewpoints, or (c) decide that such issues are out of scope and ignore them? Should he alert the management to the possible improprieties (and possible illegalities) that he heard about? Right or wrong in this situation depends on whether one gives primacy to the priorities of scholarship for creating an accurate representation, to the employer (the software company) for fulfilling the contract and not exceeding the budget, to the manufacturing firm which was hosting the field research, or to the project scope (as defined by the research institute that commissioned the field study) which was to create a document adequate for submission to the federal agency funding the contract.

This small story illustrates an elementary structure that is played out in larger, more consequential ethical controversies, such as the well-known campaign against the Ok Tedi mine in Papua New Guinea (Kirsch 2002). In this controversy, one of the world's largest multi-national mining companies, Ok Tedi, was being sued. Stuart Kirsch, a respected anthropologist at the University of Michigan, had been retained in 1991 to conduct a "social impact assessment" of a mining development. The assessment was sought by a faction within the mining company that thought it would help avoid or mitigate conflicts with the surrounding communities. When

Kirsch published his findings in 1993, his contract was not renewed. In 1994, when a lawsuit was filed against the mining company, Kirsch was threatened with a countersuit should he assist the plaintiffs. In Kirsch's words, "From a corporate perspective, neutrality does not exist" (Kirsch 2002, 182). Among the multiple parties in this situation (various factions within the mining company, an Australian law firm seeking to shake the mining company down, and not least the local indigenous peoples), the lone anthropologist was caught in the middle of multiple power struggles and priorities.

Both of these cases illustrate a common structure in fieldwork of divided obligations among academic, indigenous, and institutional values; the Ok Tedi case presents the additional feature of extreme power asymmetries and threats to the lives and livelihoods of indigenous peoples, between a multi-national corporation and indigenous villagers, with the fieldworker ostensibly caught in the middle. The study of the gear manufacturer presents a situation of enterprise complexity in which there are multiple parties, the ethnographer, his employer, the customer, the field site, the sponsoring federal agency, and numerous intersecting and cross-cutting loyalties among them. Other engagements have even more complexity, bringing together multiple (if not always dramatic) clashes of values and priorities.

Such complexities and asymmetries are the norm in the business world, and the more anthropologists are *employed* in businesses the more pointed they become. In the business world institutional complexity and contested loyalties are frequent, and the anthropologist working in a business setting or for a business client is confronted with ethical quandaries. Power asymmetries are central to the worlds of government and business. We have a few bright lines over which we must not cross, such as "Do no harm," "Protect your research subjects" and "Never misrepresent your research findings." However, as the cases we present in the third section of the chapter illustrate, even within these borders there are numerous ethical dilemmas.

In the early years of Business Anthropology in the 1990s, the ethics of Business Anthropology per se were sometimes questioned, less for any specific actions and more for the fact that we seemed to be consorting with academia's Other. Although this has largely receded, suspicions remain, and Business Anthropologists are severally developing insights and normative statements for the ethics of Business Anthropology. A survey of the current state of Business Anthropology by experienced practitioners reveals that discussions of ethical issues are alive and well. For example, Ann Jordan's 2003 textbook revised in 2011, *Business Anthropology*, devotes chapter 5 to ethical concerns; Sunderland and Denny's *Doing Anthropology in Consumer Research* discusses the ethical concerns of certain forms of representation; Malefyt and Morais's *Advertising and Anthropology* discusses in chapter 9, "Ethics in Advertising," their confrontations with ethical issues and debates in two advertising agencies. At the 2012 meetings of the American Anthropological Association, several papers in sessions on "Ethics in Business Anthropology" and "Anthropology of versus Anthropology for Business," discussed such matters as "Anthropology and

Business: Negotiating Boundaries in an Institutional Field" (Baba 2012), "Traversing the Borders: Passages Between Academia and Industry" (Lucas and Peluso 2012), "Anthropologists at Work" (Malefyt 2013), or "Lost in Translation" (Miller 2012). These presentations attest both to the growing acceptance of Business Anthropology in the corporate and academic world, and to a heightened awareness of the ethical issues this raises.

Similarly, within the American Anthropological Association, the newly published "Principles of Professional Responsibility" (2012) reflects an awareness that anthropology's writ has expanded beyond academic research and teaching. The six principles, beginning with the first (and most succinct), "Do no harm," have broad generality and reflect an awareness that anthropologists are at times working in complex and compromised situations (e.g., #4, "Weigh competing ethical obligations due collaborators and affected parties"). Within Business Anthropology, many ethical dilemmas revolve around intellectual property ownership (see next paragraph on "work for hire"), and the extensive discussion given to Principles #5 ("Make your results accessible") and #6 ("Protect and preserve your records"), reflects this (see also below Case #1, "Who owns field notes?"). Intellectual Property protection can sometimes take extreme dimensions: One of us (Batteau) had the experience of a research assistant working on a military base whose car was broken into after she refused a request by the base police to see her notes (the field notes were later found thrown in a ditch). The Association's concluding Principle, #7, "Maintain respectful and ethical professional relationships," forms the basis of our concluding thoughts on building ethical communities of practice.

From our perspective, however, it is not so much Business Anthropology per se, as it is ethnographic fieldwork in business. The confusion at some conferences between "ethnography" and "anthropology" attests to this: At earlier EPIC (Ethnographic Praxis in Industry Conference) conferences from 2007 to 2011, there was ongoing debate over the contrast between ethnographers and "real" anthropologists, and one still finds discussions of whether an "ethnographic" study can be conducted in an afternoon. Ethnographic fieldwork in business, like all fieldwork, contains a number of moral ambiguities, including the loyalties required for access, the (tacit, at least) acceptance of institutional norms, the compromised position of the fieldworker, and the need to prove himself or herself to his field site. The ethnographer has few institutional resources at hand with which to resolve these conflicts – if the fieldworker could bring along his or her entire institutional support structure, it wouldn't be fieldwork. When the conditions of field access are in terms of "work for hire" (a contractual relationship that might explicitly or implicitly include IP ownership, potentially including field notes), the potential for ethical conflict is amplified. Perhaps one could confine one's attempts at "Business Anthropology" only to the library, but in fact we abandoned "armchair anthropology" more than a hundred years ago.

However, we have yet to abandon armchair ethics. It sometimes happens that ethical pronouncements are formed at several steps removed from sites of engagement, with limited knowledge of the normative expectations or tacit understandings of the parties involved. Ethical discourse often occurs at an impracticable distance from where it is needed: Even today one finds discussions of ethics with limited knowledge of the field milieu, its institutional diversity, or the philosophical assumptions that support conflicting ethical conclusions. Conducted at such a remove, a discussion of ethics becomes "a mechanism to help regulate the behavior of those with whom they disagree" (Cassell and Jacobs 2006, 1). As an alternative, in the final section, we provide some suggestions about how Business Anthropologists might develop ethical communities of practice.

Moral Agency

A recurrent problem in moral philosophy is the ethical dilemma of conflicting moral regimes, the situation where an individual navigates among multiple institutions (including nation-states, businesses, religious communities, and universities) and social milieux (including family and community). To maintain moral agency within such situations requires an understanding of morality more developed than simply obedience to the norms or role expectations, and requires dialogue with colleagues.

Philosophical reasoning about ethics presumes a morally free agent – one that can exercise unconstrained free will. To act as a morally free agent requires first of all that one understand himself or herself as such – their moral identity is separate from their social roles:

> To understand oneself thus is to understand that one's goodness as a human being, the answer that by one's whole way of life one gives to the question "How is it best for a human being in my circumstances to live?" is not to be equated with one's goodness at being and doing what this or that rôle requires.
>
> *(MacIntyre 2006, 195)*

Sociologically, of course, the presumption of complete ethical freedom is never the case, inasmuch as there are always constraints on action, whether in terms of the resources available, the directives of the social milieu, or simply the requirement for most adults to earn a living. Within academic institutions there is ideally, at least, a sphere that is exempt from political or economic influences – the sphere of "academic freedom." However, for most anthropologists struggling along in the current era of neoliberal insecurity this academic ideal is something they will never attain. The majority of anthropologists, particularly those who have entered the discipline in the last 20 years, do not derive their primary livelihood from academic employment, instead they support themselves as consultants, corporate employees, or public servants; as such, we have necessarily agreed to barter some measure of autonomy in order to be in positions where we could create social value. Most such anthropologists live from project-to-project, necessarily accepting the base and the ignoble along with the uplifting. Choices about which projects to promote and pursue and which to reject are often left to managers, simply on pragmatic grounds.

These constraints, of course, do not exempt Business Anthropologists from ethical responsibility. Authors of this chapter have on more than one occasion, for instance, had the experience of working on projects that according to the structures of an academic moral regime might have been considered ethically troubling [improving the accuracy of naval gunnery during the Persian Gulf War (Batteau) and gathering Afghan population opinions for the US Army via the Human Terrain Systems (Trainor)]. Both of these were in contexts of armed conflict or its aftermath; questions that might and have been raised about these have less to do with specific actions or their consequences, and more with their association with anything military.

Moral philosophy can be thought of as the attempt to use philosophical methods to identify the morally correct course of action in various fields of human life. Application of moral philosophy in the consideration of ethical conduct is often derived from theory-based thinking, used by ethicists that reference their favorite ethical codes to parse whatever situation they think about – an approach that often leads to impossible-to-bridge divides developing between the practitioners of the various schools of thought. Such theoretical divides foreshadow another recurrent problem in moral philosophy – the ethical dilemma of conflicting moral regimes, the situation where an individual navigates among multiple institutions (including nation-states, businesses, and academia) and social milieux (including family and community). Conduct that may be expected in one regime can be severely condemned in another.

Jeffrey Stout, in *Ethics after Babel*, similarly examines the problems of ethics in conflicting moral regimes. In the face of diversity, one is tempted toward nihilism, skepticism, or relativism, each of which is ethically problematic. Heightened awareness of ethical issues, he suggests, and a broad sense of responsibility (not simply to one's employer or customer, or even to one's academic discipline) offers a way out of this impasse (Stout 1988).

In sum, we make a strong distinction between ethics and institutional obligations, although these latter often present themselves in the language of ethics. Business Anthropologists, *like other professionals* are obligated to navigate, mediate and arbitrate among multiple moral regimes. An alternative approach to bridging such divisions is provided by case-based reasoning that begins with the immediate facts of real and concrete cases, rather than theory or moral regime. While case-based reasoning makes use of ethical theory or social norms, it incorporates other features of moral reasoning as well. Case-based reasoning starts with the particulars of a case and then asks what morally significant features ought to be considered. Observation of medical ethics committees by researchers revealed that a consensus on the resolution of problematic cases often emerged when participants focused on the facts of the case, rather than on theory (Jonsen and Toulmin 1988). Participants might thus agree on the resolution of a particular case, while still disagreeing on the reasoning behind their particular positions.

Some Examples of Anthropological Dilemmas in Business

The infancy of this discourse is illustrated by the dearth of resources that speak directly to ethical dilemmas that Business Anthropologists confront: Of the 25 cases presented in the AAA's *Handbook on Ethical Issues in Anthropology* (Cassell and Jacobs 2006), only one deals with a situation (disputes over IP ownership) typical of the business world. More characteristically, the ethics cases presented consist of hot gifts in an urban ghetto, the sharing of personal pharmaceuticals with a dying villager, assisting a villager who was (possibly) a witness to a murder, or a shakedown by a middle eastern travel agent arranging a university tour: All very real and troubling, yet from a business perspective, well, "exotic."

More representative of the business world might be Cassell and Jacobs' case in this handbook, "Who Owns the Field Notes," in which an ethnographer conducts a social impact assessment for a federal agency. The contract contained no stipulations of ownership of data, and paid 75% of the ethnographer's salary and expenses in advance. The report that was presented stated that the planned project would have a severe impact on the community, and that no mitigation was possible. These unwelcome conclusions led to the agency demanding the ethnographer "turn over his entire research record in order that the agency could solicit another opinion on the matter." With an attorney's advice, the ethnographer refused, and was eventually paid.

From a business perspective, this is a familiar situation, abetted by power asymmetries, in which a powerful party tests the limits of a contractual understanding. Every formal contract has an informal commentary, and often one party or the other to the contract will attempt to probe its boundaries. The greater the social and cultural distance between the contracting parties, the more likely this is to happen. Somewhere between the extremes of contracting through a one-page Memorandum of Understanding and a minutely specified contract covering every conceivable contingency mutually agreeable working arrangements are possible. Part of the ethical challenge here is to determine what balance is appropriate to the field situation, and how far one should err on the side of caution.

For another example of the sort of conflicts that arise when working in institutional settings, we can consider the experience of one of the authors (Trainor) in a corporation. The ethnographer, working on organizational development issues in a 300+ person automotive design group, interviewed a number of engineers working as members of a subcontractor team. The small team was tasked with designing the vehicle's HVAC (heating, ventilation, and air conditioning) system. The interviews revealed that the team leader was actively working to suppress all attempts to pass information about his team's design problems to other design teams in the group, teams with which the subcontractor team needed to coordinate. Considering that all the parts of the automobile would eventually have to fit together, the team leader's suppression of communication about design problems was a big problem. Interviews with team members revealed that the members of the subcontractor team were doing their best to work around the obstructionism of their leader and promote the necessary communications. Further, they had already reported to the subcontracting company's higher management about the team leader's behavior. Two senior members of the subcontractor team ultimately asked the ethnographer to not report back to the group's organization development team about the situation because they wanted time to allow the subcontractor to resolve the situation in its own way. What to do?

Deontology is a popular theory of ethics that judges the morality of an action based on the action's adherence to a rule. Thus, an ethnographer would be ethical if she just follows the rule. Yet, whose rule should she follow: The rule of the company to which the design group belongs, the rule of the subcontractor to which the HVAC team belongs, the rule of the ethnographer's professional organizations, or some other? Another popular moral theory is consequentialism, which holds that an act is morally right if the consequence of the act maximizes the good. Still, what action would most likely maximize the good: Allowing the subcontractor to handle the situation, or reporting it to group leadership? Group leadership will probably force a rapid replacement of the team leader, which might improve the good of the group, but come at the expense of the team leader. Leaving things to the subcontractor might allow them time to ease the team leader into another position where he will be less liable to cause problems, and they might even be able to do it in a timely enough fashion as to not cause harm to the group, but who can say?

Another case that has several similarities to ethical dilemmas that arise in business ethnography is the "Bio-Bio Case" discussed in Whiteford and Trotter's *Ethics for Anthropological Research and Practice*. In this case the International Finance Corporation (IFC) contracted with Anthropologist Theodore Downing to conduct a social impact assessment for a dam being constructed by a Chilean energy corporation and financed by IFC. When Downing's study came up with unwelcome findings, the final phase of the contract (submission and dissemination of a report) was cancelled, and Downing filed a human rights complaint alleging violation of IFC indigenous and resettlement policies.

Whiteford and Trotter present several ethical questions raised by the Bio-Bio situation, including:

- Is practicing anthropology for a small nonprofit organization the same as consulting for large, global organizations like the IFC? Do the professional guidelines apply uniformly across the spectrum of employers ...
- What are the ethical consequences of taking a particular position? How does a particular decision affect multiple interest groups, including individual stakeholders, the community, academic and governmental institutions, the discipline of anthropology, and the larger society?

(Whiteford and Trotter 2008, 85)

As a final example, we might examine the ethical issues potentially posed by Tim Malefyt's work in developing a promotional strategy for a soft drink (Malefyt and

Morais 2012, 131). The product, "Citrus Splash" (a pseudonym) was depicted as helping:

> anxious young people overcome odds and adjust to new life responsibilities through clever humor, good spirits, and levity. The creative campaign, "Surprisingly invigorating" aired successfully in its run from 2004 to 2007, depicting savvy young consumers outsmarting "hot and compromising" social situations with clever, cool humor, and, of course Citrus Splash.
>
> *(Malefyt and Morais 2012, 132)*

Malefyt discusses his reservations about a campaign that "centered on people's insecurities" and that suggested that a commercial product "can somehow substitute for, or enhance, real human relations." Malefyt confronts head-on the ethical ambiguities in the advertising industry, noting that there are both no-go zones (advertising directed at children, advertising for harmful products like cigarettes) and grey areas (such as covert observation of consumers), but places this in the context of the changing character of consumer agency and the fact that in contemporary society the circulation of values increasingly presents itself in terms of the circulation of media images.

Ethical Intersections

One should notice that in each of these cases the ethical dilemma involved no outright illegal or dishonest or harmful act, but rather conflict between competing institutional, community, public, and professional priorities, each involving at least one powerful actor. Applied scientists working in practical (i.e., not laboratory) settings are by definition located at intersections of scientific and practical obligations, and are expected to conform to the norms and requirements both of scientific inquiry and the settings in which scientific findings are obtained and applied. The profession of engineering has been navigating such frontiers for more than a century, and has accumulated ample resources for a well-developed discourse on engineering ethics. The principles of engineering ethics are articulated by professional societies such as the Accreditation Board for Engineering and Technology (ABET), and gives attention to the teaching of ethical principles, "including an understanding of and a commitment to address professional and ethical responsibilities, including a respect for diversity" (ABET 2013).

Similarly, Business Anthropology could create practical dialogue between business and anthropological ethical practice, and use these as resources to develop a robust discourse of Business Anthropology ethics. However, we are immediately confronted with the fact of the subaltern and contested status of ethical reasoning in management literature and in business schools, and in business in general. Although this is not the place to conduct a comprehensive survey of these issues, we can take note of some general tendencies.

A series of articles collected by Julian Friedland, a philosopher at the Fordham University School of Business, *Doing Well and Good: The Human Face of the New Capitalism*, demonstrates that ethical behavior in business is not contrary to core business values of practicality and profitability (Friedland 2009). Written in the wake of Enron and Worldcom, and on the cusp of a Great Recession induced by the world's leading financial institutions, its 11 articles develop the point of view that in the long run, an ethical stance within the corporate world is, well, good business.

As anthropologists, we might take special note of section one of the book, "The Rôle of Corporate Culture." One chapter in this section, "Facing the Stakeholder Trust Gap" by Michael Pirson, describes how such behaviors as managerial inflexibility, broken promises, and hidden agendas can undermine trust, and conversely how value-based culture and ethical role models can reinforce trust. Yet as businesses become larger and more complex, and more tightly coupled, thinking through ethical issues such as product lifecycles and compensation schemes should be something to which anthropologists can contribute. In other words, it is not business per se, but rather certain business practices – the commodification of everything, institutional growth far beyond human scale, concentrations of wealth and power, over-compensation of executives, short-term thinking, predatory class relationships – that give business a bad name. All of these can be treated either as sources of pollution to be avoided, or as problems to be ameliorated or resolved.[2]

Similarly, Mark Schwartz in "Beyond the Bottom Line: A Shifting Paradigm for Business" (2009) claims that in the last few years the business world is undergoing some major paradigm shifts which include corporate social responsibility, sustainability, stakeholder management, business ethics, and corporate citizenship (Schwartz 2009, 131). However, business ethics still remains a peripheral discipline within organizational studies. J. B. Ciulla, in "Is Business Ethics Getting Better? A Historical Perspective" (2011) observes that some business schools do not commit to business ethics and keep teaching students more on "the craft of making money than on the craft of actually running a business or a sustainable business" (Ciulla 2011, 341). Steve May, in "Transforming the Ethical Culture of Organizations" observes that "Business ethics has continued to have a marginal status in the theory and practice of organizational studies" (May 2009, 89).

In the management literature, Friedland shows how top management journals' "empirical and descriptive focus leaves precious little room for ethics" (Friedland 2012, 330). Friedland points out that "much more needs to be done to address the broader epistemological crisis that is the root cause of the dearth of such genuinely business ethical articles in top-tier journals" (Friedland 2012, 343).

A preliminary survey of the syllabi from MBA programs across U.S. universities confirms John Rollert's observation that there seems to be limited agreement on what stands for "business ethics." Rollert claims that the most obvious reason for this may be that in contrast to law and medical students, MBAs do not have a norm of professional ethics they must learn and follow if they wish to practice business (Rollert 2010). Yet, numerous books on business ethics (e.g., Crane and Matten

2007) and journals on business ethics (e.g., the *Journal of Business Ethics*) attest that understanding ethics is a current concern within business.

A first-hand examination of such intersections comes from two anthropologists employed in research and development at General Motors, Elizabeth K. Briody and Tracy Meerwarth Pester, in "The Coming of Age of Anthropological Practice and Ethics" (Briody and Meerwarth Pester 2014). The authors observe that although the academic discipline of anthropology is more than a century old, the *practice* of anthropology is a relatively new phenomenon, with the consequence that anthropological ethics have not yet kept pace with the emerging realities of practice. They demonstrate that although their context of engagement, a major industrial corporation, had its own strongly developed code of ethics, there were areas in which the corporate code and the academic disciplinary code were not in alignment.

An anthropological contribution here might be an understanding of the complexity of value. The utilitarianism that dominates most economic thinking in American society in terms of "rational actor" models, and denominates value in terms of market transaction and individual gratifications, has several logical inadequacies: First, there are numerous values other than utility, values that are intrinsic to an activity rather than external to it: What, after all, is the value of true friendship? Second, most human activity, even within a capitalist society, takes place outside market relationships. Thus elevating the market as a universal measure of all human worth can oftentimes prove problematic. Even within market exchanges, value has dimensions of locality, temporality, and sociality. Values of locality are expressed in the well-known "spheres of exchange" first documented by Bohannan yet found in any society: "priceless" works of art, for example, are not sold at Costco. Values of temporality or commitment are described by Karen Ho in her study of stockbrokers: The contrast between short-term trading mentality and the long-term investment strategies needed to build products and companies is evident in the contrast between the "shareholder value" movement and corporate executives (Ho 2009). Values of sociality are described by Zelizer in her description of "social currencies," in which sums of money are "earmarked" either in terms of their origin ("Uncle Sidney's Christmas gift") or their intended purpose (Zelizer 1994). The "rational actor" of economic theory is more an article of faith than it is an empirical observation.

In sum, in the business world the content and primacy of ethics is a contested terrain, although there appear to be openings for dialogues over ethics, to which anthropology's commitments to empiricism can contribute. This dialogue can move forward only insofar as business and other institutions are no longer viewed as academic anthropology's Other, but rather as sites of legitimate participation and engagement.

Building Ethical Communities of Practice

Laura Hammershøy and Thomas Ulrik Madsen, two anthropologists with ReD Associates, a consultancy, turn the conversation of Business Anthropology ethics away from standard formulations of "do no harm" toward a positive obligation to "do good in a broader sense" (Hammershøy and Madsen 2012, 46). Echoing Alain Badiou, they argue that ethics based on universalist principles of right and wrong implicitly solidify and justify the imbalances and inequalities of the status quo (Hammershøy and Madsen 2012, 52). As an alternative to such deontological formulations they call for an "ethics of process in which ethical truths can unfold as one works toward the good." In the spirit of their formulation, we offer the following foundation for building an ethics of Business Anthropology.

First, ethics should be seen as a core part of training in Business Anthropology. Training in ethical reasoning comes not from memorizing codes but from working through difficult cases. Just as one learns to play baseball not from studying the rules, but from practice in pitching and catching and swinging and missing and hitting (even in a batting cage), one learns ethical reasoning primarily by solving ethical problems, real or simulated. Such simulations or workshops should be fundamental to professional training.

Second, part of any institutional engagement should be *due diligence* on the ethical norms (both formal and informal) of the site of the engagement. Preparation for fieldwork in business or any other formal, institutional setting should include a due diligence effort at reviewing the business's and industry's code of ethics: The conscientious ethnographer departing for the field should be more knowledgeable about his or her field site's ethical guidelines than most of his or her informants. In most cases these codes are taken seriously, although the complexity of the discourse of the codes (firm commandments, advisory documents, or window-dressing) usually mirrors the institutional complexity.

Such a due diligence review and familiarity will accomplish several things: First, it might provide an advance warning of lurking ethical hazards. More typically, it will alert the ethnographer to conflicting ethical priorities between the profession of anthropology and the business or industry in which he or she is conducting research, including both contracting parties and cooperating sites. Most importantly, it will give the ethnographer a resource for resolving ethical issues that arise *in vivo* in the course of fieldwork; the federal agency that contracted with Jerry Vaughn (Case #1) and later demanded to see his field notes would have to pause (at least) when asked "Are you asking me to break *your* rules?" Demands such as this are, of course, often power plays with no contractual or ethical foundation; ethnographers working at the intersections of multiple institutions including sponsors, field sites, and consultancies, should be aware that power asymmetries, confrontations and conflicting priorities come with the territory.

Third, such ethical processes as due diligence and ethical reviews can be built into communities of practice that embrace Business Anthropologists. The concept of "community of practice" was developed as a social learning concept by Jean Lave and Etienne Wenger (Lave and Wenger 1991; Wenger 2000; Wenger et al. 2002). Communities of practice are groups of people who engage in some common endeavor on an ongoing basis, e.g. organizational development, industrial design, or consumer research. A community of practice engages people in mutual sense-making that can be both consensual and conflicting. The mutual sense-making is founded on their engagement in the shared activity and a mutual understanding of that activity. The activity enables shared sense-making, permits meaning to be exercised, and affords the circumstances for developing conventions (Lave and Wenger 1991).

A community of practice can provide ethnographers with trusted collaborators who can help him or her work through ethical difficulties. To illustrate, when one of the authors (Trainor) was in Afghanistan in 2010–11 he worked in relative isolation from social science colleagues spread across the country, despite the fact that Internet connectivity was often available. It wasn't until he accepted a post-deployment position as a social science instructor in his program's training school that he had the opportunity to meet several other social scientists with similar experiences in Iraq and learned how they had addressed ethical issues. They all were much concerned about ethical issues because they had to teach the subject as part of the curriculum and they also sometimes had opportunities to give input to program leadership. This association presented Trainor with the chance to participate in an informal ethical community of practice that allowed him to review his ethical decison making during his first Afghan deployment and improve upon those he made during his second deployment in 2013–14 by reaching out to other social science colleagues for input.

Participation in a community of practice allows multiple perspectives to be brought to bear on any particular issue. It helps someone in the field implement ethics on an ongoing basis, avoids the easy slide into a go-along-to-get-along mode of conduct, and provides an accountability link between the individual and the group. Moreover, technology has changed what it means for communities to "be together": Email lists, wikis, blogs, and online discussion forums means that just because a Business Anthropologist is working alone that he or she does not need to grapple with ethical questions alone. Other members of the ethical community are just a mouse click away to offer insights, listen to one vent frustrations, or to provide moral support.

For a community of practice to achieve ethical ends, it must have self-awareness as one of its objectives. "We work together to figure out the right thing to do," even if unstated as such, must be at least an implicit reason for communal identity. The more a sense of "we," as a communal identity is articulated, the more natural conversations about "the right thing to do" become. Following the insights of Hammershøy and Madsen regarding creating ethical processes, we suggest the following steps to place Business Anthropology on the firmest of ethical foundations.

First, our understanding of ethics should expand beyond code compliance to embrace a larger conception of doing good, with the understanding that "doing good" often varies from one situation to another. Does "doing good" mean protecting one's informants (and which group of informants?), or the corporate interests of the field site (Case #2, *supra*).

Second, training in moral reasoning should be on par with other elements of training in field methods: Working through difficult ethical cases, such as those presented above, is no less critical to sound fieldwork than interviewing technique or pile-sorting, and should be given similar stress in methods classes.

Third, the professional life of anthropologists, business or otherwise, should include spaces for shared ethical reflection among colleagues, with the understanding that moralistic accusations contribute little and can even derail the process. Sometimes these spaces might be formalized, as in the morbidity and mortality reviews of clinical settings; in other cases they might occur as casual conversations among colleagues. The obligations of collegiality include mutual contributions to ethical reasoning, which professional societies should foster.

For most of the twentieth century Anthropology grew up in an institutional intersection between academic and colonial or quasi-colonial institutions: The Explorers Club and its social milieux, the Bureau of Indian Affairs, or the Colonial Office were as much the institutional anchors of Anthropology as Oxford or Cambridge or the Museum of Natural History. As old-fashioned colonialism fell out of favor and as universities became core institutions of post-industrial societies, Anthropology's identity and professional obligations were increasingly problematized and contested. In today's new world of neoliberal insecurity and flexible rationalization (Batteau and Psenka 2012) this is likely to continue.

The authors of this chapter and the contributors to this volume have spent decades engaging anthropological knowledge and methods in business and other institutional settings, typically far removed from tribal villages or peasant communities. Recent data (Whiteford and Trotter 2008; Baba 2009; Davenport 2007) suggest that Business Anthropology will occupy a prominent and growing place in the anthropological firmament, as academic employment recedes and as business demand increases. As many of the contributions to this volume suggest, just as is the case with the professions of law and medicine, Anthropology will increasingly find its home in the worlds of corporate work, public service, and private practice, as well as in the university. A Business Anthropology that embraces ethical commitments and communities of practice can be in the forefront of preserving Anthropology's mission in service of humanity.

Acknowledgments

The authors would like to express their appreciation to Ms. Irene Mokra for her very substantial research and editorial assistance, both of which were essential to the completion of this chapter. We also express our appreciation to the two anonymous reviewers, whose guidance gave substantially new direction to the argument. Whatever merits this chapter has owes much to these; its defects remain the responsibility of the authors.

Notes

1 We write this, of course, with a full awareness of the multiple and sometimes difficult ethical conflicts that anthropology has encountered in its traditional field sites: Knowledge of indigenous customs, social arrangements, sacred lore and objects, and many other issues can and have been used against the objects of study, and anthropology has undertaken

much soul-searching in recent years to create guidelines for ethical behavior in these situations. The extreme power asymmetries between Western institutions and actors (including professors) and their sponsors on the one hand, and indigenous peoples on the other, makes these particularly hazardous, with field anthropologists frequently caught in the middle. In the business world, by contrast, ethical dilemmas tend to be more subtle and far-reaching.

2 From a cross-cultural point of view, moralities of pollution and moralities of pragmatism are probably orthogonal; detailed prescriptions of what one is and is not permitted to touch based on semiotic properties is difficult to square with a get-the-job-done attitude. Yet as anthropologists we cannot judge which of these has general ethical applicability; we can, however, recognize the different cultural circumstances in which one or the other is more appropriate.

References

Accreditation Board for Engineering and Technology (ABET). 2013. Criteria for Accrediting Engineering Technology Programs 2013–2014. www.abet.org/DisplayTemplates/DocsHandbook.aspx?id=3150 (accessed February 14, 2013).

American Anthropological Association. 2012. Statement on Ethics: Principles of Professional Responsibility. www.aaanet.org/coe/Code_of_Ethics.pdf (accessed February 9, 2013).

Baba, Marietta. 2009. Disciplinary-Professional Relations in an Era of Anthropological Engagement. *Human Organization* 68, 4: 380–391.

Baba, Marietta. 2012. *Anthropology and Business: Negotiating Boundaries in an Institutional Field*. Paper presented at the Annual Meetings of the American Anthropological Association, San Francisco, California, November 17, 2012.

Batteau, Allen and Carolyn E. Psenka. 2012. Horizons of Business Anthropology in a World of Flexible Accumulation. *Journal of Business Anthropology* 1, 1: 72–90.

Briody, Elizabeth K. and Tracy Meerwarth Pester. 2014. The Coming of Age of Anthropological Practice and Ethics. *Journal of Business Anthropology* 1, 1: 1–27.

Cassell, Joan and Sue-Ellen Jacobs. 2006. *Handbook on Ethical Issues in Anthropology*. Special publication of the American Anthropological Association, Number 23. Washington, DC: American Anthropological Association.

Ciulla, J. B. 2011. Is Business Ethics Getting Better? A Historical Perspective. *Business Ethics Quarterly* 21, 2: 335–343.

Crane, A. and D. Matten. 2007. *Business Ethics: Managing Corporate Citizenship and Sustainability in an Age of Globalization*. New York: Oxford University Press.

Davenport, T. 2007. The Rise of Corporate Anthropology. *Harvard Business Review* November: 2–3.

Friedland, Julian, ed. 2009. *Doing Well and Good: The Human Face of the New Capitalism*. Charlotte, NC: Information Age Publishing.

Friedland, Julian. 2012. Beyond Empiricism: Realizing the Ethical Mission of Management. *Business and Society Review* 117, 3: 329–356.

Hammershøy, Laura and Thomas Ulrick Madsen. 2012. Ethics in Business Anthropology. *EPIC 2012 Proceedings*, 46–55.

Ho, Karen. 2009. *Liquidated: An Ethnography of Wall Street*. Durham, NC: Duke University Press.

Jonsen, Albert R., and Stephen Toulmin. 1988. *The Abuse of Casuistry: A History of Moral Reasoning*. Berkeley and Los Angeles: University of California Press.

Jordan, Ann T. 2013. *Business Anthropology*. Long Grove, IL: Waveland Press.

Kirsch, Stuart. 2002. Anthropology and Advocacy: A Case Study of the Campaign against the Ok Tedi Mine. *Critique of Anthropology* 22, 2: 175–200.

Lave, Jean, and Etienne Wenger. 1991. *Situated Learning: Legitimate Peripheral Participation.* Cambridge, MA: Cambridge University Press.

Lucas, Jessica L. and Daniela M. Peluso. 2012. Traversing the Borders: Passages Between Academia and Industry. Paper presented at the Annual Meetings of the American Anthropological Association, San Francisco, California.

MacIntyre, Alasdair. 2006. Social Structures and Their Threats to Moral Agency. In *Ethics and Politics: Collected Essays,* Vol. 2, A. MacIntyre, ed., 186–204. West Nyack: Cambridge University Press.

Malefyt, Timothy de Waal. 2013. Anthropologists at Work in Advertising and Marketing. In *A Handbook of Practicing Anthropology,* R. W. Nolan, ed. New York: John Wiley and Sons.

Malefyt, Timothy de Waal and Robert J. Morais. 2012. *Advertising and Anthropology: Ethnographic Practice and Cultural Perspectives.* London: Berg.

May, Steve. 2009. Transforming the Ethical Culture of Organizations. In *Doing Well and Good: The Human Face of the New Capitalism,* S. Friedland, ed., 87–111. Charlotte, NC: Information Age Publishing.

Miller, Christine Z. 2012. Lost in Translation: Ethics and Ethnography in Design Research. Paper presented at the Annual Meetings of the American Anthropological Association, San Francisco, California, November 15, 2012.

Miller, Daniel. 1997. *Capitalism: An Ethnographic Approach.* London: Berg.

Rollert, John Paul. 2010. Going Beyond Business Ethics-as-Castor Oil. Harvard Business Review Blog. blogs.hbr.org/cs/2010/10/going_beyond_business_ethics-a.html (accessed January 12, 2013).

Schwartz, Mark S. 2009. Beyond the Bottom Line: A Shifting Paradigm for Business. In *Doing Well and Good: The Human Face of the New Capitalism,* S. Friedland, ed., 131–147. Charlotte, NC: Information Age Publishing.

Stout, Jeffrey. 1988. *Ethics after Babel: The Language of Morals and their Discontents.* Princeton: Princeton University Press.

Sunderland, Patricia L. and Rita M. Denny. 2007. *Doing Anthropology in Consumer Research.* Walnut Creek, CA: Left Coast Press.

Wenger, Etienne. 2000. *Communities of Practice.* New York: Cambridge University Press.

Wenger, Etienne, Richard McDermott, and William Snyder. 2002. *Cultivating Communities of Practice.* Boston: Harvard Business School Press.

Whiteford, Linda and Robert Trotter. 2008. *Ethics for Anthropological Research and Practice.* Long Grove, IL: Waveland Press.

Zaloom, Caitlin. 2006. *Out of the Pits: Traders and Technology from Chicago to London.* Chicago: University of Chicago Press.

Zelizer, Viviana. 1994. *The Social Meaning of Money.* New York: Basic Books.

5

ETHICAL CHALLENGES AND CONSIDERATIONS IN GLOBAL NETWORKED ORGANIZATIONS

Julia C. Gluesing

Introduction

As the processes of economic integration and globalization have accelerated remarkably over the past twenty years, multinational enterprises (MNEs) stand at the center of trade, investment and the transfer of knowledge and technology. Everyday, MNEs cross many boundaries on multiple levels: political, legal, and economic boundaries at the national, regional and community level, various external and internal organizational boundaries, the boundaries of language, and multiple cultural boundaries – all of which must be recognized, negotiated, and integrated in some way to get work done on a global scale (Leung et al. 2005). Since the 1990s, anthropologists have been writing about and investigating MNEs as the primary vehicles for the movement of information, symbols, capital, and commodities in global and transnational spaces (Appadurai 1996).

For business leaders, globalization carries with it complex moral challenges that they cannot ignore. The moral challenges and dilemmas of choice they pose cannot be easily resolved through moral theory because there may be more than one right response from conscientious people who present choices that may all be justifiable according to different moral logics (Thompson 2010). There are dominant challenges that present both ethical risks and opportunities, especially in any attempt to create common moral ground (Thompson 2010, 16):

- Growing recognition of human rights norms assert the equal value of individuals as part of the human community, but also threaten to supplant norms and laws of local cultures.
- Weapons of mass destruction heighten a sense of security for some nations and the power to enforce international law, but they also threaten the safety and security of the planet.

- Transnational threats such as environmental degradation, disease, famine, water shortage, and population migration represent temporary but tractable obstructions on the pathway to global peace and prosperity for some wealthier stakeholders, but these conditions also waste human lives, threaten the world's ecosystem, and disrupt local economies.
- Global integration of markets, labor, and capital creates market efficiencies and wealth that are seen by some as promising a future of economic freedom and security for all, but these same forces expose large segments of humanity to severe economic and social risks with no effective safety net.
- Global communication networks link people and communities together, but these same technologies threaten the integrity and autonomy of local languages, customs, and cultures.

Meeting these challenges of globalization is not just the work of governments and international non-profit agencies; these challenges must also be faced and resolved in multinational enterprises.

For business and organizational anthropologists the complex global arenas of MNEs mean that there are multiple stakeholders in any research project that crosses global work contexts, creating ethical complexity in any ethnographic endeavor, whether in pursuit of business objectives or in the conduct of basic research. This chapter is about one global research project, called ATI, which illustrates from a business anthropologist's first-hand experience and perspective the reasons for and challenges of ethical complexity in the MNE multi-stakeholder work context and discusses how the multidisciplinary research team addressed these challenges. The example concludes with a discussion of current ethical dilemmas and their implications for the future of anthropological work in, and study of, business and organization in global MNE multi-stakeholder work contexts.

The Ethical Challenges of Complex Global Business

There are three primary reasons why MNEs create an ethical complexity that poses challenges for business and organizational anthropologists: (1) there is a perspective of neoliberalism in MNEs that generates the prevalent ethical principles for decision making; (2) ethical judgments are embedded in culture and are especially difficult to grasp when multiple cultural arenas are involved; and (3) ethical conduct in MNEs is also an intercultural phenomenon that requires negotiation across cultural boundaries.

The first reason for ethical complexity is the predominance in MNEs of the neoliberal perspective. Neoliberalism is based in the belief that freely adopted market mechanisms are the optimal way of organizing all exchanges of goods and services, and includes the conviction that the only legitimate purpose of the state is to safeguard individual, especially commercial, liberty, as well as strong private property rights (Hayek 1979; Bourdieu 1998; Friedman 2006). It remains a pervasive form of political rationality that is both formal and global in nature and that continually enters into new relationships with diverse value orientations and political positives (Collier and Ong 2005). The neoliberal perspective is a difficult one for anthropologists to sort out, because neoliberalism incorporates many concepts that anthropologists might agree with, such as agency and the active creation of social and economic order. But it also is universalist in its advocacy for a *corporate* form of agency, in which people should see themselves in a means–end relationship with the world, and see themselves as though they were a business (Gershon 2011, 539).

MNEs develop codes of ethics, especially ethical principles for decision making, from two main schools of thought based in formalism and utilitarianism: rules and results (Jackson 2007). Ethics in business has generally meant rules about how the company and its employees should act internally, and toward consumers and others in the marketplace because of what is "right" or simply because of what is required by law. These rules are usually made by management and are generally meant to apply corporate-wide, across the MNE. However, recently, the Code of Ethics is shifting somewhat from a universally "right" and "wrong" basis for action to one that emphasizes sustainability, such that what is ethical is that which produces a sustainable operating environment, whether it is social, economic, political, or environmental, or even all of these in combination. Ethics is becoming intertwined with responsible leadership that produces operational sustainability or results:

> The New Ethics is a conduct of business that enables a company to optimize its returns to shareholders, employees, customers, business partners, local communities, and the environment. It is a dynamic standard for pursuing profitability and growth that allows future generations an equal opportunity for growth and development.
>
> *(Laszlo and Nash 2007, 2)*

There is a move in MNEs to responsible leadership in global business to ensure positive outcomes at multiple levels, combining a macro-view of business with a micro-view of leadership. This new model of leadership places emphasis on the deliberative practices and discursive resolution of often conflicting positions on the appropriate action to take in any specific situation and couples this micro-view with the understanding that MNEs are political actors, the macro-view (Voegtlin et al. 2012). Similarly, events are thought to interact with business ethics. While there may be an institutionalized ethic in MNEs that governs or guides routine choices and behavior, unpredictable things happen in global enterprises on a daily basis, and managers are responsible for making sense of these events. The unpredictable events serve to de-institutionalize business ethics. In practice, events pose a particular problem for generalized interpretive frameworks and place emphasis on the wisdom of the manager or leader faced with unpredictability to make the ethical choice in the circumstances (Deroy and Clegg 2011).

The challenge for anthropologists in the prevalence of neoliberalism and this shift to responsible leadership and a focus on events is the very dominant and dynamic nature of this view of ethics. The "intersubjective reception of events that

2017

ETHICS IN THE ANTHROPOLOGY OF BUSINESS

Explorations in Theory, Practice, and Pedagogy

Edited by Timothy de Waal Malefyt and Robert J. Morais

Routledge
Taylor & Francis Group

NEW YORK AND LONDON

Debssmantee 20$

S3244
Watch plan ~

transform ethical interpretive frameworks and engender their dynamics" (Deroy and Clegg 2011, 638) means there is increased complexity in anthropological work as well as in managerial work. For researchers, the "New Ethics" means that within the MNEs people's views, especially managerial decision-makers', are likely to be changing in adaptation to the current global and local business environment. Ethics becomes a moving target.

The second reason MNEs create ethical complexity is the relationship of culture and ethics itself and the many cultural arenas that are likely to be involved in any research to be conducted in MNEs. There is general agreement among sociologists and anthropologists that ethical ideas, beliefs, views, or judgments and the practices that accompany them derive from general social practices and accords, or to say it another way, are "socially constructed" (Abend 2008). Why particular groups of people have the moral views that they do, and what the effects of these views are on behavior, interaction, structure, change, and institutions is a dominant topic of ethnographic work. What makes it so challenging in the context of MNEs is the sheer number of groups with whom one must become acquainted, at least superficially, in order to sort out the ethical viewpoints that must be managed to conduct a research project.

Third, the process of globalization, with MNEs as drivers of this process, can be understood as the intensification of exchange, both economic and social, across national borders (Scherer and Patzer 2011). This process increases the number of interactions of people and organizations from different cultural and national backgrounds. Ethics becomes cross-boundary and intercultural in nature, and anthropologists who want to do research in MNEs can find themselves in the challenging position of having to negotiate ethics within the MNE as well as among stakeholders outside the MNEs, such as universities and funding agencies, whose views might and do conflict with one another. Not only do anthropologists have to try to understand the different ethical standards and viewpoints of multiple stakeholders, but they also often have to become the negotiators for reconciliation of these multiple ethical standards if research is to go forward.

Ethical Complexity in the ATI Research Project

The story of a United States National Science Foundation (NSF) funded research grant called "Accelerating the Diffusion of Innovations: A Digital Diffusion Dashboard Methodology for Global Networked Organizations,"[1] provides a very real illustration of the ethical complexity in multinational enterprises, and is a good example for a discussion of the ethical dilemmas anthropologists face in conducting research, especially in interdisciplinary research teams with multiple stakeholders.

Background

The idea for the research project came about when my colleagues (from the academic disciplines of information systems, communication, and engineering) and

I had been consulting and teaching in the automotive industry for over a decade. We had observed that, despite the increasing ubiquity and sophistication of information technology (IT), organizations were not taking advantage of the capabilities inherent in their information infrastructure to manage their global innovation processes and networks. We thought that the IT infrastructure could be used to investigate the diffusion of innovation in multinational corporations, which are global networked organizations. We believed that a company could use its IT infrastructure not only to create, transmit, and store communication messages, but also to learn something about how the innovation of new technology was proceeding across the company's global product development network. These ideas formed the basis for our NSF proposal to develop a new methodology for investigating and leveraging a company's IT infrastructure to accelerate the diffusion of an innovation. We proposed to develop IT-based methods by tapping into the company's infrastructure and to validate our methods using ethnography. The NSF funded the grant for three years beginning in 2005, and the grant received a two-year extension to continue the research until 2010.

The Digital Diffusion Dashboard (DDD) NSF grant focused on one automotive innovation with several sub component systems, which had the pseudonym Advanced Technology Innovation (ATI) to comply with corporate confidentiality requirements (which will be discussed later in this chapter as part of the ethical issues faced by the researchers). The ATI product innovation was not a top-down mandatory component built into a vehicle, for example, like a safety belt or an air bag. Rather, ATI was a bottom-up innovation, which was shaped and reshaped by a team of specialized engineers from different disciplines to determine its system compatibility, and its final functional features for customer appeal and competitive advantage. An auto product development innovation team must persuade members of the social system targeted for adoption – such as engineers who specialize in the engine, transmission, chassis, and electrical subsystems for a new vehicle program – of the value of adopting its new technology, and how it will meet or exceed anticipated user needs, as well as satisfy the requirements for engineering cost, timing, weight, performance, safety, and regulatory specifications for inclusion on a vehicle.

The adoption or rejection of such innovations can be a long, difficult, and arduous path – especially when the team is globally distributed – taking anywhere from three to five years from idea to production in a vehicle that is ready for marketplace introduction. Using IT-based methods, we designed and tested a set of indicators, which we assembled into a prototype "Digital Diffusion Dashboard" (DDD) to help innovation managers visualize, monitor, and manage their global innovations and accelerate innovation in a global networked organization. We created simple, clear, and reusable dashboard indicators that we thought would help open a new frontier for both scholars and practitioners alike by demonstrating how to leverage a company's data resources – primarily email – to visually manage the diffusion network as it emerges, and to monitor the consequences of implementation efforts during the diffusion process. The indicators made visible the ATI team's network of interactions, the main topics of their conversation, and how they felt about their work over time. ATI managers linked the indicators to their own business performance metrics to get an overall sense of how the innovation diffusion process was proceeding.

The Multiplicity of Stakeholders: Study Teams, Corporate, and Government Stakeholders

Automotive product development is most certainly a complex multi-stakeholder research context. The research involved the following primary stakeholders who all had their own views about ethics and ethical behavior: two collaborating study teams, corporate management, including the legal staff and human resource departments, the study participants themselves (the ATI product development innovation team), the university institutional review boards (IRBs), and the governmental funding agency, the NSF. The research team also referenced the American Anthropological Association (AAA) Code of Ethics in considering and making decisions about ethical issues during the course of the research.

The two teams who collaborated to conduct the NSF DDD study were the university-based researchers and the internal corporate research team. The university team included two other professors and me as the principal investigators on the grant, plus graduate and undergraduate research assistants. We led the study and were responsible for the study design, software choice, indicator selection, all research approvals, and for training the internal research team how to install and use the software for the study. We were also the people who had to negotiate our way through the difficult ethical landscape. The internal corporate research team consisted of five company engineers who managed the internal corporate IT resources, databases, and security for the study. This team also performed the dashboard testing and indicator validation, and facilitated access to research subjects and settings for the ethnographic research. The members served as internal technical experts regarding the product development process and as liaisons to the university research team.

On the corporate side, the primary stakeholders were corporate management, the legal staff, and the human resource departments. The spokespersons for corporate management were the seven people who reported to the chairman as global vice presidents. They assumed the overall corporate oversight and support for the research and had very practical ethical criteria for evaluating the outcomes. Their motivation for participating as an industry partner for an NSF study was to gain access to leading edge university research. By providing in-kind resources in the form of managerial and employee time, as well as use of company facilities and equipment, they hoped to receive tools that might give them a competitive advantage. The legal staff got involved in the research to review and ensure the protection of the MNE's intellectual property and employee privacy rights, and in the implementation of regulatory compliance for the conduct of research across the multiple national locations. The human resources department was primarily concerned with protecting employee privacy rights and obtaining permissions for the research from employees.

The global ATI team members were the study participants, and consisted of 298 people distributed in locations around the world. This team was charged with navigating the innovation through the global product development process, obtaining buy-in from the component vehicle engineers, and persuading a target program team to adopt their innovation and include it in the vehicle that would eventually be produced and sold in the marketplace.

There were two university institutional review boards that had to give their approvals for the research to begin and move forward. Both of these review boards had their own systems for evaluating the research and for ensuring compliance with both university and U.S. federal government requirements.

The NSF Human and Social Dynamics program itself, which funded the study, was the last primary stakeholder. Their interest was ensuring the study would contribute to the broader societal and public good, as well as advance graduate and undergraduate education and training.

Because the research project involved anthropologists, who were responsible for investigating the "whys and hows" behind the innovation process and validating the IT-based dashboard metrics with "ground truth," the AAA Code of Ethics was the guiding reference for ethical decisions on the research team, especially when the decisions concerned human subjects. The engineers and IT specialists on the university and corporate research teams were most concerned with IT security and intellectual property protections.

The complexity presented by multiple stakeholders in the NSF research project resulted in ethical challenges throughout the five-year study, requiring that the university research team learn the ethical viewpoints of each of the primary stakeholders and also serve as negotiators across the various groups.

Ethical Challenges

The general neoliberal perspective of the corporate stakeholders in the MNE meant that ethics was reviewed according to market criteria that ensured competitive advantage and minimized the impact of governmental regulations. Ethical considerations included keeping all data gathered in the research inside the corporate IT firewall and minimizing the potential of leaks that might occur in giving "outsiders," the university research team and the NSF, access to confidential company information, especially information about a high-stakes innovation that was under development. The NSF also embodied some of the same free market concerns by seeking to ensure national advantage in the marketplace through funding of research in the corporate sector with an eye to fostering a faster development cycle of ideas to products in the nation overall; but, at the same time, the agency actively advocated a policy of open sharing of data from the research with other researchers both inside and outside the United States. In fact, one of the elements of the NSF research proposal was the development of a database of descriptive information about innovations and their diffusion trajectories, which could be accessed and used by other researchers for future studies. There was an ethical challenge presented by the corporate desire to protect its innovations, and the NSF focus on openness and sharing of research results. Was it ethical to share corporate data, or not?

The protection of human subjects was another ethical challenge for the university research team. The MNE legal staff and the human resource staff were in agreement about protecting the privacy of the MNE's employees. However, the human resources rules and regulations were different in all the countries where the ATI project was ongoing. That meant that the human resources policies in each country had to be reviewed and compared, and legal negotiations had to be undertaken. The NSF had one set of rules, based on U.S. governmental regulations regarding human subjects research, and these rules were in turn incorporated into the IRBs at the two universities as a requirement for government funding, but with different implementation practices in each. The IRBs did agree that the IT-based data gathering could be conducted, as long as no participant could be identified. The ethnographic data would have to be subjected to the approvals process for behavioral data at both universities, however.

The research team had to contend with contradictory recruitment policies regarding research participation in each country as well. The recruitment policies in MNE locations around the world varied and were often at odds. For example, in the United States the policy was one of general informed consent with employees agreeing to participate in the research with the option to "opt out" at any time. In Germany, however, it was just the opposite: employees were actively required to "opt in" to the research individually after the German Workers Council had approved the research project.

Over and above the general protection of human subjects, employees had their own personal safety and privacy concerns, which posed a challenge to both the university and the corporate research teams. The IT-based data collection methods involved the automated gathering of employee email, a sensitive matter indeed. As far as corporate management was concerned, the MNE owned all employee email and could access it and read it at any time. All employees, when they logged onto the corporate intranet, saw an automatic message saying that their email was company property and not their own and by logging on they acknowledge that fact. However, from the perspective of the employees, their email was still private, and they did not want "just anybody" accessing it and reading it, let alone analyzing it. Human resource policies also supported this position, regardless of the corporate legal position. Therefore, the university research team was faced with the task of convincing employees that their individual email would not be read by either of the two research teams, internal or university, or by anyone outside the company. The researchers gathered 45,000 emails to create the DDD and the links among more than 2,000 people across the enterprise communicating about the ATI innovation project over time. The DDD metrics were designed to answer seven important evaluative questions that a manager might want to know about an innovation:

1. Who is talking?
   - Who is talking about the innovation?
   - What group of the company do they represent?
   - What level of the company is talking about the innovation?
2. Who are the champions?
   - Who is central in the network?
3. How is the team collaborating?
   - Who is involved in the network?
   - Are the right people talking?
   - Is anyone missing?
4. What is the "buzz" about the innovation?
   - What are people saying about the innovation?
5. What is the emotion of the team?
   - Are people talking positively or negatively about the innovation?
6. What is the rate of adoption?
   - Is the innovation diffusing fast enough?
   - Is it spreading throughout the organization as it should?
7. What is the value proposition?
   - What is the value of the innovation to the organization?

While corporate management, human resources staff, legal counsel, and the universities' IRB boards considered much of this information sensitive and confidential, it was the participants themselves who especially expressed concern because their individual reputations and careers could be at risk. Ethical concerns also arose for everyone because the participants' email boxes contained email sent, forwarded, or copied from people who may not have consented to participate in the study.

Resolving the Ethical Challenges

To respect the MNE's desire for data security and protection of intellectual property and the NSF's desire for open data sharing, the university research team, in collaboration with the internal research team, agreed to keep the "raw data" inside the corporate firewall. This restriction meant that the researchers could create a database or publication that contained only the *results* of the study. The *data leading to the results* had to stay with the company. This decision specified that the researchers could not continue to analyze data after the conclusion of the study because they would not have access to it, and it meant that the NSF could receive and share results but would not have the promised database of descriptive data about the innovation. It also meant that the researchers could not call the MNE or the innovation by their real names but would have to use pseudonyms. The decision was an unusual compromise for the researchers who are accustomed to keeping the data they collect, but it applied only to the IT-based data.

The ethnographic data were another story. The anthropologists successfully presented their case to the MNE, to the university IRBs, and to the study participants for protecting and preserving their data, and not giving anyone inside or outside the corporation access to it. The AAA Code of Ethics[2] was instrumental in supporting the argument.

Human subjects, participant recruitment, personal safety, and privacy concerns surrounding the collection of email data, were all resolved by establishing four procedures with the support of the IT staff and through clear and honest communication with study participants, with approvals from corporate legal and human resources staff around the globe and the university IRBs:

1. All ATI team members received an emailed consent form, approved by the IRB, which they returned with their consent or refusal to participate, which meant that everyone had to actively choose to "opt in." Team members who elected to participate in the study could also "opt out" at any time.
2. The research teams did not gather all email, only the email that was related to the ATI innovation project. To collect only this subset of email, the ATI team members participating in the study installed and activated email rules themselves (which again meant they had to actively choose to participate), using common project keywords (emic language). They copied their email, using a "dummy" email address in the "cc" field, to a centralized, secure server email box with restricted access. They could readily see the dummy email address in their email header and delete it if they did not wish to have a particular email sent to the dummy mailbox in the secure server.
3. Two additional filters were placed in the rules. First, if an email was designated as personal, private, or encrypted, it was automatically excluded from data collection. Second, all legal email around patents that was labeled as "privileged" was excluded from data collection.
4. The university team could not read any individual email. All email content was aggregated as frequency counts for single words or word pairs for analysis. No email message could be reconstructed. Email was also anonymized for any public presentation, for example, user 1, user 2, user 3. After some deliberation, the university IRB and the company's human resource staff decided that because all the email was anonymized for analysis and no individual email could be reconstructed, there was no violation of confidentiality or privacy ethics from their points of view.

The anthropologists on the research team did know who many of the participants were because they talked with them about the ATI innovation project and shadowed them in their work, in accordance with informed consent and with all corporate and IRB approvals of data collection protocols. However, the ethnographers were not able to connect any of the emails with the ethnographic data without the participants giving the anthropologists permission to look at their specific email. The anthropologists did not remove email data from the work site, not just because of both personal privacy and corporate security reasons, but also out of respect for participants in the study. The anthropologists wanted to encourage trust in the research team and between the team and participants.

It took about eight months to resolve the challenges posed by the ethical complexity in the multi-stakeholder context of the ATI research project, and resolution was especially difficult for the anthropologists on the team who were leading this aspect of the project.[3] The project could not get started without negotiated agreements based on the various rules and regulations of the various agencies, governments, and the MNE's corporate legalities and policies. However, there were ongoing ethical decisions that had to be made as new challenges arose throughout the project. The anthropologists had to develop an approach to ethics that could serve as a reference for the project team as they encountered these challenges and worked toward their resolution throughout the life of the project. What follows is an extended discussion of this approach and the dilemmas that are before all anthropologists who do this work.

Discussion and Ongoing Ethical Dilemmas

All of the actions the stakeholders negotiated to resolve ethical issues involved both complying with rules and regulations (which include ethical considerations but cannot be equated with ethics) and considering the ethical decisions to be made within the specific circumstances of the work context. The anthropologists on the research team were the ultimate decision-makers about ethics in the project, primarily because they considered not only what was right by law and by rule, but also what was ethical according to their own ethical values, the values of the people with whom they were working, and the values of the people they were studying. In other words, the anthropologists practiced what could be called situated and relational ethics, taking a pragmatic approach grounded in what they considered to be good anthropology.

In business anthropology, research is generally conducted in the context of daily organization work, where the ethics of everyday activities are often ambiguous. Therefore, a practical and situated ethics helps clarify ethical reasoning in the course of normal problems, or ethical dilemmas that workers and managers face in doing their jobs (Alvesson and Svenningsson 2003). Explicit ethical codes espoused by organizational leaders and those who are part of formal organizational policy in an MNE, as well as the formal Code of Ethics adopted by the American Anthropological Association, were some value as guidelines. However, ethical judgments that are made as part of everyday work are emergent and practical. Ethics are embedded in the situated, particular realities of a context in all its complexity, especially in MNEs where multiple boundaries are crossed and different, often divergent, values and ways of understanding and working are likely to intersect.

To negotiate the ethical complexity in the ATI research project, the anthropologists had to use practical wisdom. In the *Nicomachean Ethics*, Aristotle (1999) outlines three types of intellectual virtue: *Episteme, Techne*, and *Phronesis. Episteme* is known as scientific knowledge (also called declarative knowledge, or know-what) and is considered to be universal and relatively context independent. *Techne*, known as craft knowledge or technical art (also called procedural knowledge, or know-how), is dependent on context, but oriented toward the production of something pragmatic. *Phronesis* is practical wisdom. It is "concerned with action about things that are good or bad for a human being" (Aristotle 1999, 89). *Phronesis* has an ethical component. It is not the "right" way of doing things as might be specified by rules and regulations, or laws in a particular community, but the ethically good action a practical, wise person would take. *Phronesis* puts practice in the foreground and closely connects ethics and action in situated circumstances, since it is "concerned with action and action is about particulars" (Aristotle 1999, 92).

In the ATI project, ethical evaluations were situated and contextualized and discussed by the research teams, both internal and external, and communicated to other stakeholders, and perhaps even negotiated and modified based on stakeholder feedback. However, these evaluations did not mean "anything goes" in a relativist sense. Some universals, such as "do no harm" or "be open and honest regarding your work" in the AAA Code of Ethics were strong points of reference to guide behavior. However, anthropologists, and other stakeholders, too, made ethical judgments and decisions based on the business, technical, and social context, which presented limited choices and possibilities for action. The identification and evaluation of ethical or unethical behavior was based on what was occurring in a specific situation within a particular context in the course of the ATI project's everyday work activities and the research activities involved. *Phronesis* guided the anthropologists, and the other stakeholders as well, through the particularities of contextual complexity.

Phronesis is developed through experience and cannot be taught as part of a university curriculum. It is gained by sharing situations, cases, and stories, and is achieved through discussion with members of different kinds of organizations and who might hold different points of view. The anthropologists working on the ATI project had to practice their trade in the MNE, and reflect and talk about their work in general (without reference to confidential information) with other anthropologists and those outside the discipline in the workplace and on research teams.

Socialization and training must occur in practice, in an emergent way, in order for business anthropologists to develop *phronesis*, and to create an ethical community of practice. As Nyberg has so rightly stated:

> Giving people time to reflect upon and discuss their activities does not necessarily change them but it does make change more likely. The alternative is to enforce disciplinary and controlling pressures to make people behave in certain ways. However, rules or principles will not get us there, since we cannot expect people to act ethically if there they are given no opportunity to exercise practical ethical judgement. This is the major point: following ethical codes does not involve choice, merely compliance; if one does not choose to act, one has not acted ethically.
>
> *(Nyberg 2008, 596)*

There will always be situations that codes of ethics cannot cover. In the complexity of life in an MNE, "universal" rules can only take one so far and one cannot know or memorize them all. Rules may even restrict the capacity to act ethically. It is the practical wisdom to handle particular situations that anthropologists wishing to work in or study complex, global multi-stakeholder organizational contexts must develop over time through practice. For academics who train anthropologists, the development of practical wisdom means that students have to be given the opportunity to practice in complex organizational settings under the guidance of experienced business anthropologists. As Muehlebach (2013, 305) has stated in her review of anthropology for the year 2012, students would benefit by experiencing the ambiguity that arises when different ethical imaginations confront one another. Students, especially graduate students, should be drawn into the conundrums they are likely to face in complex contexts. They should be required to work through the conundrums and reconcile them as part of developing an ethical stance of their own that will prepare them for the contradictions they will face in fieldwork as they move forward with their careers.

There also must be an opportunity to reflect within the larger community of practice, and this generally takes place at conferences such as the Ethnographic Praxis in Industry (EPIC). This reflection is important for students, but it is equally and especially important for business anthropologists who are already practicing in MNEs or other large complex organizations.

Doing "good anthropology" means tracking between the universal and the local, and between general and specific knowledge, "wherein specificity of insight lends credibility to general knowledge, and local knowledge holds the grains of universal wisdom" (Gershon 2011, 550). Good anthropology also means resisting the neoliberal perspective that tends to group together people, communities, or even nations in terms of business or market skills, treating them as though they were all alike, as corporate forms. Gershon (2011) has advocated an "Ethics of Imagination," in which anthropologists pay attention to social forms of organization, to epistemological differences, and to relationships with people as individuals. The ATI researchers attempted to make ethical decisions based on a consideration of how people were related to one another in their organizational networks, both formal and informal social networks, and on an understanding of how people might be personally affected by the decisions, and the multiple ways they might view the situation and the decisions. This took time, which ultimately limited the scope of the research. However, acting within a central tenet of care, in which the researchers valued and respected the connection between themselves and the people they studied, was both a "practical" and "good" anthropology in this author's opinion.

Phronesis as the basis of good anthropology is processual in nature as well as experiential and relational. Complex global work is and will continue to be rapidly changing, so there will be no wisdom that is "once and for all." As our working landscape becomes ever more digital and distributed, and we are faced with new ethical dilemmas posed by the Internet, as well as yet unforeseen technological and societal developments, as practicing business anthropologists we must develop a "discourse ethics" (Palazzo and Scherer 2006; Scherer and Patzer 2011). Discourse that includes storytelling and reflection fosters continual discussion of the situations encountered, and how best to act with wisdom where ethical dilemmas are posed and ethical decisions are required. In an almost post-national era of globalization, the complexity of our dynamic multi-stakeholder business environment requires an open and continual discourse to maintain practical wisdom in the face of the ethical challenges anthropologists face now and will face in the future. Such a discourse ethics is both a constructivist and an intercultural philosophy of ethics that encourages both relativistic and universalistic debate of ongoing situated action that leads to practical knowledge consistent with Aristotle's concept of *phronesis*.

Conclusion

This chapter highlights the three primary reasons for ethical complexity in multistakeholder work contexts: (1) the predominance of neoliberal thinking; (2) the difficulty of dealing with ethics that are situationally and culturally embedded, dynamic, and that also cross multiple boundaries at multiple levels; and (3) the intercultural nature of most interactions in these enterprises that necessitate continual negotiation in the face of unpredictable events. The example of the global ATI project provides an illustration of the ethical challenges that result from this complexity and how these challenges were resolved through eight months of negotiation. The ATI researchers considered the rules, regulations, policies, and laws in the MNE, universities, funding agencies, and various codes of ethics to reach ethical decisions over the life of the project. Which research practices are considered ethical, and in particular, what data – including corporate data – it is ethical to protect or consider confidential, is a matter of compromise across multiple views of ethics and is based in an attuned consideration of context. Acquiring local knowledge and basing decisions in a system of "common sense" (Geertz 1983, 73–93) worked for the team to resolve ethical dilemmas as they faced them.

It also was critical for the ATI researchers to realize that ethics are intertwined with identity. In practice, for organizational actors, values and the choices and behaviors they engender are situated in identities, those held by individuals and those promoted by the organizations in which they work. From this perspective, ethics can be seen as discursive resources that individuals and groups draw upon to author versions of their own identities and engage with organizational narratives. Therefore, all instantiations of ethics will be contextual and situational, often producing conflict if identities are threatened by events or subsequent actions or decisions. The potential for conflict is all the more reason why anthropologists must understand something of the identities of the organization and the organizational actors they are working with and be able to mediate or negotiate conflict when it arises.

The pragmatic nature of lived organizational life also means that explanations of events are always incomplete, allowing for new interpretations of old events as well as for the adjustment of ethical guidelines as unanticipated events occur that redefine the past and potentially remodel the future. The researchers at ATI had to pay attention to the discourse that constitutes the sensemaking surrounding unpredictable events if they were to gain acceptance for their research. The research posed much unpredictability in events that were not part of the normal organizational routine and required shared sensemaking before an "ethical" decision to proceed with the research could be made. Ethics have vitality. "The notion of ethical vitality is a means of registering the ways that ethical responsibility comes alive in organizations when people take, and are in a position to take, a reflexive responsibility for their conduct" (Deroy and Clegg 2011, 646). The explanations contain ethical interpretations that shed light on values, identities, and responsibility in the face of decision-making.

Doing "good anthropology" and making "good ethical decisions" clearly involve more than expertise in international law or the rules and regulations or formal policies of international business. Ethics in business anthropology is based on an understanding of context, in the ability of the anthropologist to dig deep to surface and learn about individuals' perspectives and their reasoning, and how they are situated in particular contexts. Ethics is about relationships and social organization, and about how people refer to the universal in making ethical decisions, while also paying attention to the particularities and constraints of the situation to know not only the right thing to do, but also the good thing to do in the circumstances under a tenet of care. As business and anthropology move more and more into the global business arena, it will be increasingly important to teach and to learn through practical experience, discourse, and especially reflection, if we are to make wise ethical decisions in our own work as it changes and adapts over time to new circumstances, and if we are to proffer "good advice" to organizational actors. A process framework, a "global moral compass" for managing ethics in multistakeholder environments that cross geographic, cultural, and organization boundaries might look something like this:

- Focus on and examine assumptions that underlie beliefs, feelings, and actions, and dig deep enough to understand the identities involved in any situation.
- Assess the consequence of these assumptions and identities.
- Identify and explore alternative sets of assumptions.
- Test the validity of assumptions and the possible ethical choices in the situation through dialogue and reflection.

Notes

1 www.nsf.gov/awardsearch/showAward.do?AwardNumber=0527487.
2 The AAA Code of Ethics contains the following major guidelines:
   - Do no harm.
   - Be open and honest regarding your work.

- Obtain informed consent and necessary permissions.
- Weigh competing ethical obligations due collaborators and affected parties.
- Make your results accessible.
- Protect and preserve your records.
- Maintain respectful and ethical professional relationships.

3 In another MNE that was part of the same National Science Foundation grant it took two years to negotiate intellectual property rights, involving the research team (especially the anthropologists who did not want to disclose interview data), corporate managers and legal staff in different countries, and both universities' legal staffs.

References

Abend, Gabriel. 2008. Two main problems in the sociology of morality. *Theory and Society* 37: 87–125.

Alvesson, Matts and S. Svenningsson. 2003. Managers doing leadership: The extraordinarization of the mundane. *Human Relations* 56, 12: 1435–1459.

Appadurai, Arjun. 1996. *Modernity at large: Cultural dimensions of globalization*. Minneapolis: University of Minnesota Press.

Aristotle. 1999, *Nicomachean ethics*, T. Irwin, trans. 2nd Edition. Indianapolis: Hackett.

Bourdieu, Pierre. 1998. L'essence du néolibéralisme. *Le Monde diplomatique*. www.monde-diplomatique.fr/1998/03/BOURDIEU/10167.

Collier, Stephen J. and Aihwa Ong. 2005. Global assemblages, anthropological problems. In *Global assemblages: Technology, politics, and ethics as anthropological problems*, A. Ong and S. Collier, eds., pp. 3–21. Malden, MA: Blackwell.

Deroy, Xavier and Stewart Clegg. 2011. When events interact with business ethics. *Organization* 18, 5: 637–653.

Friedman, Thomas. 2006. *The world is flat: The globalized world in the twenty-first century*. London: Penguin.

Geertz, Clifford. 1983. *Local knowledge*. New York: Basic Books.

Gershon, Ilana. 2011. Neoliberal agency. *Current Anthropology* 52: 537–555.

Hayek, Friedrich A. 1979. *Law, legislation and liberty: A new statement of the liberal principles and political economy. Volume III: The political order of a free people*. London: Routledge.

Jackson, T. 2007. Cross-cultural sensitivities in developing corporate ethical strategies and practices. In *Corporate ethics and corporate governance*, W. Zimmerli, K. Richter, and M. Holizinger, eds., pp. 229–250. Berlin: Springer.

Laszlo, Christopher and Jeremy Nash. 2007. Six facets of ethical leadership: An executive's guide to the new ethics in business. *Electronic Journal of Business Ethics and Organization Studies* 12, 2: 1–7.

Leung, K., R. Bhagat, N. Buchan, M. Erez, and C. Gibson. 2005. Culture and international business. *Journal of International Business Studies* 36: 357–378.

Muehlebach, Andrea. 2013. On precariousness and the ethical imagination: The year 2012 in sociocultural anthropology. *American Anthropologist* 115, 2: 297–311.

Nyberg, Daniel. 2008. The morality of everyday activities: Not the right, but the good thing to do. *Journal of Business Ethics* 81: 587–598.

Palazzo, Guido and Andreas Georg Scherer. 2006. Corporate legitimacy as deliberation: A communicative framework. *Journal of Business Ethics* 66: 71–88.

Scherer, Andreas Georg and Moritz Patzer. 2011. Beyond universalism and relativism: Habermas's contribution to discourse ethics and its implications for intercultural ethics and organization theory. In *Philosophy and organization theory, research in the sociology of organizations*, Vol. 32, H. Tsoukas and R. Chia, eds., pp. 155–180. Bingley, UK: Emerald Group Publishing Limited.

Thompson, Lindsay J. 2010. The global moral compass for business leaders. *Journal of Business Ethics* 93: 15–32.

Voegtlin, Christian, Moritz Patzer and Andres Georg Scherer. 2012. Responsible leadership in global business: A new approach to leadership and its multi-level outcomes. *Journal of Business Ethics* 105: 1–16.

6

OWNING IT

Evolving Ethics in Design and Design Research

Christine Miller

Introduction

In fall 2012 the American Anthropological Association (AAA) was wrapping up the latest revision of its Statement of Ethics.[1] The theme of the 2012 AAA Annual Meeting, "Borders and Crossings," provided an opportunity to examine issues of ethics and ethical challenges related to anthropological practice in business and organizations in a session on Ethics in Business Anthropology. Historically, ethics have been a primary concern within anthropology. Vigilance is constant and pervasive, from the education and training of students throughout all aspects of professional practice. The 2012 revision of the Code of Ethics was triggered by concerns around complex ethical questions arising from the increasing engagement of applied anthropologists in domains such as business and the military. These arenas often involve a departure from the traditional way of working as an individual researcher to working as a member of a diverse team of researchers. How would the Academy respond to the implications of these engagements relative to core ethical concerns that are deeply embedded in the history of the discipline? Implied in this question were concerns about anthropologists working in multiple disciplinary design teams where ethics had multiple and often contested meanings.

The purpose of this chapter is to examine ethics in the field of design where ethics is broadly defined as the consideration of the moral dilemmas and consequences of human action. In the first iteration of this study (Miller 2014), my perspective was colored by strictly anthropological questions such as: Have ethics accompanied the diffusion into design of anthropological forms of field research such as participant observation? Since then the lens of inquiry has widened to include a broader and deeper study of ethics influenced by "the emerging design research landscape" (Sanders and Stappers 2012) that includes user- and/or human-centered design, generative research, and other approaches. Consistent with the earlier approach, my intent is to show how the history of design has shaped designers' perspectives on ethical issues and to provide insight into how the meaning of ethics is negotiated within the field, as well as how the awareness of ethics is changing as the field evolves. My initial study was inspired by the theme of the 2012 Annual Meeting of the AAA: *What is lost, gained or in need of reevaluation in the interstices of border crossings?* In this iteration an examination of ethics in design provides a lens that informs anthropologists' concerns and questions and allows for critical reflection and self-evaluation.

Designers have continued to move into increasingly complex design and research domains. Designers working within the healthcare arena have been faced not only with ethical concerns that do not exist in the purely commercial design world, but also with a growing awareness of their responsibility to the people who will ultimately use or experience the artifacts that they design (Taylor and Dempsey 2015). The power (and hubris) of design has been recognized by designers and design theorists, as well as by anthropologists (Suchman 2011). Victor Margolin (2007) noted that:

> As creators of models, prototypes, and propositions, designers occupy a dialectical space between the world that is and the work that could be ... They operate in situations that call for interventions, and they have the unique ability to turn these interventions into material and immaterial forms. Granted that others usually define the conditions of their work, designers still create the artifacts that are put to use in the social world.
>
> *(Margolin 2007, 4)*

As the landscape of design practice has evolved and expanded, so has the awareness around ethics and accountability. Initiatives by both design practitioners and educators are challenging traditional perspectives on ethics, facilitating the emergence of ethical initiatives, standards, codes, and practices that are unique to design.

This exploration of ethics in design and design research is grounded in my experience as an anthropologist, educator, and researcher working at the intersection of anthropology, design, and business. Drawing on a range of secondary sources, interviews with design practitioners and personal experiences the chapter provides an overview of the role of ethics in the emerging landscape of design research (Sanders and Stappers 2012, 18–19). What are the conversations around ethics within the field? Are ethics integrated into the education and training of designers? What ethical guidelines are used by practicing designers in planning and conducting research with human participants? These questions have led to insights that connect the shift in focus from "object" to "user", the increasing complexity of problems that designers are being asked to confront, and a heightened sensitivity among designers regarding ethics, responsibility, and accountability.

The Diffusion of "Ethnography" and Anthropological Methods in Design

In 2000 Christina Wasson noted that "The application of anthropological methods has become strikingly popular in the field of industrial design" (2000, 377). Further in the chapter she wonders whether or not in ten years ethnography will be regarded as a "short-lived fashion from the turn of the millennium" (Wasson 2000, 384). Sixteen years after publication of Wasson's chapter methods of naturalistic inquiry (i.e., participant observation) have far from gone out of fashion within design research although they have been thoroughly recontextualized. These methods have attained a central role in design practice and design education, so much so, Wasson noted, that most young designers have never known of "a world where design happened without ethnography." Designers often refer to the method of naturalistic inquiry that they practice as "ethnography" in spite of the vast differences in the ways in which the term is conceptualized and practiced by designers (Wasson 2000, 382).

Have ethical considerations, so deeply embedded in the education of anthropologists and in professional practice, diffused along with "ethnography" and anthropological field research methods? The core principles that anthropologists are expected to uphold can be found on the AAA website, where the topic of professional ethics is included under "professional development." In this section one can read the May 1971 "Statement of Ethics: Principles of Professional Responsibility" that was written "to clarify professional responsibilities in the chief areas of professional concerns to anthropologists." The 1971 statement includes two earlier statements: The December 1948 "Resolution on Freedom of Publication" and the March 1967 "Statement on Problems of Anthropological Research and Ethics." Six areas of responsibility are addressed in the May 1971 Statement on Ethics that are reflected in somewhat different language in subsequent versions in June 1998, 2009, and – most recently – the 2012 "Statement on Ethics: Principles of Professional Responsibility," where the focus is on "core principles" that address ethical concerns that are "shared across subfields and contexts of practice" (AAA 2012). The seven principles in the 2012 statement embody the primary ethical concerns related to anthropological research. The fact that they have evolved over time reflects changes in anthropological practice, a consideration that becomes important in investigating the diffusion of ethics, "ethnography," and anthropological methods to the field of design.

It is important to call attention to the use of the term "ethnography" in design and what Ingold (2014) has referred to as the persistent blurring of the critical distinction between "ethnography" and "participant observation" within anthropology. According to Ingold "'Ethnographic' has become the most overused term in the discipline of anthropology" (383).

> I argue that to attribute "ethnographicness" to encounters with those among whom we carry on our research, or more generally to fieldwork, is to

undermine both the ontological commitment and the purpose of anthropology as a discipline, and of its principal way of working – namely participant observation.

(Ingold 2014, 383)

Ingold asserts that the misuse and overuse of the term has "done great harm to anthropology, that is holding it back while other fields of study are surging forward." This is a critical point: "ethnographic" has proliferated as the descriptor for qualitative approaches and methods (i.e., "ethnographic research," "ethnographic methods") that are applied in many areas of design research. Ingold defines ethnography by stating that "Quite literally, it means *writing about people*." Participant observation, what we do in our encounters with people "in the conduct of our research" is "our tried and true way of working" (2014, 386). Point taken. Correcting the misuse of the term as it has diffused to other disciplines requires that as anthropologists we first stop misappropriating it ourselves.

Lost in Translation?

Debates about whether or not designers have actually adopted "ethnography" are much less frequent these days. However, concerns for how anthropologists are engaging in business anthropology and the implications for ethics continue to run high. It is well known that anthropology's deep sensitivities regarding ethics grew out of its history. Since designers do not share that history, it is not reasonable to expect them to adopt the same sensitivities and perspective. Yet it is incorrect to assume that those who employ research approaches and methods appropriated from anthropology and other social sciences have no regard for ethics. There is ample evidence to argue that within design clearly articulated ethical educational concerns are emerging that reflect changes in the field over time, the particular aspects of design practice and research, and the variety of contexts in which designers work. Sanders and Stappers (2012) explain that the "shape of the design development process has changed in response to the shifting foundations in design research." Designers are now engaged at the "fuzzy front end" where "it is often not known whether the deliverable ... will be a product, a service, an interface, or something else" (2012, 22). This shift in the design process has changed the roles of the players as illustrated in Figure 6.1. The transition from "the traditional user-centered design process to a design process based on collective creativity (i.e., a co-design process) is having an impact on the roles of the players in the design process" (Sanders and Stappers 2012, 23).

Two Disciplines; Two Histories

Design has been defined in many ways. Charles and Ray Eames,[2] eminent designers and creators of the Eames Low Wood Chair (LWC), described design simply as "a plan for arranging elements in such a way as to best accomplish a particular

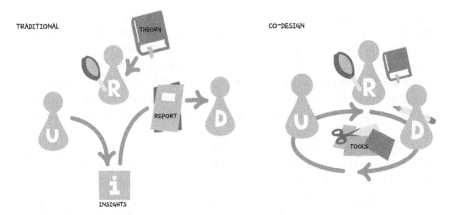

FIGURE 6.1 Roles of the Researcher, Designer, and User Change in the Transition from the Traditional Design Process to the Co-design Process.

purpose" (Eames 1972; Neuhart et al. 1989; Lunenfeld 2003). Although this broad definition encompasses both the tangible and intangible aspects of design it does not address the realm of the social. Writing about design's historical repositioning, Latour (2008) acknowledged the multiple meanings of design, noting the early French translation from English, "relooking," meaning to give something "a new and better look" (2008, 1). He uses this definition as a baseline to "fathom the extraordinary career of this term" (2008, 3). In contrast to anthropology's unwavering focus on situated human social and cultural contexts, the central focus of design has been *the process of making*, or as Latour suggests, in the more modest connotation of contemporary design, *remaking*.

> The expanding concept of design indicates a deep shift in our emotional make up: at the very moment when the scale of what has to be remade has become infinitely larger ... what means to "make" something is also being deeply modified. The modification is so deep that things are no longer "made" or "fabricated", but rather carefully designed, and if I may use the term, precautionarily designed.
>
> *(2008, 4)*

The shift within design from "object" to "user" can be traced in part to the Ulm School (1953–68) which followed in the steps of the Bauhaus movement.[3] With the emergence of the user-centered design approach designers were required to immerse themselves directly in the users' work and social contexts, "thereby giving them the richest possible data to invent from" (Holtzblatt and Jones 1995). *Contextual Inquiry* (CI), observation *in situ* that includes shadowing and intermittent questioning, is the first component in the process of *Contextual Design* (Beyer and Holtzblatt 1998) and was developed in response to the challenge "to design new kinds of systems rather than iterating existing systems" (1998, 20). The advantage of holism, anthropologists' conceptualization of systems thinking, and immersive participant observation initially gave anthropologists significant influence in designers' turn to the "user." Challenging assumptions and problematizing areas of investigation opened the way to fresh insights and potential innovations. The holistic approach, which uncovers the range of dimensions that might not be obvious or immediately relevant to someone intent on designing a new product or service, was compatible with the systems thinking approach practiced by designers and espoused by design theorists.[4]

As designers and well-known design firms began to adopt the use of "ethnographic" methods in the 1980s and 1990s they attracted significant attention from the popular business and design press (Wasson 2000). "Ethnographic-style" methods were recontextualized, merged, and adapted to design practice. The introduction of anthropological field research and participant observation facilitated the shift in focus from the "object" to the "user." Over time designers have developed a distinctive approach to naturalistic inquiry and qualitative research reflected in what Sanders and Stappers refer to as "the emerging landscape of design research" illustrated in Figure 6.2. Design research, "research to inform and inspire the design and development process" (2012, 18), encompasses the approaches and methods included in Figure 6.2.

Figure 6.2 illustrates the richness and diversity of the design research ecosystem as the emphasis has shifted from object-centered to human-centered design. Two intersecting dimensions are featured: *mindset* – "expert" as opposed to a

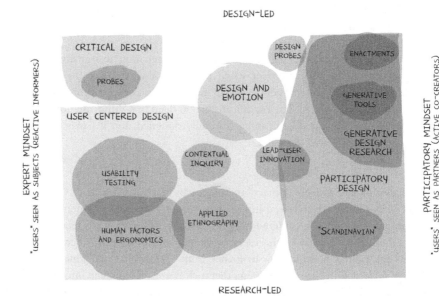

FIGURE 6.2 The Emerging Landscape of Design Research Approaches and Methods.

"participatory" mindset – and *approach* – research-led versus design-led. According to the authors, "The research-led perspective has the longest history and has been driven by applied psychologists, anthropologists, sociologists, and engineers. The design-led perspective, on the other hand, has come into view more recently" (2012, 18).

Addressing ethical considerations, Sanders and Stappers note that concerns about ethical practices vary between industry and academia.

> Design researchers in practice do not always have such "rules" to adhere to and may not even be aware that these requirements exist if they have not been trained at the university as researchers. This is not an excuse for unethical practices.
>
> *(2012, 155)*

Designers today approach their work from a variety of viewpoints. Because different factors have shaped the evolution of each discipline, the importance of ethics – when ethics matter, and for whom – is perceived differently. Within anthropology concern for ethics is deeply rooted in past ties to colonialism and the subsequent recognition of the "myriad of ethical quandaries inflected in different ways by the contexts in which they [anthropologists] work and the kinds of issues they address" (AAA 2012). Where anthropology has sought to repair the legacy of being the "handmaiden of colonialism" (Colchester 2002) design has evolved from its roots in craft and its history as a "handmaiden of industry" (Sterling 2009). As designers increasingly assume responsibility for the consequences of the artifacts they make they are turning to other fields, such as medicine, for direction and guidance in developing ethical codes that are unique to design.[5]

The context in which ethical concerns surface provides an interesting contrast between anthropology and design. The difference between "Do no harm" (non-maleficence) and "Do good" (beneficence) reflect different focuses of ethical concerns. Anthropologists' ethical concerns are focused on their primary responsibility to their human subjects and the potential impact of their work on study participants (e.g., "Do no harm"). Applied anthropologists as researchers in business and industry or the military are also concerned about protecting proprietary data and sensitive information. Designers, on the other hand, have traditionally been concerned with protecting their client's proprietary material. Today there is greater consideration of ethics in their roles as *makers*: Will designers choose to "simply do good design" or will they "do good with design"? (Scalin and Taute 2012).

Discussions within anthropology around the diffusion of anthropological methods to other fields and professions have focused on whether ethics are given sufficient attention in human-centered research, especially in situations in which anthropologists are collaborators on pluridisciplinary[6] teams. Forms of design research, such as contextual inquiry (CI), and anthropological field research are fundamentally different and vary widely in the ways they are practiced. Although both are focused on the social and cultural realms, the purpose of design and the purpose of anthropology have traditionally been distinctively different. It follows that the ways in which designers have dealt with ethics in their practice are also distinct from the ways in which anthropologists engage with ethics. However, as designers consciously move deeper into the social realm, and as anthropologists actively engage in design, this distinction is dissolving.

Ethics in the Field of Design

A distinguishing characteristic of commercial design research is that fieldwork proceeds very rapidly. Primary qualitative research is time-intensive and costly. The trend toward using Big Data and the Internet of Things (IoT) as a source of business intelligence[7] to augment or replace *in situ* fieldwork is attractive to firms that are pushed to work faster and with smaller budgets. Many clients are unwilling to fund field research since they believe that they have or can purchase all the data that is needed (usually market research studies). Consequently, field research is extremely abbreviated in comparison to traditional anthropological studies, a fact which poses a major challenge to many classically trained anthropologists who enter a process of retraining if they join design teams. The established practice of outsourcing – of using vendors to recruit and screen study participants – can pose serious questions for anthropologists. How well have participants been informed about the purpose of the study? Do they know what kinds of data will be collected and how it will be collected? Have they been informed about how data will be used, stored, how long it will be held, and whether it will be destroyed? Are they made aware of their rights, if any, to access the study findings? Since most corporate research is considered proprietary participants may never know to what end their data are used. For anthropologists, making the study accessible to a wider audience, per the AAA Statement of Ethics,[8] presents problems, since study data and findings need to be reviewed by corporate attorneys to determine what information, if any, can be shared outside the organization.

Standards of Professional Behavior in Design

Professional associations such as the American Institute of Graphic Arts[9] (AIGA) and Industrial Designers Society of America[10] (IDSA) provide guidance to design practitioners. Standards of professional practice were the initial area of concern in the field of design. For example, the AIGA's *Design Business + Ethics* series (AIGA 2009a), first published in 2001, "was created to establish consistent professional standards and define the relationship among designers, clients and content." The mission of the AIGA "includes educating designers, clients and the public about ethical standards and practices governing design." The IDSA has a "Code of Ethics"[11] that includes five Fundamental Ethical Principles and six Chapters of Ethical Practice. According to the IDSA, the Code of Ethics is based on the recognition "that industrial designers affect the quality of life in our increasingly independent and complex society; that responsible ethical decision making often requires conviction, courage and ingenuity in today's competitive business context" (IDSA 2010).

From "Can We?" to "Should We?"

The ethical questions that designers face have changed with a growing sense of personal responsibility for the impact and consequences of their work. Informal conversations, like those that convene around blog posts, reveal concerns about emerging ethical issues. David Airey[12] is a blogger and graphic designer who specializes in design brand identities. In 2007 he posted the question: "how much do ethics affect your design practices?" that generated dozens of comments over several years and provided a forum for discussions about the types of ethical decisions that confront designers.

Wide-ranging issues about the impacts of design on the environment, on specific social groups, and cultural contexts surfaced in July 2012 when Bruce Nussbaum, design commentator and Professor of Innovation and Design at Parsons New School of Design, posted an essay on *Fast Company's* blog entitled "Is Humanitarian Design the New Imperialism?" Nussbaum's post raised a firestorm when he questioned the motivations and benefits of "Humanitarian Design" through projects such as Emily Pilloton's Design Revolution Road Show (Project H), initiatives from IDEO, the Acumen Fund, and One Laptop per Child (Nussbaum 2010). The mission statement of Project H ended with the statement "WE BELIEVE DESIGN CAN CHANGE THE WORLD."[13] Not the first to question the hubris of this kind of statement, Nussbaum agreed, but went on to ask "But whose design? Which solutions? What problems?" The discussions about whether or not designers *can* change the world became whether designers *should* attempt to change the world. This level of self-reflection is directly related to the growing awareness of the role of ethics in the field.

Ethics in Design Education

The major shifts that are occurring in contemporary design present challenges for educational institutions to develop curricula and manage the proliferation of new programs and arenas of engagement such as healthcare that are explicitly focused on user- and human-centered design. Service design, interaction design, design management, design for social innovation, and design for sustainability prepare students for career paths that did not exist just a few years ago. We can imagine the emergence of new forms of design that do not yet exist today. Recognizing this potential, in 2009 the AIGA posted a series of chapters on its website that describe the skills that "the designers of 2015" will need: "a set of skills that include some beyond today's typical scope" (AIGA 2009b). Thirteen competences were ranked in order of importance through an online survey. Many of these competencies reflect a broader definition of design that moves careers into nontraditional domains. The most relevant to this chapter is number 12: "Understanding of ethics in practice."

This statement is understandably open-ended in that it does not spell out what "ethics in practice" would entail. However, it clearly signals an awareness of the need for ethics training. In institutions that receive federal funding all research involving human participants, including behavioral studies, must secure approval from an Institutional Review Board (IRB),[14] which creates external pressure to include ethics training for design students who are learning to conduct primary research with human participants. For design schools that are not research-oriented and are not required to have IRBs, there is little pressure to include ethics in their design curriculum. However, ethics training is imperative if design students engage in sponsored research projects in which they may be working under IRB oversight, or if they are working in areas like healthcare that are under federal regulations such as the Health Information Patient Privacy Act (HIPPA) and The HIPAA Privacy Rule.[15]

Concerns about the ethical dimensions of design extend beyond specific examples like healthcare and IRB compliance to the broader issues of ethics in general. Victor Ermoli, Dean of the School of Design at the Savannah School of Art and Design (SCAD), described the general lack of attention to ethics in design education curriculums, noting that ethics were "rarely if ever discussed in any of the curriculums in higher education."

> There is a lack of content on exploring the ethical impacts of being an industrial designer, the ethics of designing products, and even engaging in the dialog on how systems and services affect people. So going into a deep understanding of what ethics and ethical behaviors are and ethical decisions are and all those complex questions the subject of discussing potential impacts on society, culture, and individuals are rarely addressed.
>
> *(Ermoli 2016)*

Ermoli acknowledged that although ethics in design were being addressed from the standpoint of human factors and sometimes from the perspective of design research, the subject of ethics was not being addressed from the point of long-term impacts on society.

Schools of design are distinguished by particular pedagogical approaches and orientations toward design education, or concentration in a particular field of design. The role of ethics within schools of design that are strongly oriented toward research and publishing may differ from design schools that are oriented toward teaching and professional training. A web page associated with the Medialab at Aalto University, Finland offers "A quick primer for ethics in design" (Medialab) that takes a broad view of design. The web page lists questions under a series of subjects to "help a designer to orient herself to the problem of ethics in design." The list is not meant to be exhaustive, but instead "illustrates what kinds of problems may be embedded in [the] design process and propositions from a point of view of ethics." Rather than offering a specific set of rules, the authors assert that ethics involve multiple dimensions that require personal reflection and action.

If a designer wants to act in an ethically responsible manner, it is imperative to put forth personal effort in understanding ethical conflicts rather than trying to follow any predefined safe rules. Ethics is a process of learning – not a process of obedience.

(Media Lab)

Tom MacTavish, assistant professor at the Illinois Institute of Technology (IIT) Institute of Design (ID), explained that all ID students are required to complete the National Institutes of Health (NIH) training *Protecting Human Research Participants* that is designed to prepare *investigators*, defined as "anyone involved in conducting the research" (NIH), to understand and protect the rights and welfare of study participants. Although not all ID students are involved in projects that require rigorous formal IRB oversight, MacTavish explained the NIH training is mandatory regardless of the context of students' work with human study participants.

The thing about design teachers, especially in a human-centered design school such as ours, is that we nurture our students to have empathy for the user, especially in the sense that as designers, we are going to protect the person that we are interviewing. And, we are going to protect both of us by having an agreement that has clear boundaries. This seems like a natural connection between design and ethics.

(MacTavish 2016)

For MacTavish, having empathy for human participants means being an advocate for them. Including ethics in the curriculum (Ruecker 2016) and requiring NIH certification is an important part of students' education and training.

First, it's an opportune training moment for the students because they're going to go do this as a professional. And I know that in some companies they don't follow this very well so part of my advocacy is to train them to do this in the school context and to then ask them to be an advocate when they go to a company.

(MacTavish 2016)

Evolving Consciousness of Ethics in Design

Where and how are ethics being discussed in design today? The "call to conscience"[16] in design has a long history dating back to the late days of industrialization and the rise of consumerism to the present (Garland 1964; Papernak 1984; Poynor 1999; Dilnot 2005; Margolin 2005; Latour 2008). However, the diffusion of ethics as an area of concern has been a gradual process, influenced by factors within the field of design itself, by the nature of the work designers are being called to do, and externally by shifting social consciousness. The history of design suggests that the focus on "the user" and the transition to "human-centered design" is actually a recurring theme as designers become increasingly engaged with the social context into which their designs are introduced.

As mass manufacturing replaced one-of-a-kind craft production, design evolved from craft to become a professional occupation. The psychological and physical distance between designers and the humans who would ultimately use the designed artifact were widened by layers of management. Distributed global business practices like manufacturing meant that the designer, the output of production,[17] and the end user of the product could be literally worlds apart. The consequences brought about by objects as outputs of mass production were not perceived to be the responsibility of the individuals who designed them. The responsibility for a defective item, such as a toy or a car, rested with the firm rather than the individual who designed the product. This perceived lack of accountability has changed as public awareness of large-scale environmental and social problems resulting from designed artifacts has increased.

Multiple disciplinary teams become increasingly common in corporate environments challenging the individuals involved to articulate and integrate their work practices as well as their perspectives on ethics. Cefkin (2010) notes:

> In all areas of research, whether for primarily academic, policy, or commercial interests, issues of ethics abound. Ethical issues infuse every aspect of corporate ethnography as well, from the very constitution and formation of the research agenda to the nature of fieldwork encounters.
>
> *(2010, 18)*

Anthropologists like Cefkin who work in corporate settings bring with them sensitivity to ethical issues that may not be shared by other colleagues.

Ethics Initiatives in Design

Although the power of design and its impact on the world have been acknowledged, the global design community has yet to respond *en masse* to repeated calls for action (Margolin 2007). In spite of the decentralized nature of the design community many bottom-up initiatives are being launched. Aided by social media some of these efforts are gaining traction. New organizations are emerging that reflect the cross-disciplinary nature and "interstitial collective" of contemporary design research (Teixeira and Zimmerman 2016) in which ethics and accountability occupy a central position. The steering committee exploring the need for a new Design Research Organization for the US and Canada recognizes the diversity of design researchers:

> This group comprised a cross-disciplinary culture—an interstitial collective—of design practitioners and researchers from design, humanities, social sciences, and computer science who investigate material and symbolic interventions that shape the future. We worked to develop a culture intended to support and facilitate the entry and participation of multiple intellectual

traditions and practices. We also worked to help each other comprehend the intellectual landscape of making, doing, and exchanging design research.

(Teixeira and Zimmerman 2016)

Recognition that design research encompasses both "scholarly researchers and practitioners who share an interest in design action as a force for intentional change" turns our collective attention to bridging silos rather than furthering fragmentation.

The Designer's Oath

User Experience (UX) designers Ciara Taylor and Samantha Dempsey experienced the ethical dilemma first-hand in their work in healthcare. They recognized that, unlike healthcare professionals, designers had no clearly defined set of rules to guide their interactions with patients.

> Designers are responsible for creating more than ever before – not only designing services, but also experiences, environments, products and systems for millions of people. With this increased influence, we must take a step back and recognize the responsibility we have to those we design for.
>
> *(Taylor and Dempsey 2015)*

Between 2015 and 2016 Taylor and Dempsey partnered with designers from different disciplines and backgrounds to discuss and document what they believed were their responsibilities as designers. Through this collaboration, Taylor and Dempsey realized that their work was not about creating a single oath for all designers. Instead, it became a project about creating a tool that could be used to facilitate conversations about ethics among designers and members of multiple disciplinary teams to help define ethical guidelines for their particular engagement (Taylor and Dempsey 2015). Their project, *The Designer's Oath*, has been presented at several conferences including HxRefactored[18] in Boston (2015), Institute of Design's BarnRaise (2015), and was featured in *Touchpoint: The Journal of Service Design* (Dempsey and Taylor 2015) and online design sites.[19]

Taylor and Dempsey recently launched a second project, a role playing game (RPG) called *Ethics Quest* that was debuted at Interaction Design 2016 in Helsinki, Finland. *Ethics Quest* "brings teams together to understand, explore, and harness multiple ethical perspectives to improve collaboration and guide project outcomes

FIGURE 6.3 Designer's Oath Logo: Powered by Mad★Pow and Curated by Samantha Dempsey and Ciara Taylor.

towards the common good" (Taylor and Dempsey 2016). They argue that designers and teams are leveraging the power of design without a "common language, structure, or understanding as a professional community of our own ethical boundaries." Acknowledging that ethics are a difficult subject for cross-disciplinary teams to discuss they created *Ethics Quest* to allow people to approach the serious subject of ethics from a safe and low risk space that allows players "to experience and build empathy for ethical viewpoints beyond their IRL (in real life) selves." Individual players are able to define their personal ethical stance and develop strategies and tools for discussions about ethics in professional situations. For teams the game helps to bring out different ethical concerns and facilitates the creation of shared ethic guidelines.

Converging and Emerging Fields of Practice

This chapter has argued that as the landscape of design practice has evolved and expanded, so has awareness around ethics and accountability. The growing awareness and commitment to ethics is evident in design discourse and in the work of contemporary designers, a trend that is being driven by very practical reasons: design has become influential in ways that have necessitated reflection on the impact of the artifacts that designers create. Design anthropologists Otto and Smith (2013) note that:

> In modern societies with their emphasis on innovation and change, which are often considered intrinsic values (Suchman 2011), design has arguably become one of the major sites of cultural production and change, on par with science, technology, and art.
>
> *(2013, 2)*

Naturalistic inquiry and qualitative research methods have become staples of design research. As the scope of design has broadened designers are in direct and often intimate contact with human participants in their research. Meanwhile, in fields such as business and design anthropology the domain of practice for anthropologists has also shifted, bringing applied anthropologists into pluridisciplinary teams to work side-by-side with designers, engineers, business, and other practitioners who have distinctly different histories and training, and consequently, different ethical perspectives. Although anthropologists and designers have come to share a human-centered perspective, fundamental differences remain in the goals of their practice. The goal of design is "to conceive of an idea and plan it out, 'give form, structure and function to that idea' (Nelson and Stolterman 2003), before executing it in the world" (Otto and Smith 2013, 1). Designers engage in an iterative process to generate *design principles* that inform the design of prototypes.

The growing awareness and commitment to ethics is evident in design discourse and in the work of contemporary designers, a trend that is being driven by very practical reasons: design has become influential in ways that have necessitated reflection on the impact of the artifacts that designers create. True to the iterative nature of design, ethics in the field are undergoing a critical reframing. An approach to ethics from a perspective that aspires not only to "do no harm," but also to "do good" becomes a call to action for both anthropology and design.

Notes

1 Principles of Professional Responsibility. http://ethics.americananthro.org/category/statement/ (accessed May 25, 2016).
2 American designers Charles and Ray Eames are known for their contributions to modern architecture and furniture. They are especially notable for the design of the Eames Lounge Chair Wood (LWC).
3 Bauhaus (1919–33) is described as "the first academy for design in the world." It was a response to the Industrial Revolution and dehumanization, an attempt to keep art and craft from being lost to mass production. http://bauhaus-online.de/en (accessed May 25, 2016).
4 Tomás Maldonado (1972) who characterized the human environment as "one of the many subsytems that compose the vast ecological system of nature." Quoted in Margolin (2007, 5).
5 Product designer Laura Javier's Designer's Oath is a modification of the physicians Hippocratic Oath. http://laurajavier.com/manifesto/ (accessed May 21, 2016).
6 The term *pluridisciplinary* is used to maintain a distinction between multi-, inter- and transdisciplinary teams when the nature of the team is unknown (Miller 2016).
7 Iota Partners/Sapient Design, www.iota-partners.com/ (accessed May 21, 2016).
8 Principle (5) in the 2012 statement: "make your results accessible."
9 AIGA, www.aiga.org/about-aiga/ (accessed May 25, 2016).
10 IDSA, www.idsa.org/ (accessed May 25, 2016).
11 www.idsa.org/code-ethics (accessed May 21, 2016).
12 Airey's post was updated in 2010, 2011, and 2012. www.davidairey.com/ (accessed May 21, 2016).
13 Project H mission statement no longer ends with that statement. See www.projecthdesign.org/info/#mission (accessed May 21, 2016).
14 Cf. Michael Fischer's chapter "Emergent Forms of Life in Corporate Arenas" for a short discussion of IRBs in academic scholarship in Cefkin (2010).
15 US Department of Health and Human Services Health Information Privacy, www.hhs.gov/hipaa/for-professionals/privacy/.
16 Media Lab.
17 Final products often bear little resemblance to the original design concept.
18 HxRefactored conference, www.hxrefactored.com/ (accessed May 21, 2016).
19 Quartz, http://qz.com/456845/sick-of-selling-junk-food-and-false-promises-designers-declare-their-own-hippocratic-oath/ (accessed May 21, 2016).

References

AAA. 2012. Statement on Ethics: Principles of Professional Responsibility. Arlington, VA: American Anthropological Association. http://ethics.americananthro.org/category/statement/ (accessed May 27, 2016).
AIGA. 2009a. Design Business + Ethics. In *AIGA Design Business and Ethics*, Joanne Stone, Lana Rigsby et al., eds. New York: Richard Grefé, AIGA. www.aiga.org/design-business-and-ethics/ (accessed May 27, 2016).
AIGA. 2009b. Designer of 2015 Competencies. AIGA. www.aiga.org/designer-of-2015-competencies/ (accessed May 27, 2016).

Beyer, Hugh and Karen Holtzblatt. 1998. *Contextual Design: Defining Customer-Centered Systems*. San Diego: Academic Press.

Cefkin, Melissa, ed. 2010. Ethnography and the Corporate Encounter: Reflections on Research in and of Corporations. In *Studies in Public and Applied Anthropology*, Sarah Pink and Simone Abram, eds., 5th edn. New York: Berghahn Books.

Colchester, Marcus. 2002. Indigenous Rights and the Collective Conscious. *Anthropology Today* 18, 1: 1–3.

Dempsey, Samantha and Ciara Taylor. 2015. A Designer's Oath: Collaboratively Defining a Code of Ethics for Design. *Touchpoint: The Journal of Service Design* 7, 1.

Dilnot, Clive. 2005. Ethics? Design? In *The Archeworks Paper, Volume 1, Number Two*, Stanley Tigerman, ed. Chicago: Archeworks.

Eames, Charles. 1972. Film. Design Q&A with Charles Eames. www.eamesoffice.com/the-work/design-q-a-text/ (accessed May 27, 2016).

Ermoli, Victor. Interview by Christine Miller. Dean, School of Design, Savannah College of Art and Design. May 6, 2016.

Garland, Ken. 1964. *First Things First*. London: Goodwin Press.

Holtzblatt, Karen and Sandra Jones. 1995. Conducting and Analyzing a Contextual Interview. In *Readings in Human-Computer Interaction: Toward the Year 2000*, R.M. Baecker, J. Grudin, W.A.S. Buxton, and S. Greenberg, eds. San Francisco: Morgan Kaufman.

IDSA. 2010. IDSA Code of Ethics. www.idsa.org/code-ethics (accessed May 21, 2016).

Ingold, Tim. 2014. That's Enough About Ethnography! *HAU: Journal of Ethnographic Theory* 4, 1: 383–395. doi: http://dx.doi.org/10.14318/hau4.1.021.

Institute of Design. 2015. BarnRaise 2015: Designing for Improved Access to Care. Institute of Design. www.idbarnraise.com/#2015-section (accessed May 22, 2016).

Latour, Bruno. 2008. A Cautious Prometheus? A Few Steps toward a Philosophy of Design (with special attention to Peter Sloterdijk). *Networks of Design*. 2008 annual international conference of the Design History Society, University College Falmouth, Cornwall, UK.

Lunenfeld, Peter. 2003. The Design Cluster. In *Design Research: Methods and Perspectives*, Brenda Laurel, ed., 10–15. Cambridge, MA: MIT Press.

MacTavish, Tom. 2016. Interview by Christine Miller. Assistant Professor, Illinois Institute of Technology, Institute of Design. April 14, 2016.

Maldonado, Tomás. 1972. *Design, Nature, and Revolution*. Trans. from the Italian by Mario Domandi. New York: Harper & Row.

Margolin, Victor. 2005. The Liberation of Ethics. In *Ethics? Design?*, Clive Dilnot ed., 160. Archeworks: Chicago.

Margolin, Victor. 2007. Design, the Future and the Human Spirit. *Design Issues* 23, 3: 4–15.

MediaLab. A Quick Primer for Ethics in Design. "Medialab." http://mlab.uiah.fi/polut/Yhteiskunnalliset/lisatieto_ethics_primer.html (accessed May 25, 2016).

Miller, Christine. 2014. Lost in Translation? Ethics and Ethnography in Design Research. *Journal of Business Anthropology* 4, 1: 62–78.

Miller, Christine. 2016. Towards Transdisciplinarity: Liminality and the Transitions Inherent in Pluridisciplinary Collaborative Work. *Journal of Business Anthropology* 2: 35–57.

Nelson, Harold G. and Erik Stolterman. 2003. *The Design Way: Intentional Change in an Unpredictable World*. Englewood Cliffs, NJ: Educational Technology Publications.

Neuhart, John, Charles Eames, Ray Eames, and Marilyn Neuhart. 1989. *Eames Design: The Work of the Office of Charles and Ray Eames*. New York: H.N. Abrams.

NIH. Protecting Human Research Participants. [website]. NIH Office of Extramural Research. https://phrp.nihtraining.com/introduction/02_intro.php (accessed May 23, 2016).

Nussbaum, Bruce. 2010. Is Humanitarian Design the New Imperialism? Does Our Desire to Help Do More Harm than Good? Fast Company Design. www.fastcodesign.com/1661859/is-humanitarian-design-the-new-imperialism (accessed May 27, 2016).

Otto, Ton and Rachel C. Smith. 2013. Design Anthropology: A Distinct Style of Knowing. In *Design Anthropology: Theory and Practice*, Wendy Gunn, Ton Otto, and Rachel Charlotte Smith, eds., 1–29. New York: Bloomsbury.

Papernak, Victor. 1984. *Design for the Real World: Human Ecology and Social Change.* Chicago: Academy Chicago Pulishers. Reprint, 1992, 2000, 2009.

Poynor, Rick. 1999. First Things First Revisited. *Emigre*, 1999.

Ruecker, Stan. 2016. Email to author. *Design Ethics Syllabus*. Institute of Design.

Sanders, Elizabeth and Pieter Jan Stappers. 2012. *Convivial Toolbox: Generative Research for the Front End of Design*. Amsterdam: BIS Publishers.

Scalin, Noah, and Michelle Taute. 2012. *The Design Activist's Handbook*. Blue Ash, OH: HOW Books.

Sterling, Bruce. 2009. Design Fiction. *Interactions* 16, 3: 20–24.

Suchman, Lucy. 2011. Anthropological Relocations and the Limits of Design. *Annual Review of Anthropology* 40: 1–18.

Taylor, Ciara and Samantha Dempsey. 2015. Designing for Good: A Designer's Hippocratic Oath. www.madpow.com/insights/2015/4/designers-oath (accessed May 16, 2016).

Taylor, Ciara and Samantha Dempsey. 2016. *Ethics Quest*. Role playing game. Interaction Design 2016, Helsinki.

Teixeira, Carlos, and John Zimmerman. 2016. *Transforming Design Matters: Steering Committee Workshop to Envision Design Research Organization for US and Canada.* Chicago: Institute of Design. www.id.iit.edu/news/workshop-to-envision-design-research-organization/ (accessed February 13, 2017).

Wasson, Christina. 2000. Ethnography in the Field of Design. *Human Organization* 59, 4: 377–388. doi:10.17730/humo.59.4.h13326628n127516.

7

ADVERTISING ANTHROPOLOGY ETHICS

Timothy de Waal Malefyt and Robert J. Morais

Advertising is one of several means in the marketing mix by which advertisers convey the quality and value of goods and services to existing and potential customers. More precisely, advertising represents any "paid form of non-personal presentation and promotion of ideas, goods, or services by an identified sponsor," which, from a marketing standpoint, intends to "inform, persuade or remind" a specific target audience about a product, brand or service during a specific period of time (Kotler and Armstrong 2016, 450–451). Indeed, it is this role of advertising regarding a particular audience and/or a time period that often ignites ethical issues, since out of context, temporality or to the wrong target group, advertising can be irritating, inappropriate or even harmful. We discuss from theoretical approaches and anecdotal examples the ways that advertising "operates in a constantly shifting political, economic and aesthetic milieu, and calls our attention as an outspoken and influential mode of cultural production" (Malefyt forthcoming). The fact that scholarly discussions about advertising – whether from cultural studies, business anthropology or other disciplines – are rarely impartial to its content and purpose attests to its provocative nature as a subject of ethical interest. In this chapter, we discuss both the criticisms and benefits of advertising and address ethical concerns for anthropologists involved in the creation of advertising. We examine how ethical complexities range from the question of advertising as a necessary form of consumer–brand engagement to socially responsible advertising, to professional ethics surrounding the objects or brands being advertised, and to the work of anthropologists in advancing advertising campaigns.

For business anthropologists who investigate culture, advertising messages are about more than selling products, services and brands to consumers; they are part of cultural discourse and the exchange of ideas in society. As a way in which people acquire cultural knowledge through messages about products and services, as well a model for their lifestyle and values, advertising invests brand symbols with cultural meaning (McCracken 1986; Sherry 1987; Mick and Buhl 1992). Advertising's influence in society is powerful and can appear at times omnipresent as a "super-ideology" (Elliott and Ritson 1997). It generates meaning by appropriating extant imagery in culture and associates it with attractive consumption opportunities. Advertising's effects are so pervasive that it "invades, shapes and reflects consumer consciousness" (Hackley 2002, 212). This gathered cultural knowledge "mobilizes advertising's potentiality as a vehicle of cultural meaning, and hence enables advertising as an ideological force" (Hackley 2002, 212). The ways advertisements convey and sometimes reinforce cultural ideals and values, can also spark controversy and sharp disagreement among both target audiences and broader publics. Because advertising messages are intended to provoke consumers to take notice and purchase a product or service, they have the potential to offend some audiences on a scale and intensity greater than many other communicative and symbolic works of art, drama and literature (Hackley and Hackley 2015, 239). For all of these reasons, the power and influence of advertising sparks widespread emotional, practical and theoretical ethical discussion and debate.

Defining Advertising Ethics

What do we mean by ethics in advertising and promotion, and how might ethics be distinguished from morals in an advertising context? While the study of ethics may deal with abstract principles of what is right, good or consistent with virtue, morals can be seen as more of an applied field that regards personal behavior in specific situations (Hackley and Hackley 2015). Even though advertising is a mass form of persuasive communication, it impacts individuals, and some individuals may take issue morally with certain advertisements. In addition, since advertising messages carry symbolic meaning as a "super ideology," they require interpretation by audiences, some of whom will have differing opinions about what is appropriate or not, in addition to attitudes about the overall ad and the advertised brand itself. In other words, many ethical questions germane to marketing are mobilized in the specificities and subjectivities of advertising in contextual and temporal situations, which have to do with the framing of ads and their appropriateness (Hackley et al. 2008). For instance, it is ethically wrong to advertise to children applying the same persuasion techniques that are used on adults, since children are known to be more influenced by commercial messages. However, is it more appropriate and should it even be encouraged to market to young girls newly designed Barbie dolls that proudly express diversity in race and body type, or American Girl dolls that support ethnic heritage and pride?[1] Should advertisers be permitted to promote foods, beverages, cigarettes and other products that are deemed unhealthy or otherwise harmful to consumption, even if consumer demand for such products is strong? Is it right to use provocative imagery or words that may shock, offend, or insult a particular community or subgroup, when other subgroups find those same images humorous or even a source of pride? Should there be special aesthetic, moral and taste constraints on advertising that occupies public spaces, such as billboards on buildings or along roads, or advertising in schools, parks and other public places, or is freely available and easily accessible online to populations that might find it offensive or for whom it might be inappropriate? Is advertising even necessary in a world now informed by social media and online reviews and commentary, or is it merely a conduit for hyperbole, false illusions and misrepresentations that may underlie or even reinforce gender, class or ethnic stereotypes (cf. Goffman 1979; Zayer and Coleman 2015; Malefyt and McCabe 2016)?

Criticisms of Advertising

Advertising is not new, and nor are many criticisms of advertising recent. Ads have long occupied a contested space in the interactions of commerce, citizenship and culture (Hackley and Hackley 2015, 245). Ancient Romans and Phoenicians painted pictures on walls and rocks to announce upcoming events, and town criers in Greece were both rebuked and praised when announcing the sale of cattle to the public (Kotler and Armstrong 2016, 450). Four hundred years ago, advertising was admonished as a public form of "social pollution" on the streets of London (Hackley and Kitchen 1999) and letters of complaint about advertising were written 200 years ago in London's *Punch* magazine (McFall 2004). During the mid-twentieth century, advertising was critiqued as a subtle form of subversion and for the unethical use of ostensive subliminal messaging (Packard 1957), and cast as a modern form of "myth-making" in U.S. society (McLuhan 1951) that intended to "get inside" and manipulate the collective public mind.

Within critical scholarship, advertising has been vilified as unethical for its effects on the populace. Advertisements are critiqued for manipulating a "constellation of images" across social domains of commodities, popular culture and mass media (Jhally 1987; Leiss et al. 2005), and characterized as inherently unethical (Henry 1963) and an "uneasy persuasion" (Schudson 1984). Advertising has been blamed for distorting social values (McLuhan 1951; Ewen 1976; Pollay 1986; Pollay and Mittal 1993) and encouraging unnecessary and even "harmful" desires (Barthes 1972; Deighton 1992). Still other critics have denigrated advertising for its global dominance and widespread use of the branded sign or logo (Klein 2000), and for imparting a way of "seeing ourselves," with the aim "to make us feel we are lacking" (Williamson 1978, 8). The "unintended consequences" of advertising allegedly pollute the psychological and social ecology of society, "seducing" people into consumption through a distorted view of romanticized goods (Pollay 1986, 25). Some observers caution that "deception is the reality of AdCult" (Twitchell 1996, 3) in how advertising "colonizes relationships" into "consumption communities" (1996, 124). In these ways, advertising is positioned as fundamentally unethical; it represents an adverse force in society that distorts values, constructs partial representations (Pollay 1986; Leiss et al. 2005), and suggests misleading "social tableaus" (Marchand 1985) that undermine social life.

In Defense of Advertising

There is also relevant scholarship that rejects critical views of advertising, and sees its advantages for society. From economic, social and ideological accounts, advertising is viewed as offering numerous benefits. First, advertising is seen as contributing valuable economic functions in modern capitalistic societies. Advertising generates wealth for individuals, companies and commercial economies by performing an indispensable economic function for capitalist social systems (Hackley and Hackley 2015, 244). It allows producers of goods and services to:

- Expand their markets, enter new markets, defend market share.
- Differentiate offers to target heterogeneous consumer groups.
- Take advantage of economies of scale to reduce unit production costs.
- Increase revenue, employment, investment funds and returns to shareholders.
- Make consumers aware of various choices, product qualities and offers.
- Compete with other producers, lowering prices and stimulating innovation.
- Contribute to GDP growth and aggregate employment.

Second, advertising offers a resource by which consumers appropriate meaning for communicating explicit and implicit social functions to others. Recent investigations reveal how consumers are not passive recipients to advertising messages, but rather free-thinking agents who demonstrate creative choice and independence in interpreting advertising messages for their own use. Malefyt (2015) contends that advertising can act as a positive force in consumers' lives by creating social bonds that reinforce togetherness through consumption ideals. Advertising is also interpreted as having a purpose relative to people's particular life situations. For instance, consumers are shown to be not deceived by clever ads, but rather generate their own positive inferences of brand advertising and meaning when exposed to metaphorical advertising messages (McQuarrie and Phillips 2005). In other instances, people are found to be adept at selecting or rejecting certain celebrity characteristics in ads, processing advertising messages relevant to their own circumstances (Hirschman and Thompson 1997). Advertising can provide consumers with personal discourses to produce a range of social perspectives to suit their social needs (Thompson and Haytko 1997; Thompson 2004). Advertising is also viewed as a cultural resource for group identity formation and building social affinities such that, for example, adolescents re-interpret advertisements to promote its phatic or connection function (Ritson and Elliott 1999); or in another case, consumers use advertising images in constructing symbolic selves by drawing on selective assemblages of communicated brands (Elliott and Wattanasuwan 1998). Ads can also serve as a force to help construct notions of national identity (O'Donohoe 1999). From this perspective, consumers are not passive receptacles of ads who buy unthinkingly what they are implored to buy; rather, they are "interpretive agents" who seek to form "lifestyles that defy dominant consumerist norms or that directly challenge corporate power" (Arnould and Thompson 2005, 875). Indeed, the consumption of goods, once disapproved of as a conspicuous display of wealth (Veblen 2009), is now seen as a contributing factor in fostering social interactions and strengthening personal bonds (Belk, 1988, 2010; Belk et al. 1988a, 1988b, 1989; Wallendorf and Arnould 1991; Belk and Coon 1993). Daniel Miller (1995, 1998) contends that consumption is the contemporary means by which people express their cultural identities and relate to one another. The advertising of goods offers consumers a way to engage people toward positive ends and "apprehend the world" (Sherry 1987, 442).

Third, on a wider ideological scale, advertising and other forms of promotional communication can contribute to social and personal acceptance in capitalistic and commercial-trade societies (Wernick 1991). As an advanced form of symbolic communication that operates on syllogistic reasoning (Malefyt 2015) consumers must learn to read and interpret advertisements, either in praise or criticism, in order to make sense of them. This requires an advanced level of cognitive and cultural sophistication contingent on understanding the subtleties of humor, exaggeration, sarcasm, and so forth, any or all of which can be expressed in advertisements that make them appealing to their target audiences or not. In this way, "advertising and promotion within promotional culture constitute a self-generating system of signs that frames our experience as consumers and places our sense of social identity and economic relations within a consumption-based sign system" (Hackley and Hackley 2015, 248).

When consumers are exposed to advertisements, they become educated, consciously or not, in the nuances of culture and consumption and to values conveyed by advertising messages. Advertising does not create consumer goods, manufacturers do, but ads link social status and the attributes of goods to values held by certain social groups and individuals (Leiss et al. 1997). Moreover, advertising is not merely about selling items, but viewed more broadly, constitutes an advanced form of cultural communication that illustrates and codifies the social norms and conventional values of its time. For example, investigations have shown advertising's effects cross-culturally, when global images circulate in local cultures to advance ideas of "modern" lifestyles. Advertising in Nairobi, Caracas, Kuala Lumpur, and Colombo conveyed new forms of culture in Sri Lankan society (Kemper 2001), fostering a dynamic relationship between Sri Lankan society, its economy, local interests and new identity choices for consumers based on urban life, prosperity and modernity. Analysis of advertising in Bombay, India reveals the critical role of ads in mediating images of modernization and development of Indian society precisely at a time when the economy is transforming and opening its consumer markets to foreign brands (Mazzarella 2003). Advertising, therefore, can be analyzed as a "vehicle for understanding the structures of reality *within a culture*" (Sherry 1987, 441, emphasis added). As such, advertising represents a valuable snapshot in time that details changing tastes, fashions, norms and attitudes in particular places at particular times. "It reflects current standards of public taste and decency and modes of public discourse" (Hackley and Hackley 2015, 243).

Controversial Advertisements

Controversial issues in advertising typically emanate more from the specific nature of the product advertised, than from the operative principles of advertising or a specific advertisement per se. For instance, advertising for potentially harmful product categories like alcohol, drugs, guns and cigarettes attracts close scrutiny and special government regulations in the United States because of the polemical stance on so called personal freedoms and liberties, versus the good of society or particular subgroups (Hackley and Hackley 2015, 251). Controversies also reflect differences in views pertaining to cultural contexts and the meaning of goods advertised in particular markets. In the United Kingdom, direct-to-consumer advertising for pharmaceutical drugs is not allowed, while in the United States such advertising is permitted, though it is tightly regulated by the US Food and Drug Administration. Alcohol advertising in Muslim countries is forbidden, while in parts of Europe it is allowed with restrictions (Hackley and Hackley 2015, 252). Moreover, within many countries, specific ethnic, religious or other cultural groups may find generally permitted advertising offensive. In other words, the reception to and regulation of advertising is highly contingent on cultural norms and specific audiences.

The intentions and benefits of advertising are confounded when analyzing the long- and short-term effects of advertising for certain audiences and in particular categories. What may appear clearly dangerous or harmful in advertised goods may show residual cultural benefits when examined over time. Cigarette advertising is currently banned in the United States for its unequivocal harmful effects on smokers. Yet, cultural historians point to the benefits of cigarette advertisements in the past, particularly their role in advancing the liberation of women from social constraints and for advocating women's independence in the 1960s, when women were inspired by advertising messages that encouraged positive social change (Williamson 1978). While advertising has justly been criticized for emphasizing gender stereotypes of power and dominance (Goffman 1979), in other cases, the advertising of some alcoholic beverages is viewed as helping to define and promote gender identities as a discursive resource for the construction of masculine and feminine social identities (Griffin et al. 2012). Viewed through a longitudinal lens, ads framed for a specific time, culture and audience may eventually – and unexpectedly – provide social benefits. Thus, the effects of advertising to promote sales of "risky" products might not be so clearly determined as categorically right or wrong when taking a variety of perspectives and cultural contexts into account. In fact, advertising is more complex today with increased diversity within and among traditional and emergent populations. What John Stuart Mill might view as a natural freedom of unfettered expression and a prerequisite of a progressive modern society, might also offend the same "freedoms" of other cultural segments within that society. If advertisements that promote safe sex though condoms, or alcohol advertised as a form of socialization for young people, or pork advertised as the other "white meat" resonate with positive values for some audiences, the same ads might also be deemed unethical or problematic for devout Catholics, observant Muslims, orthodox Jews, and so run counter to the notion of freedoms shared by all. Again, the issue of appropriateness of message in framing context, temporality and audience are resonant themes in advertising. Judgments on the ethics of advertising are not simply an issue of product category and truth, transparency, or clarity of message, but rather of context and community values when different moral systems apply various standards to advertising messages.

Another ethical issue in advertising has less to do with the consequences of messages from companies, and more to do with regulatory requirements and legal permissions. By law, firms that advertise must avoid false or deceptive advertising. Advertisers cannot make false claims, such as state a health product can cure an illness when it cannot, or an automobile can achieve 40 miles per gallon under normal driving conditions when it cannot. Deceptions that once were acceptable, such as claiming a brand of diet bread has fewer calories than regular bread simply by slicing the bread thinner, are now illegal (Kotler and Armstrong 2016, 441). A company's trade promotion activities are closely regulated, so that, for example, under the Robinson-Patman Act certain customers cannot be favored in contests or sweepstakes over others (Kotler and Armstrong 2016, 441). Guidance for ethical conduct in marketing and advertising has been codified by a number of industry organizations. For example, the Marketing Research Association's Code of Marketing Research Standards "is designed to promote an ethical culture in the marketing research profession where principles of honesty, professionalism, fairness and confidentiality combine to support the profession's success."[2] In creating ads, a company, therefore, must be aware of the legal and ethical issues surrounding its communications. Still, some advertising circumvents legal guidelines and enters into questionable ethical areas. For example, parity superiority claims such as "Nothing cleans better than Brand X" may pass through formal legal advertising codes but they can mislead consumers. For many consumers, "Nothing cleans better than Brand X" conveys that Brand X is the best brand rather than simply no better or worse than Brand Y.

Doing Good and Doing One's Job

Anthropologists who weigh ethics in their commercial endeavors must also consider whose good their labors advance. Engaging in marketing and advertising research and strategic planning necessitates doing good on behalf of one's clients. What does this mean, precisely? At best, advertising helps clients design brands and create advertising messages that add value to the lives of consumers. "Doing good" for clients also entails helping firms that advertise increase market share, introduce a new product successfully, and achieve market sales that generate an acceptable return on their investment (ROI). Equally important, "doing good" builds long-term sustainable relationships, in which consumers not only are loyal to a product or service, but also advocate others on the brand's behalf. We and others (such as Briody and Meerwarth Pester in Chapter 2, this volume) have established that such positive approaches to commerce can enrich culture symbolically and interactionally as well as economically. Moreover, while marketing and advertising help drive consumption, leveling exclusive critiques at corporations for consumer over-consumption, unsustainability, inequalities in wealth and inequities in access to commercial goods is unmerited. These are not marketing or advertising issues exclusively, but rather human problems; responsibility is shared by societal institutions as well as by individual behavior, and consumers are increasingly calling for more accountable marketing practices and products that stand for something of positive "value." In present-day marketplace behavior as we discussed at length in our introduction to this volume, consumers co-create brands and brand messaging, including advertising.

Increasingly, marketers aim to benefit society by enlisting in a new movement of *Purpose Marketing* initiatives (also called pro-social marketing). These initiatives promise, and often deliver, consumers and society benefits beyond profit, charitable contributions or selling a product in recyclable packaging. *Purpose Marketing* is becoming popular on Madison Avenue, writes Stuart Elliot, because of the growing number of consumers who say that "what a company stands for makes a difference in what they do and do not buy" (Elliot 2013). Many companies use advertising and other forms of promotion to communicate and advocate for programs that are socially responsible. For instance, Nature Valley, owned by General Mills, promotes a strong commitment to preserving nature on its website. The Nature Valley website and accompanying social media site describe a "Preserve the Parks" initiative that supports park restoration through donations and volunteer efforts, and uses "street-view" technology to inspire enjoyment and preservation of the natural environment (see Kotler and Armstrong 2016, 441). Other examples of firms involved in Purpose Marketing include Tom's of Maine, Patagonia, Body Shop, Newman's Own, Zappos and Amazon, among others (see Richards 2015 for more examples). Many corporations now adhere to responsible business practices by engaging in fair trade with coffee growers, working with organizations such as Feeding America and open-donation community restaurants, or developing recycling or donation programs that engage with communities in need (Elliot 2013). Other companies, such as Whole Foods, The Container Store and First United Bank, support movements such as Conscious Capitalism,[3] as a force for good in society. In addition to these corporate efforts, advertising has promoted healthier eating habits, informed the pubic in Public Service Campaigns about fire safety, anti-drug, diversity and inclusion, among other social issues, and offered awareness of new drugs that improve the quality of life for some people. In the early twenty-first century, more marketers are helping to repair the world because consumers demand it to be so, and because through the transparency afforded by the Internet, bloggers and social advocacy groups, the best (and the worst) practices of corporations are easily accessible by critical consumers.

And yet sometimes, for some clients, doing good or at least the right thing in practice is a clouded decision-making process, if not an ethical debate. Even if one is convinced of the economic and societal value of advertising and marketing in general, arguments for the cultural benefits of Jif peanut butter, Campbell's

Soup, Duncan Hines Cake Mix or Comet Cleanser seem strained. All of these brands can, and often do, enhance interpersonal relationships and/or a consumer's quality of life. But, is it reasonable to suggest that an anthropologist who is helping these marketers build their consumer share of sales is doing society good, or, more candidly is the practitioner advancing the commercial aims of the corporation his/her work serves? If the answer is the latter, is that unethical as long as the consumer and society at large are not harmed? For Jordan, a corporation's profit motive and the potential for harm make her decision-making process clear, stating unequivocally: "if it appears the corporate bosses are only interested in increasing profit for the shareholders at the expense of the employees or the community, then I do not undertake the work" (Jordan 2012, 21). Jordan's thought process is admirable, but determining "harm" in a given context is often complex, ambiguous and multi-dimensional. The challenge of such a decision is due in part to the way marketing and advertising work in the world. Marketing and advertising, different from the anthropological open-ended and holistic approach to research, are goal-oriented in actions that aim to influence or modify consumer behavior toward specific ends: "Marketers are interested in developing explicit ongoing relations with consumers within which individual transactions may occur, and customers play a role in creating these exchanges" (Brenkert 2008, 14). In other words, relationships with customers in marketing practice are predicated on influencing their behavior in some way, so that the question is not if marketers impact behavior, but rather how such "change" in desired behavior is ethically interpreted. Are directed influences for what consumers may want or desire, harmful or beneficial? Alternatively, the anthropological prerogative of "do no harm" might imply a passive or neutral position toward affecting change. We must also consider that consumers often reject marketers' overtures. A marketplace product inspired by an anthropologist-led design study will not generate significant sales if consumers choose not to buy it, and marketers will not launch a new product into the marketplace before it is tested and found to have potential for success.

How does an anthropologist align his or her responsibility with ethical conduct in a corporate world that is designed to influence and even change consumer behavior? Does working for or in an organization that produces questionable or even harmful products determine one's complicity? Morais has worked in advertising for products such as cake mixes, and Malefyt on carbonated soft drinks for Pepsi. Likewise, Briody and Meerwarth Pester, while improving the effectiveness of the GM corporation, have also contributed indirectly to the development of unsafe vehicles (i.e., Cobalt ignition switches) and vehicles with dubious social value (i.e., Hummers). Lucas writes about anthropologists teaching in the Armed Services; their goal is to "increase cultural awareness" and "cultural sensitivities" of students, and develop "regional studies" programs for the Department of Defense (2009, 6). While all such associations may be argued as unethical, the tasks of building a client's business, creating ads, or teaching cultural relativism to soldiers can, in the spirit of Briody and Meerwarth Pester's (2015) concept, contribute toward "a more effective system" or "the use of anthropological theories and methods to help improve the human condition," from within the system. As networked and connected individuals in a modern world, we are all complicit, to some extent. Yet, in many cases how we determine complicity is a "matter of framing" (Borofsky 2016, 29). Reviving a classic anthropological debate, if Chagnon "did harm" to the Yanomani by casting them as "fierce and violent," writes Borofsky, which led to their incarceration in small patched reserves, it also had a positive effect of reducing exploitive mining, which may have otherwise occurred on the occupied land. By focusing only on "harm," Borofsky states, people tend to argue past one another, blaming this or that individual or institution rather than claiming responsibility to make a difference, and attempting to work positivity within the system (2016, 29).

Perhaps anthropologists engaged in for-profit enterprises can agree that doing good entails doing one's job without *intending* to do purposeful harm. We ask: Can the mandate for anthropologists in business to work on behalf of their subjects be mutually compatible with the interests of the corporate sponsor for whom research is conducted? As Blomberg likewise queries in her investigation of design research: Can a researcher be simultaneously a consumer advocate while supporting the "purveyors of technology?" (Blomberg 1993, 140). Our own work intends to strengthen consumers' choices for products as honestly as we can provide, while we work closely and affirmatively with our clients, even if and when consumers choose unhealthy beverages, cakes and other marketplace offerings. Anthropologists in our professions help their clients deliver what consumers want, and consumers retain the right to accept or reject marketplace offerings.

Consumer rejection of brands is high not because of or in spite of persuasive advertising, but because the marketplace is highly competitive. Consumers choose among multiple options when they consider buying products and services, and they are more informed than ever of product strengths, weaknesses and user experiences because purchase decision-making is mediated by online search and social networks. In fact, after purchase, consumers are shown to enter into an "open-ended relationship with the brand," sharing their experiences with it online to others (Edelman 2010, 64). The growing importance of empowered consumers is evident in the different forms of brand dialog behaviors and brand communities they form (Maslowskaa et al. 2016). Anthropologists who work in industry are cognizant of such consumer savvy. Marietta Baba notes: "Consumers are not passive adopters of products" (Baba 2006, 44); John Sherry observes that consumers are neither "cultural dopes nor cultural dupes" (Sherry 2008, 90). Still, much of advertising points consumers toward heightened consumption of brands and tends to offer simple solutions to even complex problems. This requires that just as consumers should make informed purchase choices, ethical business anthropologists should make thoughtful professional choices about the assignments they accept. But doing the right thing, especially when harm can be indirect and inadvertent, or when one's livelihood depends upon keeping a job or taking a particular assignment, can be challenging intellectually and emotionally. The American Anthropological

Association's Code of Ethics is of limited utility for anthropologists in business but practitioners may find the RICE Guide valuable (Bohren and Whiteford 2013; also see Whiteford and Trotter 2008). Ladner (2014) suggests that a business ethnographer might advise a client on the morality of an initiative based on research findings (Ladner 2014, 96), while Kitner (2014) is "the anthropological burr under the saddle" of her employer, arguing that "the anthropologist should be the one to constantly nudge in the right direction" (Kitner 2014, 318). In our experience, on-the-job ethical discussions and negotiations carry little weight and may even irritate clients. Anthropologists in business should be applauded whenever they have succeeded with such endeavors.

Drawing from our own experience in the advertising industry, we have described cases of on-the-job ethical thinking in detail elsewhere (Malefyt and Morais 2012, 121–135). Morais was approached recently by a former client from a dental products company who moved to the R.J. Reynolds Tobacco Company. Morais declined a series of potentially lucrative marketing research cigarette projects on personal moral grounds. Rather than engage in an argument on the morality of cigarette marketing and in order to reduce damage to his relationship with the former client, Morais framed his response as a conflict of interest for his company, which has multiple clients in the health and wellness marketplace. This instance aligns closely with the decision-making process engaged in by Jordan (2012, 21) and, we suspect, by most anthropologists in business. We also know that there is latitude in such decision-making. Morais refuses to accept projects for cigarettes, but has worked on advertising research for Post Foods' breakfast cereals and Malefyt has contributed to advertising research for Pepsi-Cola's carbonated soft drinks. If an anthropologist in advertising or marketing defines professional ethics narrowly in terms of explicitly and directly doing good for society, his or her clients would consist of companies focused on positive marketing. He/she might actively support the work of enterprises such as the Advertising Council, whose mission is to "identify a select number of significant public issues and stimulate action on those issues through communications programs that make a measurable difference in our society" (www.adcouncil.org) or contribute to academic initiatives such as Fordham University's Center for Positive Marketing. For most anthropologists in advertising, the brands to which they contribute during long careers will be highly varied. Some assignments might confront the practitioner with ethical challenges, ethically unmovable colleagues and clients, and difficult career choices. A practitioner can attempt to negotiate with the client and, if that fails, refuse to work on a project and risk derailing an advertising career. He or she might engage in personal justification – or rationalization – concerning the dubious cultural and economic value of certain products and the advertising that champions them or argue that the consumer can and will make an informed purchase decision. In the end, like Jordan, we believe that ethical actions for anthropologists in advertising are best guided by personal values, individual cases, and the principal of inflicting no harm upon the subjects of study or consumers at large, however the practitioner defines those aims.

Notes

1 Controversy of expressing racial pride or rebellion was recently stirred over an image circulated of raised fist by Black Army female graduates (Phillipps 2016).
2 See www.marketingresearch.org/issues-policies/mra-code-marketing-research-standards. For ethical guidelines specific to advertising see, for example: https://ams.aaaa.org/eweb/upload/inside/standards.pdf and www.aaf.org/institute-advertising-ethics.
3 www.consciouscapitalism.org/.

References

Arnould, E.J. and C.J.Thompson. 2005. Consumer Culture Theory (CCT): Twenty Years of Research. Journal of Consumer Research 31, 4: 868–882.

Baba, Marietta. L. 2006. Anthropology and Business. In *Encyclopedia of Anthropology*, H.J. Birx, ed., 83–117. Thousand Oaks, CA: Sage Publications.

Barthes, R. 1972. *Critical Essays*. Evanston: Northwestern University Press.

Belk, Russell. 1988. Possessions and the Extended Self. *Journal of Consumer Research* 15, 2: 139–168.

———. 1989. Materialism and the Modern U.S. Christmas. In *Interpretive Consumer Research*, E.C. Hirschman, ed., 136–147. Provo: Association for Consumer Research.

———. 2010. Sharing. *Journal of Consumer Research* 26: 715–734.

Belk, Russel and Gregory S. Coon. 1993. Gift Giving as Agapic Love: An Alternative to the Exchange Paradigm Based on Dating Experiences. *Journal of Consumer Research* 20, 3: 393–417.

Belk, Russell, John F. Sherry, Jr. and Melanie Wallendorf. 1988a. A Naturalistic Inquiry into Buyer and Seller Behavior at a Swap Meet. *Journal of Consumer Research* 14: 449–470.

Belk, Russell, Melanie Wallendorf, John Sherry, Morris Holbrook and Scott Roberts. 1988b. Collectors and Collecting. In *Advances in Consumer Research*, Michael Houston, ed., 548–553. Provo: Association for Consumer Research.

Belk, Russel, Melanie Wallendorf and John Sherry Jr. 1989. The Sacred and the Profane in Consumer Behavior: Theodicy on the Odyssey. *Journal of Consumer Research*, 16(June): 1–38.

Blomberg, Jeanette. 1993. Ethnographic Field Methods and their Relation to Design. In *Participatory Design: Principles and Practices*. Hillsdale, NJ: Lawrence Erlbaum Associates.

Bohren, Lenora and Linda Whiteford. 2013. Ethics and Practicing Anthropology – Pragmatic, Practical and Principled. In *A Handbook of Practicing Anthropology*, R.W. Nolan, ed., 123–155. Malden, MA: Wiley-Blackwell.

Borofsky, Robert. 2016. Maybe "Doing No Harm" is Not the Best Way to Help Those Who Helped You. *Anthropology News* 57: 29.

Brenkert, George. 2008. *Marketing Ethics*. Malden: Blackwell.

Briody, Elizabeth K. and Tracy Meerwarth Pester. 2015. *"Do Some Good" and Other Lessons from Practice for a New AAA Code of Ethics*. American Anthropological Association Ethics Blog.

Deighton, John. 1992. Sincerity, Sham and Satisfaction in Marketplace Performance. In *Advances in Consumer Research*, J.F. Sherry, Jr. and B. Sternthal, eds., 462–464. Provo, UT: Association for Consumer Research.

Edelman, David C. 2010. Branding in the Digital Age. *Harvard Business Review*, 63–69.

Elliot, Stuart. 2013. Selling Products by Selling Shared Values. *New York Times, Business Section*.

Elliott, Richard and Mark Ritson. 1997. Post-structuralism and the Dialectics of Advertising: Discourse, Ideology, Resistance. In *Consumer Research: Postcards from the Edge*, Stephen Brown and Darach Turley, eds., 190–219. London: Routledge.

Elliott, Richard and Kritsadarat Wattanasuwan. 1998. Brands as Symbolic Resources for the Construction of Identity. *International Journal of Advertising* 17, 2: 131–144.

Ewen, Stewart. 1976. *Captains of Consciousness*. New York: McGraw-Hill.

Goffman, Ervine. 1979. *Gender Advertisements*. New York: Harper & Row.

Griffin, Ch., A. Bengry-Howell, Ch. Hackley, W. Mistral and I. Szmigin. 2012. Inhabiting the Contradictions: Hypersexual Femininity and the Culture of Intoxication among Young Women in the U.K. *Feminism and Psychology* 23, 2: 184–206.

Hackley, C. 2002. The Panoptic Role of Advertising Agencies in the Production of Consumer Culture. *Consumption, Markets and Culture* 5, 3: 211–229.

Hackley, Chris and Rungpaka Amy Hackley. 2015. *Advertising and Promotion*. London: Sage Publications.

Hackley, Chris and P.J. Kitchen. 1999. Ethical Perspectives on the Postmodern Communications Leviathan. *Journal of Business Ethics* 20, 1: 15–26.

Hackley, Chris, R. Tiwsakul and R. Preuss. 2008. An Ethical Evaluation of Product Placement: A Deceptive Practice? *Business Ethics – a European Review* 17: 109–120.

Henry, Jules. 1963. *Culture Against Man*. New York: Random House.

Hirschman, Elizabeth and Crag Thompson. 1997. Why Media Matter: Toward a Richer Understanding of Consumers' Relationship with Advertising and Mass Media. *Journal of Advertising* 26: 43–60.

Jhally, Sut. 1987. *The Codes of Advertising*. London: Frances Pinter.

Jordan, Ann. 2012. The Importance of Business Anthropology: Its Unique Contributions. *International Journal of Business Anthropology* 1: 15–25.

Kemper, Stephen. 2001. *Buying is Believing: Sri Lankan Advertising and Consumers in a Transnational World*. Chicago: University of Chicago Press.

Kitner, Kathi R. 2014. The Good Anthropologist: Questioning Ethics in the Workplace. In *Handbook of Anthropology in Business*, Rita M. Denny and Patricia L. Sunderland, eds., 309–320. Walnut Creek, CA: Left Coast Press.

Klein, Naomi. 2000. *No Logo: Taking Aim at the Brand Bullies*. New York: Picador.

Kotler, Philip and Gary Armstrong. 2016. *Principles of Marketing*. Sixteenth Edition. Englewood Cliffs, NJ: Pearson.

Ladner, Sam. 2014. *Practical Ethnography: A Guide to Doing Ethnography in the Private Sector*. Walnut Creek, CA: Left Coast Press.

Leiss, William, Stephen Klein and Sut Jhally. 1997. *Social Communication in Advertising: Persons, Products and Images of Well-Being*. London: Routledge.

———. 2005. *Social Communication in Advertising: Persons, Products and Images of Well-Being*. 3rd Edition. New York: Taylor & Francis.

Lucas, G.R. 2009. *Anthropologists in Arms: The Ethics of Military Anthropology*. Lanham: Rowman & Littlefield.

McCracken, Grant. 1986. Culture and Consumption: A Theoretical Account of the Structure and Movement of the Cultural Meaning of Consumer Goods. *Journal of Consumer Research* 13, 1: 71–84.

McFall, L. 2004. *Advertising: A Cultural Economy*. London: Sage.

McLuhan, Marshall. 1951. *The Mechanical Bride*. Boston: Beacon.

McQuarrie, Edward F. and Barbara Phillips. 2005. Indirect Persuasion in Advertising: How Consumers Process Metaphors Presented in Pictures and Words. *Journal of Advertising* 34: 7–20.

Malefyt, Timothy de Waal. 2015. Relationship Advertising: How Advertising Can Enhance Social Bonds. *Journal of Business Research* 68: 2494–2505.

——. Forthcoming. Advertising. In *The International Encyclopedia of Anthropology*. London: Wiley-Blackwell.

Malefyt, Timothy de Waal and Maryann McCabe. 2016. Women's Bodies, Menstruation and Marketing "Protection": Interpreting a Paradox of Gendered Discourses in Consumer Practices and Advertising Campaigns. *Consumption Markets & Culture*. http://dx.doi.org/10.1080/10253866.2015.1095741.

Malefyt, Timothy de Waal and Robert J. Morais. 2012. *Advertising and Anthropology: Ethnographic Practice and Cultural Perspectives*. Oxford: Berg.

Marchand, Roland. 1985. *Advertising the American Dream: Making Way for Modernity, 1920–1940*. Berkeley: University of California Press.

Maslowskaa, Ewa, Edward C. Malthouse and Tom Collingera. 2016. The Customer Engagement Ecosystem. *Journal of Marketing Management* 32, 5–6: 1–33.

Mazzarella, William. 2003. *Shoveling Smoke: Advertising and Globalization in Contemporary India*. Durham, NC: Duke University Press.

Mick, David Glen and Claus Buhl. 1992. A Meaning Based Model of Advertising Experiences. *Journal of Consumer Research* 19, 3: 317–338.

Miller, Daniel. 1995. *Acknowledging Consumption*. London: Routledge.

——. 1998. *A Theory of Shopping*. London: Routledge.

O'Donohoe, Stephanie. 1999. Nationality and Negotiation of Advertising Meanings. In *Advances in Consumer Research*, E.J. Arnould and L.M. Scott, eds., 684–689. Provo, UT: Association for Consumer Research.

Packard, Vance. 1957. *The Hidden Persuaders*. New York: McKay.

Phillipps, Dave. 2016. West Point Won't Punish Cadets in Raised-Fist Photo. *New York Times*, May 10. www.nytimes.com/2016/05/11/us/west-point-cadets-raised-fist-photo.html.

Pollay, Richard. 1986. The Distorted Mirror: Reflections on the Unintended Consequences of Advertising. *Journal of Marketing* 50: 18–36.

Pollay, Richard and Banwari Mittal. 1993. Here's the Beef: Factors, Determinants, and Segments in Consumer Criticism of Advertising. *Journal of Marketing* 57: 99–114.

Richards, Katie. 2015. Doing Well by Doing Good. *Adweek* 14: 8.

Ritson, Mark and Richard Elliott. 1999. The Social Uses of Advertising: An Ethnographic Study of Adolescent Advertising Audiences. *Journal of Consumer Research* 26: 260–277.

Schudson, Michael. 1984. *Advertising: The Uneasy Persuasion*. New York: Basic Books.

Sherry, John, F. Jr. 1987. Advertising as a Cultural System. In *Marketing and Semiotics, New Directions in the Study of Signs for Sale*, J. Umiker-Sebeok, ed., 441–461. New York: Mouton de Gruyter.

——. 2008. The Ethnographer's Apprentice: Trying Consumer Culture from the Outside In. *Journal of Business Ethics* 80: 85–95.

Thompson, Crag. 2004. Marketplace Mythology and Discourses of Power. *Journal of Consumer Research* 31: 162–180.

Thompson, Crag J. and Diana L. Haytko. 1997. Speaking of Fashion: Consumers' Uses of Fashion Discourses and the Appropriation of Countervailing Cultural Meanings. *Journal of Consumer Research* 24: 15–42.

Twitchell, James. 1996. *AdCult USA: The Triumph of Advertising in American Culture*. New York: Columbia University Press.

Veblen, Thorsten. 2009. *The Theory of the Leisure Class*. Oxford: Oxford University Press.

Wallendorf, M. and E.J. Arnould. 1991. "We Gather Together": Consumption Rituals of Thanskgiving Day. *Journal of Consumer Research* 18, 1: 13–31.

Wernick, A. 1991. *Promotional Culture: Advertising, Ideology and Symbolic Expression*. London: Sage.

Whiteford, Linda and Robert T. Trotter II. 2008. *Ethics for Anthropological Research and Practice.* Long Grove, IL: Waveland Press.

Williamson, Judith. 1978. *Decoding Advertising.* London: Marion Boyars.

Zayer, Linda Tuncay and Catherine A. Coleman. 2015. Advertising Professionals' Perception of the Impact of Gender Portrayals on Men and Women: A Question of Ethics? *Journal of Advertising* 44, 3: 264–275.

8

ETHICAL AMBIGUITIES IN A DESIGN ANTHROPOLOGY CLASS

Jo Aiken, Victoria Schlieder, and Christina Wasson

Introduction

In recent years, business anthropologists have increasingly turned their attention to the issue of training the next generation of practitioners (Ikeya et al. 2007; Mack and Squires 2011;Tian 2011;Wasson and Metcalf 2013).[1] While the first generation of business anthropologists was largely trained in traditional academic programs that provided no guidance on the challenges of working in industry, a number of master's and PhD programs have recently emerged that focus specifically on preparing anthropology students for careers in the business context (Sachs 2006; Squires et al. 2014). Examples include programs at Wayne State University, the University of Copenhagen, and the University of North Texas (UNT).

Training in ethics is an essential component of any graduate program in anthropology (Fluehr-Lobban 2003; Kingsolver et al. 2003). And while learning about professional codes of ethics is a valuable starting point, programs need to go further. Students need to learn how to navigate ethical complexities, contradictions, and ambiguities that cannot be fully captured by such codes. Fluehr-Lobban argues that recognizing the *limitations* of ethics codes is the "real job of ethics education through the critical study of the history of the discipline and … the review of cases, past and present, for the lessons they offer regarding fieldwork methods, relations with people and materials studied, and with stakeholders" (Fleuhr-Lobban 2003, 23).

In this chapter, we examine how a consideration of ethics has been incorporated into one course in the UNT business anthropology program, namely Design Anthropology. This course is a core elective in the UNT business anthropology specialization, and it is the only course on design anthropology offered by an anthropology department in the United States (Wasson and Metcalf 2013). Specifically, we focus on the course as it was taught in fall 2011. Authors include two students from the class (Aiken, Schlieder) and the instructor (Wasson).

Students in the Design Anthropology course learned about ethics through initial class discussions, safeguards that the instructor built into the course, and guidelines on the disclosure of findings. Most importantly, they gained hands-on experience in negotiating ethical challenges through the experience of conducting ethnographic fieldwork for a client project. In this chapter, we focus on one particular example of an ethical challenge faced by student researchers, and its pedagogical value as an extreme case (LeCompte and Schensul 1999, 113; Yin 2009, 47). In this example, a team of student researchers was faced with multiple pressures and challenges simultaneously, and had to navigate a course in the face of ambiguity and an inability to communicate with each other privately. While this kind of "perfect storm" of problems may not occur frequently, it provided a valuable learning experience for the class. As the students in the class collectively analyzed the case afterwards, they came to recognize that gray areas inevitably arise in the course of fieldwork, and that such areas do not always have tidy solutions. Nonetheless it is important for researchers to be sensitive to all of the ethical dimensions of their field activities, and to search for the most ethical path possible through them.

The dilemma that provides the case study for this article contributes to a long tradition of anthropologists writing about ethical challenges encountered during fieldwork. Often these narratives are found in books that present personal stories of the author's experience (Bowen 1954; Moeran 1985; Armbruster and Laerke 2008). These stories highlight the experiential, emergent dimensions of fieldwork in which researchers are fully, often anxiously, engaged in trying to understand local people, activities, and contexts, but often unsure about their meanings. In this sense, fieldwork encounters may be analyzed as "modes of ethical engagement wherein the ethnographer is arrested in the act of perception. This arrest can lead both to a productive doubt about the ongoing perception of the phenomena in interaction and to the possibility of elaborating shared knowledge" (Borneman and Hammoudi 2009, 19). In this sense, the examination of an ethical dilemma may produce broader insights about the cultural worlds of both the anthropologist and the research participants, and the complex, imperfect, and emotionally laden process of attempting to create translations between them.

Overview of Course and Client Project

A key aspect of the pedagogy of the Design Anthropology course, as Wasson has designed it, is that students engage in a semester-long research project for a real client. Usually about half the class time is devoted to project activities, while the other half is taken up with critical analysis of the design anthropology literature. The research project provides a rich forum for students to debate ethical issues during the planning stages, and to gain practical experience in solving ethical challenges during fieldwork.

In fall 2011, the client for the project was Motorola Mobility's Applied Research Center, represented by Crysta Metcalf, Anthropologist and Manager of Experiences

Research. Metcalf was an active partner throughout the process; she played a strong role in shaping the project goals and design before the class started, and provided feedback during the semester to keep the class focused on what was most useful to Motorola Mobility. Metcalf participated in weekly class meetings via phone and shared computer applications, and visited the class in person three times over the course of the semester. The fall 2011 project was in fact the fifth such collaboration between Metcalf and Wasson (Wasson and Metcalf 2013).

The research conducted for Motorola Mobility was an exploratory study of how people use media to enhance their cooking experience. The goal was to elicit new ideas for Motorola applications and services in the kitchen. Metcalf believed that there was an opportunity to discover and understand people's needs and desires around the specific activity of cooking, and to invent new applications and services that could address those needs. Students investigated how multimedia devices were being used in the kitchen/cooking context before, during, and after the food-making process. Findings included, for example, a set of sample trajectories of cooking experiences (see Figure 8.1) that Motorola could use to understand where the

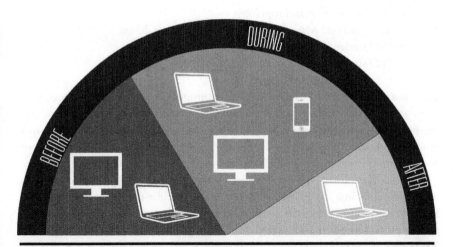

MICHAEL'S OMELET TRAJECTORY

BEFORE
- **Television**
  - Cooking shows
- **Laptop**
  - AllRecipes.com

DURING
- **Television**
  - Good Eats
- **Laptop**
  - AllRecipes.com
- **Smart Phone**
  - Stopwatch for Timer

AFTER
- **Laptop**
  - Future Ideas

FIGURE 8.1 The "Omelet Trajectory," Showing the Before, During, and After of a Cooking Event.

most media usage occurred. The "Omelet Trajectory" shown in Figure 8.1 indicates that before beginning to cook, many participants looked up a recipe on the Internet (using any kind of media device). During a cooking experience, they might have the television on for background noise, or even to watch a cooking show. Similarly, some participants watched instructional videos on the Internet during a cooking experience, to learn the skills needed. After someone was done with a particular cooking experience, they might use the Internet to share their story, especially if they were proud of their final product.

Wasson generally restricts admission to the Design Anthropology class to anthropology and design students, both advanced undergraduates and master's level students. However, she also allows PhD students in related fields to participate. In fall 2011, the 16 students consisted of:

- five undergraduate anthropology majors;
- two undergraduate communication design majors;
- one undergraduate interdisciplinary arts and design/anthropology double major;
- three MA students in anthropology;
- two MFA and one MA students in communication design;
- one PhD student in marketing;
- one PhD student in education.

The class was therefore mainly a mix of anthropology and design students, with a few students from other fields for additional diversity and insights. In conducting fieldwork, students were required to work in interdisciplinary pairs. This mix produced a productive learning experience for all participants, and the project benefited from the expertise of each discipline.

The interdisciplinary diversity of students had implications with regard to ethics, since each discipline has evolved ethical norms particular to its concerns (Balsamo and Mitcham 2012). While the centerpiece of anthropological codes is the imperative to protect research participants from harm (AAA 2012; NAPA 2013; SfAA 2013), design codes do not address the treatment of research participants at all, since historically human research was not a part of design activities (AIGA 2010; IDSA 2010). However, the Department of Design at UNT focuses on the emerging field of design research, which borrows extensively from anthropology and other social sciences. Therefore, while most anthropology students were probably more familiar with the topic of ethics, the design students had already been sensitized to the challenges of conducting fieldwork.

The most recent code of the American Anthropological Association (AAA) recognizes the challenges of interdisciplinary collaboration, stating that "conflicting, competing or crosscutting ethical obligations" may result from "differing ethical frameworks of collaborators representing other disciplines" (AAA 2012, 9). We would not go so far as to say that students experienced conflicts between disciplinary ethical principles. However, they did encounter a rich learning environment in which they were exposed to new ideas. Additionally, due to the practice-driven nature of the course and the opportunities students had to conduct actual field-work, the students were able to experience the complex challenges of ethics in practice, not just as bystanders. This chapter seeks to share the experiences of these budding practicing anthropologists so they can be used as a learning tool for generations to come.

How Ethics Were Incorporated Into the Course Design

Initial Class Discussion of Ethics

Ethical considerations were incorporated into the course design in several different ways. First, during the initial planning of the research project, Wasson invited students to identify and discuss the possible ethical issues that might be involved in conducting an applied project for a business client. This was one way in which students from different disciplines were brought into a shared conversation on ethics as practiced in the anthropological tradition.

Students focused on two main ethical issues. One was the recognition that a client like Motorola sponsors research for the purpose of increasing its sales. So, in a way, the class project would be promoting consumption. Students noted critiques of American society as being too consumption-oriented already, and expressed concern about contributing to this trend (Miller 2001). However, as their discussion progressed, they ended up differentiating among the consumption of different kinds of products; students concluded that while they would not want to promote the consumption of some items, they felt comfortable promoting media use to support cooking activities. More generally, they reflected on how to draw the line between products whose promotion would be ethical and those that would not be ethical. They realized that it was a personal decision; each anthropologist would probably draw the line a bit differently based on their biases and priorities. Students discussed whether or not it would be ethical to promote products which had the potential to cause harm to a person's health, if consumed in large quantities, such as sugary drinks, junk food, and alcohol. Other students noted that the decision to abuse products remained with the consumer, and ethical practitioners could contribute in a positive way to counteract misuse such as in the design of responsible advertising. An important outcome of this discussion was their realization that they should reflect *now* on where they wished to position their personal ethical boundaries, so that they would be prepared later when they were hired for work.

A second potential ethical issue that students raised was the payment of research participants. Students initially wondered whether it might bias study results. After discussion, they concluded that it was actually more ethical to pay research participants than to impose on their time without any form of recompense, as would be more common in traditional kinds of anthropology. This discussion opened a broader critique of the historical model of anthropological fieldwork in which researchers benefit by obtaining material for publication, while the research participants do not receive reciprocal benefits (Fluehr-Lobban 2008).

Safeguarding the Confidentiality of Study Participants and Fieldwork Data

In developing courses that include client projects, Wasson always builds a set of ethical safeguards into the design of the course. One important consideration is to make sure that the client recognizes and is willing to honor the ethical concerns and commitments of anthropological research, with regard to the confidentiality of study participants, the protection of fieldwork data, and indeed the ownership of the data. When the main client contact has a background in engineering or business studies, this may require a process of education and relationship development. Fortunately, the client for this project was an anthropologist, Crysta Metcalf, so Wasson did not need to go through the kinds of explanations that she might need to with someone from another background. Metcalf herself was highly sensitive to ethical concerns and had educated her multidisciplinary work group in anthropological norms concerning the treatment of study participants.

A second ethical safeguard that Wasson built into the course was to obtain approval for the client project from UNT's Institutional Review Board (IRB). The IRB process is mandated by American federal regulations for the protection of human research participants (DHHS 2009). All studies conducted by U.S. university faculty that constitute "research with human subjects" as defined by the regulations must be approved by the university's IRB before the research can begin. The application process is fairly detailed and somewhat bureaucratic, but it is valuable in ensuring that study participants go through a thorough informed consent process. From a pedagogical point of view, the IRB application process provided students with useful exposure to ethical regulations beyond anthropology. All students were required to complete an online training course developed by the U.S. National Institutes of Health on "Protecting Human Research Participants" as a condition for IRB approval of the class project. The IRB application form and informed consent form were shared with students, and they were invited to suggest improvements. These forms became useful models for some students later when they prepared IRB applications for their master's thesis research.

On a more practical level, Wasson safeguarded the confidentiality of study participants and fieldwork data by creating a data storage site that was password-protected. She also taught students the importance of making sure that all of the information they uploaded was protected. In order for students to be able to access data from any location, the storage site was created in WordPress. Students were quite vigilant about protecting data and on one or two occasions policed each other when someone forgot.

Finally, Wasson asked the class to use pseudonyms for the research participants. These pseudonyms were used on written documents, such as fieldnotes, as well as for the filenames of video clips, photos, and maps that were uploaded to the data storage site. Furthermore, in class discussions, students were asked to refer to the study participants exclusively by their pseudonyms. This was important as extensive class time was spent comparing data from different study participants in order to identify patterns in the fieldwork.

Disclosure of Findings

A third kind of ethical consideration that was built into the course design was the sharing of research findings. This can be a challenging issue in business anthropology, since corporate sponsors of research often regard the findings as providing a competitive advantage that they do not wish to share with potential competitors, at least for several years. The secrecy of anthropological findings has been a controversial issue in debates about the ethical code of the AAA (Baba 2009).

Wasson and Metcalf developed an approach to this issue that accommodated the needs of both Motorola and UNT. They worked with lawyers from both organizations to develop a legal agreement, which protected Motorola's right to profit from the findings of the class, and the students' and Wasson's right to publish freely. No restrictions were placed on what could be described in publications. Motorola did not require any non-disclosure agreements to be signed. The current chapter illustrates the publishing freedom that students and professor enjoy.

The Class Project: Fieldwork and Analysis

In this section we outline the fieldwork process used for the class project, as a context for the ethics case study in the following section. To take advantage of the range of disciplines in the class, as well as support a collaborative environment, students worked in cross-disciplinary pairs; usually this resulted in an anthropologist and a designer being partnered. This allowed for a greater level of learning, especially while in the field conducting the interview. The student pairs first selected a research participant from a list of names provided by a recruiter hired by Motorola. The teams of two then contacted their selected participant via email and/or phone call. It was during this first contact that the student researchers discussed with participants what would be expected of them. The research methodology had three main components: photo narratives, kitchen maps, and in-depth interviews.

Photo Narratives

Photographs were used to discover what media devices participants were using in the kitchen and how those devices affected the cooking process. During the initial phone call, participants were instructed to take photographs of all the ways they use media devices throughout their cooking experiences for about a week and email them to the student researchers. A date and time for an in-home interview with the participant, during which the students could further explore the meaning behind the photographs, were set up during this initial correspondence. Figure 8.2 provides some examples of photos taken by the study participants.

Kitchen Maps

Research participants were also asked to draw a map of their kitchen during one particular cooking process. This was important for tracking the movement and use of media devices in the kitchen while cooking. Some participants used mobile devices (iPads, phones, and laptops), while others used more stationary devices (desktop computers and televisions). The kitchen maps allowed the students to see to what extent different media devices were being used. The maps were discussed during the interview with the research participants and were accompanied by a kitchen tour. Figure 8.3 provides an example of a map; noted on the map is the placement and movement of the participant's computer while cooking.

Interviews

After receiving the photos and maps, student researchers conducted an in-home semi-structured, in-depth interview with the research participant to explore his or her cooking process and the roles that media played in it. An effort was made to schedule the interview no later than a week after the participants had submitted their photographs and kitchen map. In class, the students developed an interview guide that was used, along with the photo narratives and the kitchen maps, to conduct the one-and-a-half- to two-hour interviews. The interviews were video recorded so they could later be re-watched and summarized by students. In the interviews, students paid special attention to how media devices were used at each stage of the cooking process, before, during, and after.

Analysis

Analysis of the interviews began with each team presenting their individual participant findings to the rest of the class, using a PowerPoint with video clips, maps, and photos. This allowed each team to present to the class what they found interesting and pertinent from their personal interview experience and allowed the rest of the class to begin identifying common patterns and themes throughout all of the interviews. All participant photos, important video clips, field notes, interview transcripts, and kitchen maps were posted on the password-protected data storage site described earlier. This provided the students, professor, and Motorola contacts with easy, secure access to all of the project documents.

As the student teams started to present their findings, a Word document was created in which all themes and patterns that emerged in class discussion were logged. During subsequent weekly class meetings, this Word document was expanded and

FIGURE 8.2 Examples of Participant Photographs.

FIGURE 8.2 Continued

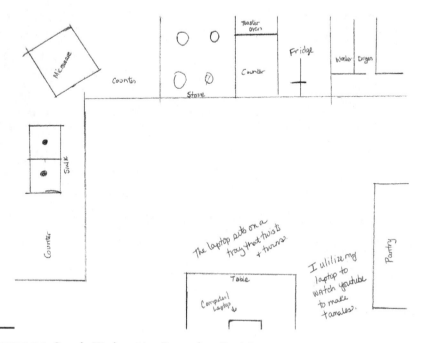

FIGURE 8.3 Sample Kitchen Map Drawn by a Participant.

reworked until the most important and valid patterns across the interviews were identified. It was very important for each of the 16 students' voices to be heard; the analysis was truly a class effort. The input and insights from the designers and anthropologists melded together to form the most complete picture possible.

Ethical Challenges of Fieldwork: An Extreme Case

Ethics has been a frequent topic of deliberation for business anthropologists since the resurgence of applied work concerning organizations during the 1980s. In the inaugural issue of the *Journal of Business Anthropology*, Marietta Baba noted that ethics is one of "our discipline's major issues at this time" (Baba 2012, 24). While most debates concerning ethics in business anthropology focus on the issues of conducting proprietary research and balancing the client–researcher relationship (Hammershøy and Madsen 2012), ethical dilemmas concerning fieldwork are common topics of discussion throughout the field of anthropology (Arnould et al. 2012).

The AAA, the National Association for the Practice of Anthropology (NAPA), and the Society for Applied Anthropology (SfAA) have adopted codes of conduct and guidelines to address ethical considerations of ethnographic fieldwork which uphold the standards issued by the United States Code of Federal Regulations on the Protection of Human Subjects (DHHS 2009). However, while ethical codes provide important guidance, they cannot predict every situation that arises in the field. Their seeming clarity may mask the murkier reality that is inevitably experienced by every ethically concerned fieldworker. In the complex, multifaceted encounters that arise between research participants and anthropologists, identifying the right course of action is not always easy. There may be complex trade-offs, multiple potential sources of harm to participants that cannot all be avoided.

We describe one such case, and its value as a learning experience for the Design Anthropology class, as well as for readers of this chapter. The case constituted a kind of "perfect storm" of problematic elements, and as such may be characterized as an extreme case. The notion of the extreme case has a long history in the social sciences. It formed the basis for Mauss's argument in "Seasonal Variations of the Eskimo" that he could develop generalized social laws from a single case study (Mauss [1904–1905] 1979).

> We have chosen this remarkable people as the special object of our study precisely because the relations to which we wish to call attention are exaggerated and amplified among them; because they stand out, we can clearly understand their nature and significance. As a result, it is easier to recognize them even in other societies where they are less immediately apparent.
>
> *(Mauss [1904–1905] 1979, 19)*

Subsequently other ethnographic studies have been organized around extreme cases. For instance, Dumont developed a conceptualization of "homo hierarchicus" by examining caste in India as an extreme form of social hierarchy (Dumont [1966]

1980). Klinenberg examined the dangers of urban life for vulnerable populations by analyzing causes of the record-breaking mortality rate of the 1995 Chicago heat wave (Klinenberg 2002). The value of extreme cases is regularly described in books on social science methods (LeCompte and Schensul 1999, 113; Yin 2009, 47). We apply the notion of the extreme case to the topic of fieldwork ethics.

Research Participant "Rev" as an Extreme Case

Rev was the last study participant interviewed by the class, and her team of student researchers had faced a number of obstacles before even getting to that point. The team consisted of Jo Aiken, an MA anthropology student and one of the authors of this article, and Rebeca Carranza, an MFA design student. Both were first semester graduate students and had attended Texas A&M University as undergraduates. They instantly connected due to their shared alma mater and developed a deeper rapport due to their shared challenges early on in the project.

Aiken and Carranza were never able to reach the first study participant they were assigned due to insufficient contact information. The second participant they were given withdrew from the study after twice cancelling scheduled interviews. By the time they were given their third research participant, Rev, the project was nearing the end of its data collection phase, and obtaining this final interview had become urgent. Aiken and Carranza scheduled an interview with Rev in late November, at the earliest possible opportunity, even though the time overlapped with the weekly class meeting.

The face-to-face interview with Rev proved to be an on-the-job learning experience for both Aiken and Carranza. From the moment Rev greeted them at the door of her home, it was obvious to both students that their interviewee seemed exceptionally happy about participating in the study. Aiken's initial impression was that Rev just had a bubbly personality. However, both students gradually developed the impression that Rev might be intoxicated. Aiken and Carranza each struggled internally, without the ability to speak to one another openly in front of their participant, with the decision of whether to carry on with the interview. They proceeded with it because, in their best judgment, Rev still had the capacity to understand the research activities she was participating in. However, the situation was ambiguous. Later, both students admitted that they could not know for sure if in fact Rev was intoxicated or at what level. Her speech was slightly slurred in comparison to their two previous phone conversations, and the open bottles and empty martini glass on the bar adjacent to the dining table where they conducted the interview supported their suspicion. Yet the two phone calls Carranza had with Rev did not offer any indication that she was intoxicated on a regular basis.

With reservations, Aiken and Carranza continued Rev's interview. Halfway through it, Rev's daughter joined her mother at the dining room table where the interview was taking place. The daughter appeared to be approximately 11 to 13 years of age. She came to the table of her own accord, seemingly bored and hungry – coming to the kitchen wondering when dinner would be ready. Sitting down next to Rev, the daughter first listened quietly and then joined in the conversation when prompted by her mother to answer certain interview questions. The exchange between the mother and daughter was casual. It appeared that Rev was trying to include her daughter in a friendly conversation with visitors, rather than encouraging her to participate in a study. Aiken, the primary interviewer, was immediately concerned when Rev began redirecting questions to her daughter since the class had not obtained IRB consent for interviewing minors. Even though her mother was present and apparently consenting to her daughter's involvement in the study, Rev's possibly inebriated state brought the circumstances into question. Carranza, in charge of video-recording the interview, was also concerned about the consequences of a minor being on record for the study. Again, without the ability to communicate openly with each other, Aiken and Carranza continued with the interview as planned, making sure to redirect fielded questions back to their adult participant, Rev.

Aiken and Carranza repeatedly reflected on whether they should continue the interview while it was taking place. Each of them felt it was best to continue. Most importantly, to stop the interview would have meant passing judgment on Rev as a responsible adult and as a mother. As they later shared with each other, they felt it was a moral obligation to withhold their own judgments about Rev's unconfirmed inebriated state and her parenting choices, and that to stop the interview would have caused more harm to the participant's feelings than would continuing. Another consideration for Aiken was that Rev would not receive compensation for participating in the study if they stopped the interview. The students were instructed to present the research payment to participants only at the conclusion of the interview. Stopping it did not seem fair to Rev, who had already devoted hours of her week to completing the other tasks she was assigned, such as taking photos and mapping her kitchen experiences. Also, Aiken and Carranza felt a responsibility to report their findings to Motorola and the Design Anthropology class. Aiken felt confident that Wasson would allow them to make up the grade for the interview, but she did not want to let down Metcalf and the class by decreasing the total population of the study.

First Ethically Gray Area: A Potentially Intoxicated Research Participant

The ethically gray area surrounding Aiken and Carranza's dealings with their participant Rev in her possible intoxicated state can be examined in terms of vulnerability and research design. Since the drafting of the Nuremburg Code in 1947, obtaining the fully informed consent of research participants has been at the forefront of concerns in ethical research. As a result, if the research design necessitates the inclusion of vulnerable participants incapable of providing informed consent, special provisions have to be made. Guidelines to these provisions are laid out in federal policies and professional codes.

There are many varying guidelines within medical research and healthcare aimed at protecting the vulnerable. While various definitions exist, the federal regulations which generally impact the research of business anthropologists in the United States are the Code of Federal Regulations for the Protection of Human Subjects (DHHS 2009) and, if conducted within academia, the Office for Human Research Protections (OHRP) IRB Guidebook (OHRP 1993). The Federal Policy for the Protection of Human Subjects – often referred to in government documents as the Common Rule or simply, Federal Policy – sets forth the basic guidelines for research concerning human subjects. Under the term *vulnerable populations*, the Common Rule states that special provisions have to be made to protect the rights and welfare of these groups when involved in research. The Common Rule classifies children, prisoners, pregnant women, mentally disabled persons, and economically or educationally disadvantaged persons as vulnerable populations. The OHRP, which governs the IRBs for all universities that accept federal funding, reaffirms the vulnerable populations identified in the Common Rule in its IRB Guidebook, but also reclassifies populations as *special classes of subjects* (OHRP 1993).

The dilemma surrounding Rev's intoxication can be evaluated according to both clinical and ethnographic standards. Chapter VI of the OHRP's IRB Guidebook specifies "mentally disabled persons" to include cognitively impaired individuals with "psychiatric, cognitive, or developmental disorders, or who are substance abusers" (OHRP 1993, Chapter VI, part D). The Guidebook states that persons under the influence of drugs or alcohol should be evaluated according to their competency in providing consent, but the OHRP does not set specific regulations for these persons except in the case of known, active abusers. The IRB Guidelines of the University of North Texas go further by stating that "all adults, regardless of their diagnosis or condition, should be presumed competent to provide informed consent unless there is evidence" (UNT ORED 2013). In accordance with the OHRP's IRB Guidebook, Rev's competency to provide informed consent should then be determined based on the researchers' judgment of her capacity to understand information in her intoxicated state if she was not an active substance abuser. The Guidebook does not outline the means by which a researcher independently determines a participant to be an active substance abuser. At the time of the interview, and previous phone calls did not give the research team any indication of institutionalization, cognitive impairment, or active substance abuse. Therefore, the question of Rev's competency could only be answered by Aiken and Carranza by evaluating her capacity to understand information. Rev had no difficulty in understanding the interview questions, the photo narrative, or the kitchen tour, and at no point indicated incapacity to consent to the process.

Mirroring the guidelines of the Common Rule and OHRP's Guidebook, the AAA, NAPA, and SfAA professional associations also place the judgment of a participant's capacity to consent, outside general circumstances, with the researcher without providing the means of determining capacity. Keeping in mind anthropological paradigms of building rapport and reflexivity, it is doubtful that these associations would support researchers administering breathalyzer tests to their participants, nor would they encourage researchers to question participants based on a hunch. In fact, intoxication is often an important part of the ethnographic research design. Cultural and applied anthropologists often conduct studies of drinking cultures and other groups in which drinking plays a vital role (Frake 1964; Spradley 1999; García 2008; Sandiford and Seymour 2013). When alcohol is not pertinent to the research question, ethnographers have noted that intoxication often aids in building rapport with participants (Joseph and Donnelly 2012). Anderson and De Paula (2006) describe a significant experience they had with an intoxicated group of Portuguese locals on an inter-island boat ride home after a long day of work. Even though their research in Salvador da Bahia, Brazil was not targeted toward partakers of alcohol and even though the encounter was unintentional, the experience added to their research on the collective nature of the culture (anderson and De Paula 2006).

Like anderson and De Paula's study, the kitchen media study did not intend to include intoxicated participants. Aiken and Carranza were not uncomfortable with the interview because of a moral judgment against alcohol in and of itself, but because they were unsure about Rev's mental state and how it would affect their findings. The question of how to handle cognitively impaired participants did not come up in the ethical discussions in class because the research design did not specifically target such populations. Since the interview posed no more than the least amount of minimal risk to the participant, the student researchers completed the interview with the understanding that Wasson or Metcalf could choose to eliminate the data from the study.

Second Ethically Gray Area: An Unapproved Child Joins the Interview

The ethical dilemma concerning Rev's questionable demeanor during the interview was magnified when her daughter joined the interview. Rev's daughter was undoubtedly a minor by federal standards. There was no question that Rev's daughter was a minor, and there was no question in the minds of the student researchers that special precautions should be taken to protect children participating in research.

As described earlier, Rev's daughter sat down at the table voluntarily. Rev introduced the girl to Aiken and Carranza as the students conducting the kitchen study, and mentioned that her daughters, plural, found the week fun because their mom was taking pictures of all their meals. As for the daughter's mental capacity to understand the research situation, there was no question that she had already been aware of the study and was capable of understanding her surroundings and the risks involved from participating in the research. However, the Federal Policy (DHHS 2009) concerning the involvement of children as subjects stipulates that legal consent be obtained in writing by at least one parent or guardian. Rev had not provided written consent for her daughter's participation, even though she was the one who instigated the daughter's involvement in answering the interview questions.

Nevertheless, the flow of the interview brings into question whether or not the child was actually participating in the kitchen media study, and if the student researchers were in violation of federal policy. The Federal Policy states that "no investigator may involve a human being as a subject in research … unless the investigator has obtained the legally effective informed consent of the subject or the subject's legally authorized representative" (DHHS 2009). The Federal Policy notes the involvement of a *research subject by an investigator*. Rev's daughter was not at any point considered by the student researchers to be a subject of the study. Consent was not obtained prior to the study because there was no intention of involving the daughter, or any child, in the study. The Federal Policy and the IRB Guidebook outline provisions for studies in which the intent of the use of human subjects changes as a result of the research design. However, the student researchers did not involve the child in the interview. The mother, Rev, repeated an interview question, or portions of a question, to her daughter and asked for her thoughts on the subject. The daughter, it could be argued, was engaging in conversation with her mother rather than engaging in a research study. The responses from the child were not transcribed, or included in the research findings or the final report. Although glimpses of the child appeared in the video of the interview due to the close proximity of the interviewee and her daughter, no images of the child were used in any presentation or publication. Rev's daughter contributed in no way to the kitchen media study.

Aiken and Carranza's decision to continue with the interview weighed heavily on their minds during the three to four minutes she was present. Even though the mother apparently consented to her daughter's involvement and the child was apparently capable of providing assent, they were aware of the ethical issues in involving children in research studies. One issue, susceptibility to coercion, did not appear to be of concern in this particular situation. The child sat down at the dining room table where the interview was being conducted without being asked to by her mom. When the child responded to *her mother's* questions with the typical adolescent "I dunno," Rev did not scold her daughter or entice her in any way. Based on Aiken and Carranza's judgment of the situation, the child was in no danger or was in any way harmed by their presence.

Conclusion: Navigating the Gray Areas

The extreme case of the participant Rev not only provided a learning experience to the student team that conducted her interview, but also opened class discussion on navigating the ethically gray areas in ethnographic research. Based on class discussions as well as further conversations at the 2012 AAA session on ethics in business anthropology where this research was initially presented, we offer three conclusions regarding ethical encounters in anthropological research.

1. *Ethically gray areas can occur in any research, no matter how well planned.* Prior to the start of fieldwork, the kitchen media study was carefully reviewed for its ethical soundness by Metcalf, Wasson, the UNT IRB, and the students in the design anthropology class. Everyone agreed that it did not pose risks to the research participants. The population of research participants did not include categories

of vulnerable persons such as children, prisoners, mentally disabled persons, or economically or educationally disadvantaged persons (DHHS 2009). The fact that the situation with Rev nonetheless occurred illustrates the point that any study involving human subjects, no matter how carefully designed, can produce ethically gray areas. There is always an unpredictable aspect to human interactions due to the complexity and multifacetedness of human agency as well as the diverse institutions and social processes we navigate.

2. *Ethically gray areas occur for seasoned anthropologists and students alike.* Much to Aiken and Carranza's relief, Wasson assured her students that even the most seasoned anthropologists are not exempt from dealing with ethically gray areas. Students and their mentors share in the agony of ethical dilemmas encountered in the field. Anthropologists, perhaps more than any group of researchers, understand and appreciate the diversity and often unpredictable nature of human behavior. As long as humans remain diverse and unpredictable, ethically gray areas are sure to arise. Ethics will remain a subject of concern as humans continue to evolve and adapt their behaviors. In fact, the publication of this volume proves the prevalence of ethical debate within anthropology today.

3. *Ethically gray areas are experienced across disciplines.* Although this research was originally presented in a 2012 AAA session on ethics in business anthropology, gray areas are not limited to business anthropology. The lively discussion that followed the presentation of papers in this session included audience members who specialized in a range of different areas. Yet they shared a broad agreement on the kinds of ethical challenges they faced. Furthermore, the discipline of anthropology shares ethical considerations with other social and biological sciences as well as with any discipline that seeks to engage with human participants.

Ideas for Solutions: Preparing for the Unpredictable

The kitchen media study conducted for Motorola during the fall 2011 Design Anthropology course at UNT resulted in valuable findings for the client and valuable lessons in ethics for the class. In particular, the interview with Rev opened the class to multidisciplinary conversations regarding ethically gray areas of field research. The practical lessons learned are not only applicable to a class of interdisciplinary students, but also serve as points of discussion for seasoned researchers. Although ethically gray areas are by definition ambiguous, the authors offer ideas for solutions in preparing for the unpredictable.

First and foremost, we suggest that researchers should strive to avoid complacency as they move forward in their careers. Where students have the advantage over seasoned anthropologists is the advantage of novelty. Shocking stories of human research programs that initiated the development of ethical guidelines are usually heard first in the classroom. As ethics continues to be taught in graduate programs, students are exposed to ethical considerations through coursework and classroom discussions. For many students, the classroom is the first and possibly the last environment that requires their review of literature regarding ethics.

In order to avoid complacency, professional anthropologists should endeavor to regularly review ethical standards. As students are constantly reminded by their coursework, seasoned anthropologists should stay up to date on ethical debates, including the consistent revisiting of professional guidelines such as the AAA's Statement on Ethics and the SfAA's Ethical and Professional Responsibilities as well as those of other disciplines with which they work.

Furthermore, as anthropologists, we are aware that the cultures of our study participants may have different conceptualizations of ethical behavior from the American-based AAA Statement on Ethics. The debate between cultural relativism and universalism is ongoing in anthropology in relation to topics such as human rights.

> Should not global research be met by global ethics or a vigorous discussion and debate of what our universal standards of ethical conduct are? … Have non-Western anthropologists achieved agency in the international discourse of ethics and professionalism, or is this yet another piece of the unfinished business of colonialism and its fallout?
>
> *(Fluehr-Lobban 2013, 18)*

While there are no simple answers to such questions, it is useful for practitioners to reflect on them and develop their own personal guidelines.

Finally, we suggest that anthropologists share their stories of encounters with ethically gray areas within their communities of practice. Although it is unlikely that extreme cases of ethically gray areas will be experienced repeatedly in the same manner, storytelling is a valuable tool in preparing researchers in any discipline for adventures in the field. Sharing Rev's story provided a learning opportunity for all the students in the design anthropology class on how to manage ethical dilemmas, and allowed the class to discuss ways in which to handle ethically gray areas. Such stories of extreme cases not only offer lessons learned to students, but can also open lines of communication among experienced anthropologists. By sharing stories, students and professional anthropologists are given the opportunity to learn from another's experience in the field while also discovering that ethically gray areas are a shared, acceptable subject of discussion.

Note

1   We would like to extend our deep appreciation to Tim Malefyt and Robert Morais for organizing the 2012 session on ethics in business anthropology where this research was originally presented, and for guiding us gracefully through the editing process. The comments of our anonymous reviewers improved the original article and this subsequent chapter immeasurably. Finally, we wish to thank Crysta Metcalf, our research participants, and all of the other students in the 2011 Design Anthopology class for collaboratively creating such a rich and rewarding learning experience.

References

American Anthropological Association (AAA). 2012. Statement on ethics: Principles of professional responsibility. www.aaanet.org/profdev/ethics.html (accessed February 3, 2013).

American Institute of Graphic Arts (AIGA). 2010. Standards of professional practice. www.aiga.org/standards-professional-practice.html (accessed February 14, 2013).

Anderson, Ken, and Rogério De Paula. 2006. We we we all the way home the we affect in transitional spaces. *Ethnographic Praxis in Industry Conference Proceedings* 2006, 60–75. Blackwell Publishing Ltd. for the American Anthropological Association.

Armbruster, Heidi, and Anna Laerke, eds. 2008. *Taking sides: Ethics, politics and fieldwork in anthropology.* New York: Berghahn Books.

Arnould, Eric J., Howard S. Becker, Dominic Boyer, Ulf Hannerz, Marianne Lien, Orvar Löfgren, George E. Marcus, Robert J. Morais, Hirochika Nakamaki, and Alan Smart. 2012. Opinions: What business anthropology is, what it might become… and what, perhaps, it should not be. *Journal of Business Anthropology* 1, 2: 240–297.

Baba, Marietta L. 2009. Disciplinary-professional relations in an era of anthropological engagement. *Human Organization* 68, 4: 380–391.

Baba, Marietta. 2012. Anthropology and business: Influence and interests. *Journal of Business Anthropology* 1, 1: 20–27.

Balsamo, Anne, and Carl Mitcham. 2012. Interdisciplinarity in ethics and the ethics of interdisciplinarity. In *The Oxford handbook of interdisciplinarity.* R. Frodeman, J.T. Klein, and C. Mitcham, eds. Oxford: Oxford University Press.

Borneman, John, and Abdellah Hammoudi, eds. 2009. *Being there: The fieldwork encounter and the making of truth.* Berkeley: University of California Press.

Bowen, Elenore Smith. 1954. *Return to laughter: An anthropological novel.* New York: Harper and Brothers.

Department of Health and Human Services (DHHS). 2009. 45 CFR 46. www.hhs.gov/ohrp/regulations-and-policy/regulations/45-cfr-46/index.html (accessed February 13, 2013).

Dumont, Louis. 1980 [1966]. *Homo hierarchicus: The caste system and its implications.* M. Sainsbury, L. Dumont, and B. Gulati, trans. Chicago: University of Chicago Press.

Fluehr-Lobban, C. 2003. Ethics and anthropology 1890–2000: A review of issues and principles. In *Ethics and the profession of anthropology: Dialogue for ethically conscious practice.* 2d ed. C. Fluehr-Lobban, ed. Walnut Creek: AltaMira Press.

Fluehr-Lobban, C. 2008. Collaborative anthropology as twenty-first-century ethical anthropology. *Collaborative Anthropologies* 1: 175–182.

Fluehr-Lobban, C. 2013. *Ethics and anthropology: Ideas and practice.* Walnut Creek: AltaMira Press.

Frake, Charles O. 1964. How to ask for a drink in Subanun. *American Anthropologist* 66, 6: 127–132.

García, Victor. 2008. Problem drinking among transnational Mexican migrants: Exploring migrant status and situational factors. *Human Organization* 67, 1: 12–24.

Hammershøy, Laura, and Thomas Ulrik Madsen. 2012. Ethics in business anthropology. *Ethnographic Praxis in Industry Conference Proceedings,* 2012, 67–73. Blackwell Publishing Ltd. for the American Anthropological Association.

Ikeya, N., E. Vinkhuyzen, J. Whalen, and Y. Yamauchi. 2007. Teaching organizational ethnography. *Ethnographic Praxis in Industry Conference Proceedings,* 2007, 270–282. Blackwell Publishing Ltd. for the American Anthropological Association.

Industrial Designers Society of America (IDSA). 2010. Code of ethics. www.idsa.org/content/content1/code-ethics.html (accessed February 14, 2013).

Joseph, Janelle, and Michele K. Donnelly. 2012. Reflections on ethnography, ethics and inebriation. *Leisure/Loisir* 36, 3–4: 357–372.

Kingsolver, A., G. Wagner, R. Barrera, J.C. Bennett-Brown, D. Clark, V.D. Gerald, D. Goodrich, M. Hewlett, M. Hughes, J. Leader, L. Liger, T. Little Water, C. Loftlin, D. Parra-Medina, D. Rymer, C. Scott, C. Shumpert, G.N. Thompson, and T. Wilson. 2003. Teaching anthropological ethics at the University of South Carolina: An example of critical ethical dialogues across communities. In *Ethics and the profession of anthropology: Dialogue for ethically conscious practice.* 2d ed. C. Fluehr-Lobban, ed. Walnut Creek: AltaMira Press.

Klinenberg, Eric. 2002. *Heat wave: A social autopsy of disaster in Chicago.* Chicago: University of Chicago Press.

LeCompte, Margaret D., and Jean J. Schensul. 1999. *Designing and conducting ethnographic research: Ethnographer's toolkit 1.* 1st edn. Walnut Creek: AltaMira Press.

Mack, Alexandra, and Susan Squires. 2011. Evolving ethnographic practitioners and their impact on ethnographic praxis. *Ethnographic Praxis in Industry Conference Proceedings,* 2011, 18–28. Blackwell Publishing Ltd. for the American Anthropological Association.

Mauss, Marcel. 1979 [1904–1905]. *Seasonal variations of the Eskimo: A study in social morphology.* J.J. Fox, trans. London: Routledge & Kegan Paul.

Miller, Daniel. 2001. *The dialectics of shopping.* Chicago: University of Chicago Press.

Moeran, Brian. 1985. *Okubo diary: Portrait of a Japanese valley.* Stanford: Stanford University Press.

National Association for the Practice of Anthropology (NAPA). 2013. NAPA ethical guidelines. www.practicinganthropology.org/about/ethical-guidelines.html (accessed January 10, 2013).

Office for Human Research Protections (OHRP). 1993. IRB guidebook. www.hhs.gov/ohrp/archive/irb/irb_guidebook.html (accessed February 20, 2013).

Sachs, Patricia. 2006. Bushwacking a career. *NAPA Bulletin* 26: 152–162.

Sandiford, Peter John, and Diane Seymour. 2013. Serving and consuming: Drink, work and leisure in public houses. *Work, Employment & Society* 27, 1: 122–137.

Society for Applied Anthropology (SfAA). 2013. SfAA ethical and professional responsibilities. www.sfaa.net/sfaaethic.html (accessed January 10, 2013).

Spradley, James P. 1999. *You owe yourself a drunk: An ethnography of urban nomads.* Long Grove, Ill: Waveland Press.

Squires, Susan, Christina Wasson, and Ann Jordan. 2014. Training the next generation: Business anthropology at the University of North Texas. In *Sourcebook of anthropology in business.* R. Denny and P. Sunderland, eds. Walnut Creek: Left Coast Press.

Tian, Robert G. 2011. We need business anthropology education: Editorial commentary. *International Journal of Business Anthropology* 3, 1.

University of North Texas Office of Research and Economic Development (UNT ORED). 2013. IRB guidelines. www.research.unt.edu/faculty-resources/research-integrity-and-compliance/use-of-humans-in-research.html (accessed February 14, 2013).

Wasson, Christina, and Crysta Metcalf. 2013. Teaching design anthropology through university-industry partnerships. In *Design anthropology: Between theory and practice.* W. Gunn, T. Otto, and R.C. Smith, eds. London: Berg.

Yin, Robert K. 2009. *Case study research: Design and methods.* Los Angeles: Sage Publications.

9

REFLECTIONS ON REFOCUSING BUSINESS EDUCATION

A Human-centered Approach

Dawn Lerman

While it is a tradition at many academic institutions not just to welcome but to embrace a wide diversity of people and perspectives, many of us at Fordham University like to think that it is woven more tightly into the fabric of our institution than it is at others. One might think that embracing a wide diversity of people and perspectives is a direct result of our location in New York City, one of the most diverse cities on earth. Certainly the two are not unrelated. New York City offers endless lessons about diverse people and perspectives but I like to think that we are here in New York because we value diversity and not just that we value diversity because we are in New York.

This chapter focuses on this idea of value, or more specifically human value in the context of business education. I argue that business education needs what I would call a human-centered approach. That is, we need to infuse an understanding of people, a respect for their diversity and a commitment to upholding human dignity into the fabric of business education. It is incumbent on us to do this because of the central role of commerce and consumption in society as well as the changing educational landscape – and not just the changing business education landscape but a changing landscape in higher education across the board. Business education is already being refocused, but we need new ideas for how to continue to push it forward.

Searching for the Human Value of Business

There are a number of assumptions underlying my main idea, the biggest of which is that there is human value in business. I do not extol the human value of business in part because that has been addressed elsewhere (e.g., Allinson 1998; von Kimakowitz et al. 2011; Erisman and Gautschi 2015), but also because readers of this chapter may themselves work in business, either as academics or practicing professionals, and believe in the value that such work creates for people. That value may be to you, yourself, by giving you a sense of accomplishment, pride and purpose in what you do, to your colleagues for the same reasons, and to your customers by providing to them products and services that make their lives easier and more enjoyable. Even so – even if we believe in the human value of business – we do need to recognize the debate, if not also the evidence that we are not fully living up to the promise of that value.

Marketing is one of the places where that value should come across loudly and clearly. Marketers are trained to help consumers solve their problems, from mundane decisions such as what to eat for dinner to complex matters such as how to care for an aging parent. In return for this help, individuals willingly give back to the marketing organization in the form of monetary payment, word of mouth, loyalty or other considerations. This exchange process is – or at least, should be – at the heart of marketing as a philosophy, a discipline, and an organizational function (Lerman and Shefrin 2015).

Yet, we increasingly hear of an imbalance, one that is typically described as favoring marketers and hurting ordinary citizens. Think of Occupy Wall Street and perhaps more directly relevant, Occupy Black Friday, a movement that encouraged American consumers to boycott publicly traded retailers because they do not serve local communities (Rabinowitz 2011; Thompson 2011). Think of criticism of the pharmaceutical industry over the high prices of their life-saving drugs. Think of former Mayor Bloomberg's proposed ban in New York City on the sale of sugary drinks larger than 16 ounces. The evidence appears endless. I have not even mentioned, for example, the havoc wreaked on our planet by efforts to bring innovative well-priced products to market.

Listening to this criticism, it sounds like marketers are driving the revenue and profit of firms that have become increasingly perceived as out of touch with ordinary people and the needs of society. And they – we – have been collecting vast amounts of personal data to boot, which can feel like an invasion of privacy.

Of course, consumers benefit by having food and clothes to satisfy basic needs, technological products to help satisfy communication or social needs, amusement parks, video games and movies to help satisfy experiential needs (Lerman and Kachersky 2012). But at what cost? The United States ranks relatively far from the top on measures of gross national happiness (Helliwell et al. 2016). To what degree is consumption, at least in part, to blame?

We already have evidence that as consumers turn to marketers to help fulfill their needs, the resultant clutter can and does have a negative impact. A growing body of consumer research suggests that the plethora of product and brand choice in the developed world clouds consumer decision making. It creates inefficiencies in the decision-making process and contributes to cognitive dissonance (Chernev 2003; Iyengar 2010). At the same time, the steadily increasing number of reality TV shows that "declutter" subjects' homes reflect how popular culture recognizes the challenge that too much consumption can raise.

Yet criticism of marketing is not new. And it comes from many camps.

It comes from cultural critics in the form of books like Naomi Klein's *No Logo* or Eric Schlosser's *Fast Food Nation*.

It comes from social scientists such as the prominent sociology professor from another institution who, in a conference held at Fordham University, said, "Is marketing good or evil? My professorial mode would be to say that it is good and evil. Basically I think it's evil."

It comes from respondents in a consumer panel, who in the data collection for the Center for Positive Marketing's V-Positive report on the value of brands warm up with a sentence completion task and tell us that marketing is "invasive," "lies," "fooling the public, legally" and yes, "evil."

And it comes from respondents in a survey commissioned by Adobe. According to an article in *Advertising Age* (Parekh 2012), only 35% of marketers responding to the Adobe study deem their profession valuable. *Even marketers* question the value of their profession!

Yet, it is not just marketers. Our colleagues in management and finance can and often do struggle with the same question as to their value (e.g., Pfeffer 2007, 2011; Brocklehurst et al. 2009).

Consider Salman Khan. He is the hedge fund analyst turned founder of the Khan Academy, the non-profit educational organization whose use of video has helped spark a new way of thinking about learning and classrooms. In one of his TED talks (Khan 2011), he reads a letter from the very thankful parents of an autistic child. Their child came to understand decimals from a math video that Mr. Khan had put on YouTube, and this child was *very* excited to have mastered decimals. The story took place before the founding of Khan Academy, and he speaks in his TED talk about his reaction to the parents' letter. He says, "Here I was an analyst of a hedge fund. It was very strange for me to do something of social value."

In 2014, EPIC, the self-proclaimed "premier international gathering on the current and future practice of ethnography in the business world" (http://epiconference.com/2014/) collaborated with the Center for Positive Marketing at Fordham University to bring its annual conference to New York City. This was the first time that EPIC was to be hosted at a business school. For those of us at Fordham University's Gabelli School of Business, EPIC was a natural fit. The global financial crisis of 2007 and 2008 left many of us – and I am referring to a collective us that goes well beyond our campus or our university – grappling not only with the question "what is the role of business in society," but also "what *should* the role of business in society be." Of course, higher education professionals have also had to ask how we should be educating future business leaders to help ensure that business plays a *positive* role in society.

It is quite likely that the architects of the financial crisis – those individuals whose decisions and actions contributed to its occurrence – held business degrees. It is even possible that the coursework required for those degrees included a course in business ethics. Gallenga (2016, 9) argues that "business ethics encounters an increasing social demand for responsibility from companies, which should act as role models for society and make their inner workings more humane" and is presumably recognized and discussed in business ethics courses. Nonetheless, the study of business ethics was not sufficient for ensuring the integrity of their actions.

In an op-ed entitled "Becoming a Real Person" published in the *New York Times* the same week that we hosted EPIC, David Brooks (2014) debated to what degree educators are responsible for moral as well as spiritual and emotional growth. He points out that many educators do not think it is their place, and as Steven Pinker, a well-known psychology professor at Harvard University, seems to suggest, perhaps it is just that we do not know how to facilitate such growth in an explicit and direct way (2014).

That may be arguable but let us leave that aside and think about this ethics course – and I will do some *very* unfair math in order to make a point. Let us suppose that as students, these folks needed to complete 60 credits to obtain their MBA degree. And let us suppose that each course in their program carried 3 credits. This means that 5% of their program – 3 credits out of 60 – were dedicated to people and planet, whereas the other 95% – 57 credits out of 60 – were dedicated to profit. What is amazing about this is that business is really about people – employees and customers and, yes, individual shareholders. As we like to say at the Center for Positive Marketing, markets are people too.

Unfair math, I know – I warned you. It is unfair for a whole number of reasons including the fact that a number of business disciplines *are* about people – management and marketing, for example.

Let us reflect on marketing. Since that is my own discipline, I feel most comfortable choosing it for critique.

Marketing as a discipline is squarely focused on responding to concerns about people's well-being. Job number one for any marketer is to understand the market. One of the first lessons in any marketing course covers what we call the marketing concept, which I would argue is intended to be both a philosophy and a practice. The idea is that marketers should start with human needs – what *people* need – and then design products and brands, along with whole marketing programs around those products and brands. As marketers, we must study individuals and society with great care in order to identify their needs and to determine how those needs can best be satisfied – marketing is about people.

Now here is the rub: Marketing curricula typically do not teach much about people! We do teach research design which gives students a toolkit for studying people. And it is true that consumer behavior – essentially consumer psychology – is a regularly offered course at most schools. But as any social scientist knows, psychology does not explain it all.

It is for this very reason that I and so many of my marketing colleagues encourage students to learn as much as they can from the social sciences. It is also why we developed an interdisciplinary undergraduate marketing minor that includes courses from psychology, sociology and anthropology. It is why we jumped on an opportunity to create a special marketing track that focuses on consumer insights as part of a new bachelor of science program in global business. And it is why we developed a master of science program in marketing intelligence that combines quantitative and qualitative approaches for understanding consumers and using that understanding to drive marketing strategy. Simply put, consumers are served better by marketers who understand people.

This focus on people is not unique to our marketing faculty, although it is true that my marketing colleagues and I do like to think that we are a unique bunch. It is a hallmark of Fordham and deeply intertwined with our Jesuit tradition. As an institution, we are guided by principles that speak directly to this focus on people, and I would like to call out two of them: *homines pro aliis*, meaning men and women for others, and *cura personalis*, or care for the whole person.

Men and women for others. As our university website will tell you, our students live this by contributing their time and talent in service to the community: tutoring the disadvantaged; feeding and clothing the homeless; planning outings for an orphanage; and spending vacation periods in distant corners of the world, from New Mexico to Calcutta, as part of Fordham's Global Outreach Program. To us in the Gabelli School of Business, men and women for others also means teaching our students to think about customers and colleagues, teaching them to contribute their time and talent *in service* to customers and colleagues. It is *not* about *selling* to customers. It is about being *in service* to them. And if you do it well, they will *want* to buy. The sales will come.

Care for the whole person. This implies individualized attention. It implies a dedication to promoting human dignity and care for the mind, body and spirit. In the Gabelli School of Business, this means – returning to an earlier point – *thinking* about how the plethora of consumer choice breeds indecision and cognitive dissonance. It means thinking about how in a garment factory setting a target for number of pieces produced per minute can create a disincentive for exceeding the target, while also making elusive the feeling of a job well done. More generally, it means understanding oneself and the impact that one has on the thoughts, behaviors, feelings and actions of others with whom we engage at work and in the marketplace.

In 2014 we launched a new MBA program with a revised curriculum and a variety of other new features. One of those features is a series of self-awareness assessments, the idea being that only through self-knowledge – knowledge of one's style and strengths, and knowledge of how one's approach to work and to people impacts others and is impacted by others – can one achieve excellence as a manager or a leader. A management colleague who was instrumental in helping to design this program suggested an exercise whereby we ask students to think about some of the best leaders and then spend a few minutes brainstorming what makes them so great. Her predication was that the vast majority, perhaps as much as 90%, of the answers would be about emotional intelligence. We tried it, and she was right.

Men and women for others and care for the whole person. At no time has the need for these principles been greater, whether within the context of an ever shrinking middle class, political unrest in a far-away land or closer to home, or the social isolation that results, ironically, from social media.

Higher education is under intense scrutiny, and is experiencing tumultuous change – from pressures put upon us from technology to government to the students themselves and their parents. For many of us in today's professional ranks, going to college meant getting a liberal arts education, and majoring in something that could be broadly classified as arts and sciences. I, for example, majored in French language and literature and I have business faculty colleagues who majored in psychology, sociology, politics, English and physics just to name a few. For us, business came later in the form of on-the-job training, MBAs and doctoral degrees.

But as a 2012 article in *The Wall Street Journal* pointed out, "with tuition increases far outpacing inflation and graduates entering a bad job market with record debt, students and parents are demanding a clearer – and quicker – return on their investment" (Weber 2012). Less than a year later, the same newspaper reported that business majors now outnumbered liberal arts majors in the United States by two-to-one, and that the trend is for even more focused programs targeted to niches in the labor market (Cappelli 2013).

The Wall Street Journal cited clear and quick return on investment as the driving force behind this shift. Whether real or perceived, this is likely a key component. Concerns are widespread that today's children and young adults will not necessarily be better off than their parents. But perhaps there are other contributing factors as well such as modes of communication and related technologies that have raised our expectations for instant gratification. Perhaps our increased capacity to collect data and distribute information somehow plays a role. And how about the increasingly global world with global brands that have helped put commerce at the forefront? Or not unrelatedly, our increasingly consumer-oriented – or for those more cynical, materialistic – society?

With an undergraduate degree in business, the career opportunities are obvious, or so they seem. Major in finance and you will be positioned to land a job in finance. Major in marketing and you will be positioned to land a job in marketing. But are learning the concepts and tools in finance or marketing enough to prepare students for a successful career in these fields? When we think of the whole person, are we serving these students well? Are we serving business well? And what about society at large?

A quick read of the headlines in the popular press would suggest that we are not. Consider David Glenn's *New York Times* article (2011) entitled "The Default Major: Skating Through B-School." The default major? When I was in college, the default major was psychology, and not because it was considered easy but because it seemed to be relevant to almost any field of endeavor. Talk to business faculty and you will often find that they strive to deliver an education rooted in critical thinking and an understanding of the world. They want their students to think, and not simply apply a standard formula. They seek rigorous intellectual exchange in the classroom just like their counterparts in the liberal arts.

At Fordham, we go a step further. We believe that business leadership – the kind that will make business a positive force in society – requires that a person know more than business itself. For this reason, our students take more than half of their core curriculum courses – 13 out of 25 – in liberal arts. We believe in the need for this foundation because of what it delivers for them and for business. We believe that business leaders need to write well. They need to know how to tell meaningful stories that not only captivate their audiences but inspire them to act. They need to understand other cultures, have exposure to humanity's greatest thinkers, and grasp how the lessons of the past influence our world today (Gabelli School of Business Academic Bulletin 2014–2016).

And while we may require more than many or even most business schools, we are not alone in recognizing the importance of liberal arts as part of a business education. In April 2014, a *Business Week* article entitled "Business Schools Embrace the Liberal Arts" cited the growing number of business schools experimenting with liberal arts components in the curriculum.

But I would say that even this is not enough to bring a human focus to business education.

Let us return to Salman Khan, the hedge fund analyst turned social change agent who helped an autistic boy master decimals. What Mr. Khan has done is called flipping the classroom. In a traditional classroom, students come to class to hear a professor give a lecture, and then they go home to work on applying what was covered in a class as part of a homework assignment. In a flipped classroom, students typically watch a video of the professor's lecture at home and then come to class to discuss, debate and work together and with the professor on the types of problems and assignments that students would have otherwise done by themselves at home. This puts greater control of the learning process into the hands of the student who can rewind and review lecture videos on their own as many times as they need, and allows the instructor to serve in class more as a facilitator of learning rather than distributor of knowledge. The result is deeper, richer active learning experiences for students.

Mr. Khan (2011) argues that to flip the classroom is to humanize the classroom because it gives every student the opportunity to master the material. He claims that a traditional classroom does not do this. In a traditional classroom, the lecture happens once, the homework assignment is completed by each individual student following that single lecture, and once it is graded or at least submitted, we move on to the next topic. That next topic probably builds on the first, and we move on to it whether the student got a 95% or a 75% on the test of the first topic. This approach does not expect mastery and does not provide adequate opportunity for all students to achieve mastery. Research shows that in a flipped classroom, a student who struggles with a topic will spend the required time to master it.

Flipping the classroom falls within a broader classification of pedagogy that we refer to as applied learning. Applied learning has a long history in business school where the use of case studies and simulations is the norm. At Fordham we take applied learning further by stepping out of the classroom and using New York and the world as our campus.

Consider the Fordham Foundry, a mixed-use business incubator developed to assist promising entrepreneurs in launching new businesses. This unique partnership between Fordham University and the City of New York marries the aspirations and needs of the Fordham community, most specifically our entrepreneurially minded students, with those of the Bronx community, resulting in opportunities that we believe will solidify the Bronx as the next hub of growth and renewal in New York City. This is not only applied learning but applied learning in the context of men and women for others.

The soapstone rams that many of us have on our desks and that we offer as gifts to guests of our university are another example. These rams were born out of a service learning program designed by former Fordham faculty member Kate Combellick. It started in 2006 when a group of six students traveled to Kenya over winter break and toured fair-trade businesses in the outskirts of Nairobi and in the western village of Nyabigena. As Fordham reporters have wonderfully documented in articles which are available online (e.g., Sassi 2011), the group consulted with business managers, strategizing ways to improve economic conditions in the villages they visited and devised plans to help women in these villages start new enterprises. But when they visited a soapstone collective in Nyabigena, they learned how difficult it can be to start even the smallest business in the developing world. Because women are not allowed to inherit land or money in Kenya, most in the collective could provide no collateral for a loan from a Kenyan bank.

The students were challenged to find another way to assist – and they did. They bought thousands of dollars of soapstone goods, which they sold at Fordham. Now, years later, those same women at the soapstone collective have a regular customer and a commissioned product –Fordham and the soapstone ram.

A practical business experience *and* a first-hand look at the economic and social issues that affect people in the third world – learning cannot get much more applied or humanly focused than that.

The beauty of these kinds of applied experiences is that our students often live them as a kind of participant-observer or ethnographer. This is something that we encourage. We also regularly encourage students to reflect on their experiences and come to understand why they experienced what they did. I think back to a consulting project for IBM that paired our students with students in London and for which I served as faculty advisor. My students wrestled with some of the speedbumps and what they perceived as oddities in working with the London students and faculty, even after the deliverables were submitted to the client. I used these speedbumps and my students' reaction to them as an opportunity to talk about culture, meta-communication and the power of language, none of which I could have done if I did not have the background that I do in language and culture.

It may seem odd for business school professors to be interested in such topics, let alone incorporate them into their teachings. But many business school faculty – and not just at Fordham – were similarly trained as liberal arts faculty, at least as undergraduates. And we have carried that training into our doctoral programs, into our classrooms, and also into our research where it is now common to incorporate interdisciplinary perspectives, a use of both qualitative and quantitative methods, including ethnography and a focus not just on profit but also people and planet. Arnould and Thompson (2014) cite, for example, "the growing host of colleagues invested in the cultural turn throughout the world" (p. 125), the institutionalization of Consumer Culture Theory (CGT) as a track at the annual American Marketing Association conferences, and the interest by "mainstream" marketing researchers in "identity, brand community, status consumption, consumer co-creation, and the hedonic, emotive, and social properties of consumption experience," topics of "path-breaking cultural work" (p. 126) by consumer culture theorists whose work sits at "the nexus of disciplines as varied as anthropology, sociology, media studies, critical studies, and feminist studies" (Joy and Li, 2012, p. 1).

The Role of the Learning Environment

Curriculum and faculty, along with their approach both to the classroom and to research, play a central role in building a human-centered approach to business education. Another critical piece deserving of consideration is the learning environment. Those with a background or interest in design likely know how important that can be.

FIGURE 9.1 Hughes Hall at Fordham University.

Pictured above is Hughes Hall, the building that houses Fordham University's undergraduate business programs at its Rose Hill campus in the Bronx. Both the building and the campus are beautiful – true oases in the hustle and bustle and grit of our great city.

As the picture might suggest, this is a very old building – built in the 1890s. It served many functions over the years, including as a dormitory, but was recently gutted and rebuilt on the inside as part of our transformation of the business school. It still looks old on the outside, but step inside and the message is clear – this is not business as usual.

Stoelker (2012) gives a sense as to what one will find inside:

> At first glance, the renovation would almost appear to be a restoration, but a studied view reveals a surgical approach that didn't shy away from the contemporary. Wide marble steps lead up to sliding glass doors that swoosh open beneath a clean-lined glass canopy, where a lobby cuts straight through the building on a north-south axis. Architects used a white Vermont marble on the stairs to harmonize with original stonework, but the glass openings bring the visitors into another realm entirely.
>
> Inside, most rooms are enclosed in glass, reflecting the current design trend in businesses to portray transparency. Stairwell landings and administrative offices provide large lounge areas to foster spontaneous collaboration.

Something not mentioned in the article is the glass rooftop, which for us embodies so many meanings – soaring ambition and the sky's the limit for our students, and a higher purpose for business.

While we do not have hard data, we believe that as a result of this building and the environment it creates, students have a new spring in their step, a renewed motivation and sense of purpose. And I like to believe that the same can be said for our faculty and staff who work in this building.

Academia may be criticized for pouring money into buildings and architecture that are perceived as being undesirable, unnecessary and perhaps even outside of the educational mission (e.g., Carlson 2011; Pearlstein 2015). However, to the degree that facilities and their design can aid or impede learning, they are mission critical. Controlling for variables such as students' socio-economic status, Berner (1993) found a positive correlation between the condition of school buildings and student achievement as measured by test scores. More recent research suggests that design is also an essential element. A plethora of studies indicate, for example, that seating arrangements affect both academic and behavioral outcomes in K-12 classrooms (e.g., Wannarka and Ruhl 2008). More recently, a study by Zhu and Argo (2013) demonstrated how various shaped seating arrangements can prime two social needs, a need to belong or a need to be unique, and that this in turn influences responsiveness to persuasive information. To the degree that today's students will need to inspire their future colleagues to remain human-focused and encourage consumers to make choices that are in their best interest, which they do not always do, then the onus is on us to create the learning environments that prepare them to do so.

Conclusion

Research by Piff et al. (2012) reveals a positive association between social class and unethical behavior. In their studies, upper-class people were more likely to engage in behaviors such as breaking the law while driving, taking valued goods from others, endorsing unethical behavior at work, and cheating to increase their chances of winning a prize. An earlier study by some of these same authors (Piff et al. 2010) found that individuals in lower social classes "orient to the welfare of others as a means to adapt to their more hostile environments and that this orientation gives rise to greater prosocial behavior" (p. 771). Specifically, lower class individuals proved to be more generous, charitable, trusting, and helpful compared with their upper class counterparts.

Study results such as these led Grewal (2012) to the conclusion that wealth reduces compassion. If this is indeed true, does at least some of the fault lie with education, which has long been seen as providing a path away from poverty and toward wealth (Card 1998)? This may sound counterintuitive, especially for those of us whose education was – or whose education career is – focused on understanding people. Perhaps as individuals put their education to work and see the outcomes of that education as measured by sales, revenue, profit or share price, which would be the case for a marketer, a manager or a financier, they become distanced from the very people they served in order to yield this outcome. Oh, the irony if this is to be true! It is clearly dangerous for society, but also for business. If a marketer, for example, becomes too distant from his customers, then he will cease to serve customer needs well, and since customers – at least in developed and many developing markets – have a choice as to which brands to buy, the business will suffer. Thus, it is the responsibility of business schools to provide a human-focused education not just for the benefit of society but also for the viability of the businesses that do and should serve society.

References

Allinson, Robert E. 1998. Ethical values as part of the definition of business enterprise and part of the internal structure of the business organization. *Journal of Business Ethics* 19, July: 1015–1028.

Arnould, Eric J. and Craig J. Thompson. 2014. Living in business schools, writing consumer culture. In *Handbook of Anthropology in Business*, Rita Denny and Patricia Southerland, eds. Walnut Creek, CA: Left Coast Press.

Berner, Maureen M. 1993. Building conditions, parental involvement, and student achievement in the District of Columbia public school system. *Urban Education* 28, April: 6–29.

Brocklehurst, Michael, Chris Grey and Andrew Sturdy. 2009. Management: The work that dares not speak its name. *Management Learning* 4, 1: 7–19.

Brooks, David. 2014. Becoming a real person. *The New York Times*, September 9: A29.

Cappelli, Peter. 2013. Why focusing too narrowly in college could backfire. *The Wall Street Journal*, November 15: www.wsj.com/articles/SB10001424127887324139404579016662718868576.

Card, David. 1998. The causal effect of education on earnings. In *Handbook of labor economics*, Orley Ashenfelter and David Card, eds. New York, NY: Elsevier.

Carlson, Scott. 2011. Cooper Union, bastion of free arts education for the deserving, mulls tuition. *The Chronicle of Higher Education, November* 13: http://chronicle.com/article/Cooper-Union-Bastion-of-Free/129749/.

Chernev, Alexander. 2003. When more is less and less is more: The role of ideal point availability and assortment in consumer choice. *Journal of Consumer Research* 30, September: 170–183.

Erisman, Albert and David Gautschi, eds. 2015. *The purpose of business*. New York, NY: Palgrave Macmillan.

Gabelli School of Business Academic Bulletin. 2014–2016. Fordham University.

Gallenga, Ghislaine. 2016. The anthropology of business ethics: Worth thinking about! *Journal of Business Anthropology* 3, Spring: 7-19.

Glenn, David. 2011. The default major: Skating through b-school. *The New York Times*, April 17: ED16.

Grewal, Daisy. 2012. How wealth reduces compassion. *Scientific America*, April 10: www.scientificamerican.com/article/how-wealth-reduces-compassion/.

Helliwell, John, Richard Layard and Jeffrey Sachs. 2016. *World happiness report 2016, Update (Vol. I)*. New York, NY: Sustainable Development Solutions Network.

Iyengar, Sheena. 2010. *The art of choosing*. New York, NY: Grand Central Publishing.

Joy, Annamma, and Eric P. H. Li. 2012. Studying consumption behaviour through multiple lenses: An overview of Consumer Culture Theory. *Journal of Business Anthropology* 1, Spring: 141-173.

Khan, Salman. 2011. *Let's use video to reinvent education*. TED. March: www.ted.com/talks/salman_khan_let_s_use_video_to_reinvent_education?language=en.

Klein, Naomi. 1999. *No logo*. New York, NY: Random House.

Lavelle, Louis. 2014. Business schools embrace the liberal arts. *Business Week*, April 11: www.bloomberg.com/news/articles/2013-04-10/business-schools-embrace-the-liberal-arts.

Lerman, Dawn and Luke Kachersky. 2012. Seven ways to think of your marketing in human terms. *Forbes*, April 30: www.forbes.com/sites/gyro/2012/04/30/seven-ways-to-think-of-your-market-in-human-terms/#401216a66e62.

Lerman, Dawn and Hersh Shefrin. 2015. Positive marketing: Introduction to the special issue. *Journal of Business Research* 68, December: 2443–2445.

Parekh, Rupal. 2012. Marketers rate below politicians, bankers on respectability scale. *Advertising Age*, October 24: http://adage.com/article/news/marketers-rate-politicians-bankers-respectability/237937/.

Pearlstein, Steven. 2015. Four tough things universities should do to rein in costs. *The Washington Post*, November 25: www.washingtonpost.com/opinions/four-tough-things-universities-should-do-to-rein-in-costs/2015/11/25/64fed3de-92c0-11e5-a2d6-f57908580b1f_story.html.

Pfeffer, Jeffrey. 2007. A modest proposal: How we might change the process and product of managerial research. *Academy of Management Journal* 50, 6: 1334–1345.

Pfeffer, Jeffrey. 2011. Management a profession? Where's the proof? *Harvard Business Review*, September: 2.

Piff, Paul K., Michael W. Kraus, Stéphane Côté, Bonnie Hayden Cheng and Dacher Keltner. 2010. Having less, giving more: The influence of social class on prosocial behavior. *Journal of Personality and Social Psychology* 99, 5: 771–784.

Piff, Paul K., Daniel M. Stancato, Stéphane Côté, Rodolfo Mendoza-Denton and Dacher Keltner. 2012. Higher social class predicts unethical behavior. *Proceedings of National Academy of Sciences of the United States* 109, 11: 4086–4091.

Pinker, Steven. 2014. The trouble with Harvard: The Ivy League is broken and only standardized tests can fix it. *The New Republic*, September 4: https://newrepublic.com/article/119321/harvard-ivy-league-should-judge-students-standardized-tests.

Rabinowitz, Marco. 2011. What is occupy Black Friday? *Forbes*, November 25: www.forbes.com/sites/benzingainsights/2011/11/25/what-is-occupy-black-friday/#43b82ad5d2af.

Sassi, Janet. 2011. The human side of business. *Fordham Business*, Spring: 10.

Schlosser, Eric. 2012. *Fast food nation*. New York, NY: Houghton Mifflin Harcourt.

Stoelker, Tom. 2012. Architecture brings digital age to Hughes Hall. *Fordham News*, October 1: http://news.fordham.edu/university-news/architecture-brings-digital-age-to-hughes-hall-video-2/.

Thompson, Cadie. 2011. Demonstrators plan to occupy retailers on Black Friday. *CNBC*, November 22: www.cnbc.com/id/45402815.

von Kimakowitz, Ernst, Michael Pirson, Heiko Spitzeck, Claus Dierksmeier and Wolfgang Amann, eds. 2011. *Humanistic management in practice*. Houndmills: Palgrave Macmillan.

Wannarka, Rachel and Kathy Ruhl. 2008. Seating arrangements that promote positive academic and behavioural outcomes: A review of empirical research. *Support for Learning* 23, 2: 89–93.

Weber, Lauren. 2012. Colleges get career-minded: More liberal-arts schools stress skills development, ruffling academic feathers. *The Wall Street Journal*, May 22: www.wsj.com/articles/SB10001424052702303448404577410592488795980.

Zhu, Rui Juliet and Jennifer J. Argo. 2013. Exploring the impact of various shaped seating arrangements on persuasion. *Journal of Consumer Research* 40, August: 336–349.

INDEX

References to figures are shown in *italics*. References to tables are shown in **bold**. References to endnotes consist of the page number followed by the letter 'n' followed by the number of the note, e.g. 101n4 refers to note no. 4 on page 101.